Conducting Online Research on Amazon Mechanical Turk and Beyond

Conducting Online Research on Amazon Mechanical Turk and Beyond

Leib Litman
Lander College

Jonathan Robinson
Lander College

Los Angeles | London | New Delhi
Singapore | Washington DC | Melbourne

FOR INFORMATION:

SAGE Publications, Inc.
2455 Teller Road
Thousand Oaks, California 91320
E-mail: order@sagepub.com

SAGE Publications Ltd.
1 Oliver's Yard
55 City Road
London, EC1Y 1SP
United Kingdom

SAGE Publications India Pvt. Ltd.
B 1/I 1 Mohan Cooperative Industrial Area
Mathura Road, New Delhi 110 044
India

SAGE Publications Asia-Pacific Pte. Ltd.
18 Cross Street #10-10/11/12
China Square Central
Singapore 048423

Printed in the United Kingdom by Ashford Colour Press Ltd.

ISBN 978-1-5063-9113-7 (pbk)

This book is printed on acid-free paper.

Acquisitions Editor: Leah Fargotstein
Editorial Assistant: Claire Laminen
Production Editor: Olivia Weber-Stenis
Copy Editor: Amy Marks
Typesetter: Exeter Premedia Services
Proofreader: Scott Oney
Indexer: Exeter Premedia Services
Cover Designer: Janet Kiesel
Marketing Manager: Shari Countryman

20 21 22 23 24 10 9 8 7 6 5 4 3 2

BRIEF CONTENTS

DETAILED CONTENTS

Chapter 3 • Conducting a Study on Mechanical Turk   48

Jonathan Robinson and Leib Litman

Chapter 9 • Conducting Longitudinal Research on Amazon Mechanical Turk 198

Michael P. Hall, Neil A. Lewis Jr., Jesse Chandler, and Leib Litman

PREFACE

Science is shaped by the tools at hand. When Galileo Galilei sought to measure the weight of air, for example, he used a glass bottle, a leather stopper, a syringe, and a bellows. But in the biological and social sciences the right tools can be much more difficult to obtain. In antiquity, Egyptian physicians were highly sought-after by people from all corners of the ancient world because they had acquired a knowledge of anatomy through their practice of mummification. But in the Roman world and during much of the Middle Ages, progress in medicine had all but halted because the use of cadavers was illegal. In the 19th century, before teaching hospitals and before people could donate their bodies to science, students interested in human anatomy used what they could find: amputated limbs, deceased relatives, and often a corpse taken from a fresh grave. More recently, before public opinion permitted the use of cadavers in crash test research, scientists who wanted to understand how the body reacts in collisions so that they could design safer cars sometimes jumped into the crash simulators themselves, risking life and limb to quell their curiosity.

Whereas progress in the medical sciences has been shaped by access to human bodies (or the lack thereof), progress in the social sciences is dependent on researchers being able to interact with human minds. The way in which social scientists sought to do this can be characterized as having proceeded through five stages. In the first stage, roughly spanning the 19th century, pioneering researchers like Gustav Fechner and Hermann Ebbinghaus used themselves as their own research subjects. The second stage began once psychology laboratories were established in German universities. From 1879 through the first decades of the 20th century, Wilhelm Wundt, Edward Titchener, and their students used highly trained professionals, who were usually psychologists themselves, as participants for their studies. By the middle of the 20th century, psychology was an established science. This marked the third stage, during which psychologists mostly used community recruitment to gain access to research participants. For example, in the early 1960s, Stanley Milgram performed what are perhaps some of the most famous psychological experiments ever conducted. To recruit subjects for his studies, Milgram followed what was a standard procedure at the time: he posted fliers around town and asked people interested in the study to mail in slips of paper with their contact information, basic demographic data, and an indication of when they might be able to come to the lab. Once Milgram received people's responses, he called prospective participants, scheduled a time for the experiment, and ensured that research staff were in the laboratory to conduct each experimental session. Clearly, finding people to participate in the study and actually running them through the protocol was a demanding process, requiring significant time and resources.

Because of the labor-intensive nature of community recruitment, beginning in the 1960s (marking the fourth stage), the vast majority of academic institutions created subject pools through which students were required to participate in research studies. Other sources of information about human beings, such as national datasets, probability surveys, and field research, were also commonly used and still are. By the 1990s close to 80% of all studies in psychology and consumer behavior consisted of participants who were recruited through the university subject pools (Peterson, 2001; Sears, 1986).

The 21st century brings us to the fifth stage of data collection with human participants, which makes up the subject matter of this book. Over the past several decades, technology has rapidly refashioned the tools of social scientists. The personal computer, the Internet, and various forms of browser-based software have made it easier than ever before to find research participants, create engaging study materials, and observe people's natural behavior in direct and indirect ways. In a relatively short period of time, technology has supplanted the university subject pool and largely replaced paper-and-pencil measures as the primary means of gathering data about people's thoughts, feelings, and behavior. This change has had a profound effect on all of social science research.

The catalyst for this change was Amazon's Mechanical Turk, an online platform that began to receive significant attention from research scientists starting in 2010. Since that time, thousands of scientific papers have been published using Mechanical Turk participants. But Mechanical Turk is not the only online platform from which participants can be recruited. Although Mechanical Turk provides many unique advantages, other platforms have much to offer as well. Overall, a variety of platforms are currently available to research scientists, giving them access to tens of millions of participants from around the world.

The proliferation of these online resources brings with it many questions and concerns. How good is the data quality of online studies? Are the data representative? What is the best way to recruit hard-to-reach samples? Can participants be trusted to provide accurate information about themselves? When should one platform be preferred over another? What ethical issues are unique to the online environment? On top of all of that, sometimes just getting started with a new technological tool can seem daunting and raises additional questions.

This book aims to answer these questions. It aims to be a resource for both the beginner and the seasoned online researcher. For beginners, this book contains multiple illustrated step-by-step guides for how to get started with online research on Mechanical Turk. This basic material is presented in the first four chapters. The first chapter provides a historical overview of online platforms, focusing on Mechanical Turk and market research panels. Chapter 2 provides an overview of concepts that are unique to Mechanical Turk and describes the Mechanical Turk culture and ecosystem. Chapter 3 provides an introductory discussion of stimulus development platforms, shows how to set up a study on Mechanical Turk, and discusses best methodological practices for study setup. Chapter 4 provides a conceptual introduction to the Mechanical Turk application programming interface (API), discusses several third-party apps that make Mechanical Turk research more effective, and describes several features of the CloudResearch (formerly Turk-Prime) app. These chapters also contain much advice about best practices that even experienced researchers will find helpful.

Later chapters address many topics that are critical for getting the most from online research. Chapter 5 deals with issues of data quality on online platforms. Chapter 6 describes the demographic composition of Mechanical Turk, including the size of the MTurk population. Chapter 7 discusses issues of sampling, focusing on standard practices, the bias that such practices engender, and ways to avoid such bias. Chapter 8 discusses the representativeness of data collected on Mechanical Turk and other convenience samples. Chapter 9 describes best practices for conducting longitudinal research, and Chapter 10 provides an overview of market research platforms and discusses the advantages and disadvantages of using Mechanical Turk over other platforms. Finally, Chapter 11 discusses the ethics of conducting research on Mechanical Turk and other online platforms.

Many topics in this book—including demographics, sampling, and ethics—are informed by the CloudResearch database, which consists of hundreds of thousands of participants and tens of millions of completed assignments. This database provides many insights about Mechanical Turk participants, who they are, how they have been changing over time, and how they work.

Finally, this book is associated with a companion website, where many of the how-to guides will be continually updated to keep up with the changes inevitable on all online platforms. You can access supplementary resources for Amazon Mechanical Turk, CloudResearch, and Qualtrics at https://www.cloudresearch.com/resources/book/.

REFERENCES

Peterson, R. A. (2001). On the use of college students in social science research: Insights from a second-order meta-analysis. *Journal of Consumer Research, 28*(3), 450–461.

Sears, D. O. (1986). College sophomores in the laboratory: Influences of a narrow data base on social psychology's view of human nature. *Journal of Personality and Social Psychology, 51*(3), 515.

ACKNOWLEDGMENTS

There are many people to thank for making this book possible. We both would like to thank several colleagues who created many of the datasets and database systems referenced in this book. Tzvi Abberbock helped build the CloudResearch system as a whole and also designed many of its databases. Yisroel Peikes carefully crafted and optimized many of the database queries that generated much of the data discussed throughout this book. Their contributions are greatly appreciated. We would like to thank Cheskie Rosenzweig, whose research on data quality of online samples has been instrumental in informing our thinking going back to 2011. We would like to thank Tommy Roggina and Tova Borowski for editorial comments on the manuscript and Aaron Moss and Zohn Rosen for significant input on several of the book's chapters.

We would particularly like to thank Fred Conrad for reviewing Chapter 8 and providing extremely helpful feedback and suggestions. We would like to thank SAGE and acquisitions editor Leah Fargotstein for her tremendous patience as this book was developed over several years. We would also like to thank all the reviewers for their invaluable comments and suggestions:

- Alice M. Brawley, Gettysburg College
- Krista Casler, Franklin & Marshall College
- Joshua R. de Leeuw, Vassar College
- Susan Fant, The University of Alabama
- Azriel Grysman, Hamilton College
- David J. Hauser, University of Michigan
- See-Yeon Hwang, Sam Houston State University
- Philip Lemaster, Concordia College
- Kevin Munger, New York University
- Casey B. Nixon, USAA
- Michaela Porubanova, Farmingdale College
- Stian Riemers, City University London

—J.R. & L.L.

My PhD adviser, Robert Goldberg, has been a shining example of what it means to be a scientist, researcher, academic, and, most of all, friend. Through the many phases of my dissertation and defense he was always there to challenge, support, and bring out the best in me.

My parents, Dr. Myron and Esther Robinson, continue to be sources of inspiration and sage advice in navigating the complexities of life and relationships. From the very beginning, they have been the finest of role models and have helped me cultivate my capacity to be persistent and see my projects through to their bright conclusions. I thank them for always offering all they have to help me succeed!

My deepest appreciation goes to my wife, Rivka. She has truly been my "better half" for over 20 years of marriage and raising our six beautiful children. Thank you, Rivka, for being with me and offering your guidance and a listening ear, and for being the best life partner I could ever have.

—J.R.

Many thanks to Arthur Reber, from undergraduate to graduate advisor, to colleague, friend and sparring partner. Thank you for over twenty years of mentorship and support and for being the first to help me find my spark and passion for psychology. I still have my mid-term from our History of Psychology class where you wrote a note asking me to join your lab—you have believed in and challenged me since then. To my postdoctoral advisor Lila Davachi, thank you for giving me the opportunity to learn new tools and expand my thinking. Thank you to my parents for their support. To my lifelong friend Mark Zelcer, thank you for the countless New York City coffee shop discussions spanning thirty years. To my girls Bella and Rebecca, thank you for reminding me what really matters and how to love boundlessly. And most of all, thank you Sarah, for your unwavering love and support over all these years. Without you this book would not be possible.

—L.L.

ABOUT THE AUTHORS

Leib Litman received a PhD in experimental psychology from the City University of New York. His early research was in the area of implicit learning, focusing on the relationship between conscious and unconscious information processing. After receiving his PhD, he was a postdoctoral fellow and research scientist in cognitive neuroscience at New York University, where he studied episodic memory using fMRI. Leib's current methodological research interests are in the area of online data collection, especially in the application of online data collection tools to complex research designs, such as dyadic studies, experience sampling, intensive longitudinal designs, qualitative video and focus group interviews, and global data collection.

Leib is currently an associate professor of psychology at Lander College in Queens, New York, and director of research at CloudResearch.com (formerly TurkPrime). Leib lives in Riverdale, New York, with his wife, Sarah, and their two girls, Bella and Rebecca.

Jonathan Robinson has been creating software since he was 12 and started his first software company with a few high school friends at age 15. He continued to develop his software skills and apply his expertise to more complex problems as he completed his BA at Queens College, and his MS and PhD with a dissertation in the field of robotic vision and digital curve fitting while at the City University of New York. Jonathan conceived of using Amazon's Mechanical Turk for participants before there was public academic discussion of its application to research. He designed and implemented the core CloudResearch.com (previously TurkPrime) system together with his coauthor, Leib Litman. CloudResearch was the first cloud-based participant management system that successfully adapted Mechanical Turk for research by designing the features researchers need and managing the complexity that may get in the way of collecting high-quality data.

Jonathan is the co-CEO and chief technology officer of CloudResearch. He is also currently an associate professor and chair of computer science at Lander College, a division of Touro College. In that capacity, he mentors, inspires, and educates the next generation of software engineers and introduces them to his passion for melding cutting-edge technologies with solving real-world problems in the areas of academic and corporate research, digital image computation, approximation, and web application engineering.

ABOUT THE CONTRIBUTORS

Jesse Chandler is a survey researcher at Mathematica, where he works on measurement and data-quality projects related to health, disability, and education. He received his PhD in social psychology from the University of Michigan, where he worked under the supervision of Norbert Schwarz before completing a postdoc at the Woodrow Wilson School of Public and International Affairs at Princeton University. His methodological research interests include best practices in online survey methodology, with a particular interest in crowdsourcing platforms like Amazon Mechanical Turk.

Michael P. Hall received his PhD in social psychology from the University of Michigan, Ann Arbor. His graduate research focused on political information-seeking and moral judgments, with a focus on how contextual and situational factors affect political and moral judgments. In particular, Michael's work includes research on people's metacognitions about their own political beliefs; how people choose and appraise political information in dyadic relationships; how moral factors influence political judgments in presidential voting decisions; situational factors in judgments of performance-enhancing behavior; and how context influences attitudes about climate change. Michael currently lives in Washington, DC, with his partner and works as a consultant with the Boston Consulting Group.

David J. Hauser is an assistant professor of personality–social psychology at Queen's University in Kingston, Ontario. He received his PhD in social psychology from the University of Michigan in 2017 and completed a postdoctoral research associateship at the University of Southern California in 2018. He is also an op-ed contributor for *The Guardian* and segment contributor for NPR's *On the Media* podcast. Dave's research focuses on how seemingly minor aspects of communication impact reasoning and behavior. For instance, his work has examined the impact of word collocations and semantic prosody on inferences of word meaning and has uncovered several unintended effects of battle metaphors for cancer on health beliefs.

Neil A. Lewis Jr. is assistant professor of communication and social behavior at Cornell University and assistant professor of communication research in medicine at Weill Cornell Medical College. His content area research examines how people's social contexts and identities influence their motivation to pursue their goals, and their success in goal-pursuit efforts. He studies these processes most often in the domains of education, health, and environmental sustainability, in the hope that the knowledge generated from his research can provide useful insights for developing interventions to help people achieve their education, health, and sustainability-related goals. His methodological research focuses on meta-scientific issues surrounding the (lack of) diversity in samples and settings in social scientific research and the implications of those issues for both theory and practice. Neil earned his BA in economics and psychology at Cornell University and his MS and PhD in social psychology at the University of Michigan.

Gabriele Paolacci is an associate professor of marketing at Rotterdam School of Management (RSM), Erasmus University. He joined RSM after graduate studies at Ca' Foscari University of Venice (where he got his PhD) and at Ross School of Business, University of Michigan (where he was a visiting scholar). Gabriele's research investigates substantive and methodological questions in behavioral research. Within the substantive domain, he conducts research in the field of consumer judgment and decision-making. In particular, he studies how people's decisions seemingly contradict the assumptions and prescriptions of rational choice theory. He also conducts empirical research on the practice of online data collection in the behavioral sciences. He has investigated whether crowdsourced samples (e.g., Mechanical Turk workers) provide data of high quality, and how to attenuate their distinctive threats to experimental validity (e.g., nonnaive participants, study impostors).

Cheskie Rosenzweig is completing his PhD in clinical psychology at Columbia University. He recently completed his internship at the Cambridge Health Alliance while a clinical fellow at Harvard Medical School. Cheskie is now writing his dissertation on the underlying impact of approach-avoidance motivation on negativity bias as it relates to psychological distress. He also continues to investigate how different methodological choices in online data collection affect data quality, generalizability, and representativeness. In his clinical work, Cheskie has experience working with a diverse group of people struggling with mood and personality-related difficulties, as well as patients with severe and persistent mental illness.

INTRODUCTION

Leib Litman and Jonathan Robinson

A SCIENTIFIC REVOLUTION IN THE MAKING

Research in the social and behavioral sciences is undergoing a profound transformation that is nothing short of a revolution. This revolution consists of an explosion in online participant recruitment practices as well as a proliferation of resources for creating methodologically diverse studies and disseminating them online. Online research makes it possible to study human behavior in exciting and novel ways, at scales not possible in more traditional research settings. The applications of online technologies are limited only by the imagination of the researchers who use them.

At the heart of the web-based research revolution is Amazon's Mechanical Turk (MTurk)[1]. The MTurk platform gives social and behavioral scientists real-time access to thousands of participants from all over the United States and other countries. In traditional laboratory settings, collecting data from 500 participants can take months. On Mechanical Turk, a researcher can launch a study requiring 500 participants, go to lunch, and come back to find a complete dataset that is ready to be downloaded and analyzed.

Mechanical Turk is, however, more than just a way to quickly collect survey responses. MTurk workers write essays for open-ended qualitative research (Schnur, Dillon, Goldsmith, & Montgomery, 2018), grant access to personal data such as from their Fitbits (Brinton, Keating, Ortiz, Evenson, & Furberg, 2017) and Twitter accounts (Braithwaite, Giraud-Carrier, West, Barnes, & Hanson, 2016), allow researchers to study infants by video (Tran, Cabral, Patel, & Cusack, 2017), and engage with other participants in interactive games and group-based social experiments

---

[1] Note: Amazon Mechanical Turk is a registered trademark of Amazon.com, Inc.

(Arechar, Gächter, & Molleman, 2017). MTurk workers also participate in longitudinal studies, including studies that require intensive, daily tracking (Boynton & Richman, 2014). The limits of what is methodologically possible on Mechanical Turk have by no means been fully explored.

The popularity of Mechanical Turk among social and behavioral scientists began skyrocketing in 2011 following the publication of a seminal paper by Buhrmester, Kwang, and Gosling (2011), which showed that high-quality data can be collected on Mechanical Turk quickly and inexpensively. Since then, thousands of published studies have used Mechanical Turk to recruit participants. But interest in online research among scientists began long before 2011. To understand what led to the meteoric rise in the scientific community's adoption of Mechanical Turk, it is helpful to trace the history of online research to its very beginnings. In this chapter, we describe the range of tools that were available to researchers prior to Mechanical Turk and highlight how the limitations of those tools made Mechanical Turk the right platform at the right time for social and behavioral science.

A BRIEF HISTORY OF ONLINE RESEARCH IN THE SOCIAL AND BEHAVIORAL SCIENCES: FROM HTML 2.0 TO MECHANICAL TURK

Research in the social and behavioral sciences is currently shifting from traditional lab-based practices to the web at an ever-increasing pace. But enthusiasm for the opportunities that online research has to offer is nothing new. As early as 2000, researchers were talking about the potential of online research, writing that "the web presents researchers with an unprecedented opportunity to conduct experiments with participants from all over the world rather than with the usual student samples from their local universities. It thus has the potential to serve as an alternative or supplemental source of subjects and research environments for traditional psychological investigations" (Birnbaum & Reips, 2000). Indeed, even before the existence of the World Wide Web, scientists envisioned the vast potential that a global network of interconnected individuals would offer social and behavioral science (Kiesler & Sproull, 1986).

To understand why social scientists were interested in using the internet for research, it helps to consider the nature of human behavioral research. The social and behavioral sciences consist of a wide range of disciplines whose goals are to understand human cognition, behavior, personality, social interactions, health, and lifespan development. These disciplines include psychology, sociology, linguistics, marketing, business, economics, public health, behavioral medicine, and many others. Scientific progress across all of these disciplines depends on having access to human subjects who are willing to participate in research studies. However, gaining access to human participants is often challenging in traditional research settings. A lack of participants limits research opportunities and the speed with which research projects can be completed. For these reasons, scientists have always sought novel venues that offer access to a diverse population of research participants, provided that such venues do not compromise the quality and validity of collected data.

It is not surprising, then, that when the internet started being widely used in the early 1990s, interest in leveraging the web for participant recruitment in scientific studies developed almost immediately. Researchers quickly realized that the web offers access to countless people around the world who may be interested in participating in research studies.

Although the World Wide Web was introduced to the world in 1990, up until 1995 internet browsers were implemented using what is now referred to as HTML 1.0. At that time, web pages were static and did not allow users to interact with the page. Starting in 1995, "fill-out forms" provided the substrate on which online survey software was constructed. Fill-out forms allowed users to enter information on a web page and send that information over the internet. With the introduction of forms, it became possible for the first time to conduct rudimentary online research studies, such as online surveys.

The subsequent introduction of Java and JavaScript provided researchers with additional flexibility to control stimuli over the internet. With JavaScript, researchers were able to randomly assign subjects to different experimental conditions, control the order of stimulus presentation using conditional logic, and create studies that were more sophisticated than simple surveys. With these tools in hand, it did not take long for researchers to start using the web to conduct research studies. As early as 1995, the web was being used for classroom experiments and educational demonstrations in psychoacoustics (Welch & Krantz, 1996). The first published paper using online research participants appeared in *Behavior Research Methods* in 1997 (Smith & Leigh, 1997). Laying out the specifics of this study will highlight the advantages and the limitations of online research at the time, and show how online research has evolved since then.

What the First Online Study Demonstrated About the Benefits of Web-Based Participant Recruitment

The first paper published using online research participants was positioned at the intersection between health psychology and social psychology and addressed the topic of eating disorders. In the 1990s, the rate of eating disorders was on the rise, especially among women. Sociocultural theories suggested this was due, in part, to the influence of the media, which portrayed an ideal of beauty and thinness that is unattainable for most people. The messages portrayed by the media are important because women and men who internalize the ideal of thinness portrayed in magazines and movies are at a higher risk of developing eating disorders. To gain insight into this phenomenon, Smith and Leigh (1997) sought to better understand how the ideal female form is perceived and, in particular, how the perception of female beauty may differ across age groups. The challenge they faced, however, was recruiting participants to study psychological phenomena across the lifespan.

Limitations of the Undergraduate Subject Pool

Although thin ideal internalization had been studied extensively in prior research, the majority of those studies were conducted on college samples using what are referred to as university subject pools. These subject pools typically consist of undergraduate students who participate in research studies either to fulfill a course requirement or for extra credit. Although such undergraduate subject pools provide university faculty with easy access to research participants, they also have many drawbacks that have been discussed extensively in the scientific literature (Gosling & Johnson, 2010). Laboratory-based research with subject pool participants involves scheduling appointments and requires research staff to conduct one-on-one sessions with students. This process is labor intensive and is often time consuming. Another drawback is availability. Commonly, few people are available in the summer and during vacations. Perhaps the most important limitations are methodological. Studies using undergraduate participants are limited by the demographics of the undergraduate population at the institution where the research is taking place (Gosling, Sandy, John, & Potter, 2010; Henrich, Heine, & Norenzayan, 2010). This is especially true for finding older participants, as the average age of undergraduate subject pool participants is approximately 23 years (Gosling, Vazire, Srivastava, & John, 2004).

Therefore, a key motivation of Smith and Leigh (1997) for conducting the study online was to expand the age range of participants so as to examine whether the perception of female beauty remains constant with age. A second motivation was to examine whether any differences in the results would emerge between the online sample and the subject pool sample. An obvious concern with conducting online research is that researchers lose control over several aspects of the study that may affect participants' experience and attentiveness. As the first research study conducted online, this study sought to examine how the quality of online samples compares to a more well-established approach.

Conducting the First Online Study

The stimuli for the study consisted of black-and-white drawings that varied in the hip-to-bust ratio. Color images could not be accommodated by most monitors at the time and so were not used. Each image was rated by participants on how attractive it appeared. Participants were not recruited from any particular platform, as participant recruitment platforms did not exist. Instead, the researchers hoped that random people surfing the web would come across the study and be intrigued enough to spend 10 minutes or so completing the task.

The data collection was slow. Only around 25 people per day initiated the study. Of those who started, more than 70% dropped out. Nevertheless, after a few months the authors collected data from more than 550 participants. Comparing the web-based and college samples revealed a remarkable similarity in the results among younger participants. Most important, the online study found a systematic difference between the way in which older and younger people perceived the attractiveness of the female form. Younger participants tended to find the thinner images more attractive than did older participants. The spectrum of attractiveness ratings was shifted toward the heavier figures for the older participants, who found the heavier body types more attractive. These findings raised the intriguing possibility that younger individuals are more susceptible to beauty ideals presented by the media, or perhaps that older individuals prefer heavier body types.

This initial study demonstrated two key principles of online data collection. First, the quality of data collected online could be comparable to the data collected in more traditional research settings. Second, the demographic diversity of online samples could open significant opportunities to pursue novel research questions in a way that would be less time consuming and expensive than more traditional methods.

It was of course possible to claim, as many did (see, for example, Gosling et al., 2004), that such clean results may not be obtained for other types of online studies. A major concern was that participating in a study in an unregulated environment, as opposed to a laboratory, would increase distractibility, which would surely invalidate the results of studies that required sustained attention. Furthermore, the initial study did not reveal whether online participants could be relied on to carefully read instructions or long questionnaires, participate in tiring or tedious tasks, or complete reaction-time tasks. But this initial study did show that it was possible to collect high-quality data online, at least in some circumstances.

At the same time, this initial study demonstrated many of the limitations of online research. Data collection was generally slow, and the dropout rate was high. Significant technical limitations inhibited the range of stimuli that could be reliably presented online. Finally, significant expertise was required to program and implement the study. Indeed, within a few years, multiple books would be published describing the programming necessary to create online studies because the initial technological hurdles were steep (Birnbaum, 2004; Fraley, 2004; Hewson, 2003). Despite these challenges, this pioneering study established the feasibility of collecting data online and highlighted a key advantage of the demographic diversity of online samples—thus launching a new era in online data collection methodology.

The Emergence of Large-Scale Online Projects

Starting in 1997, the number and scale of online studies in the social and behavioral sciences rose dramatically (see Krantz & Dalal, 2000). In 1998, Mahzarin Banaji and her colleagues initiated an online data collection project called Project Implicit (Nosek, Banaji, & Greenwald, 2002). This project examined implicit prejudice by allowing online participants to complete a short version of the Implicit Association Test (IAT). Project Implicit dwarfed previous online studies in its scope, collecting an average of more than 1,000 responses per day. Within the project's initial year and a half, more than 600,000 responses were collected. And more than two and a half million responses were collected over a five-year period. An important methodological advancement of Project Implicit was that implicit prejudice was measured by reaction time.

In the most popular version of the IAT task, positive words like *good* and *happy* are sometimes presented with White faces or stereotypically White names, and at other times with Black faces or stereotypically Black names. On other trials, negative words like *bad* and *evil* are shown together with either White or Black faces. Participants are asked to press a key with their left index finger as fast as they can if the word is positive and with their right index finger if the word is negative. Implicit prejudice is revealed when responses to positive words are faster when those words are paired with White faces than if those same words are paired with Black faces. What was methodologically critical here is that in order to detect these minor differences in reaction times subjects had to be highly attentive and carefully follow instructions. Prior to Project Implicit many researchers assumed that a controlled laboratory environment was necessary to detect such reaction-time differences.

Like the Smith and Leigh (1997) study, access to demographically diverse samples allowed Project Implicit to examine implicit prejudice among groups that are difficult to access in traditional research settings. Due to the scale and diversity of the sample, Project Implicit was able to establish that implicit prejudice exists among all age groups, all ethnic groups, all political parties, and all education levels. At the same time, the data revealed that social group membership moderates both implicit and explicit prejudice in important ways. Implicit prejudice toward African Americans was higher among Whites compared to Blacks. The implicit prejudice effect was significantly higher for participants over age 50 than it was for younger people. Thus, a widely diverse group of participants provided unprecedented opportunities to examine group differences as moderators of implicit and explicit prejudice and with a sample size that could not be imagined with traditional lab-based approaches.

At the same time Project Implicit launched, large-scale studies in personality psychology began to be conducted online. Gosling and his colleagues (Gosling et al., 2004) collected a dataset of more than 350,000 participants who filled out the Big Five inventory. Because large extant lab-based datasets of the Big Five were available, it was possible to examine the data quality of online surveys with a high level of fidelity. Gosling and colleagues examined the internal reliabilities and correlation patterns among the five major personality traits in comparison to published datasets. Additionally, they conducted the first systematic examination of the diversity of internet samples relative to samples that were published in the *Journal of Personality and Social Psychology*, one of the most prestigious psychology journals.

In terms of diversity, Gosling et al.'s findings reinforced results previously presented by Nosek et al. (2002) and Smith and Leigh (1997), demonstrating that online samples were considerably more diverse across all demographic variables compared to samples of college students. In addition, they found that internal reliabilities of all personality dimensions were within a few decimal points of published norms, and that convergent and discriminant validity of all of the personality measures were consistent with published data.

Together, these early studies spoke to the concern among researchers that the quality of data collected online and outside of a well-controlled laboratory setting could not be trusted. The data from reaction-time tasks and the internal reliabilities of surveys were similar in quality to more traditional lab-based studies. Combined with the opportunities that diverse online datasets had to offer, by the early 2000s the web was beginning to look more and more appealing as a place to conduct research in the social and behavioral sciences.

THE USE OF ONLINE SAMPLES IN APPLIED BEHAVIORAL RESEARCH

As the popularity of online data collection was increasing within basic social science, web-based data collection methods were also being adopted in applied areas of behavioral science such as market research. Market research helps organizations better understand the needs of customers by collecting data about customers' opinions, their experiences and satisfaction with products, and the effectiveness of advertising messages. For example, Volvo conducted a study of female drivers living in California to help with the development of a new Volvo model (Parasuraman, Grewal, & Krishnan, 2006).

Before the market research industry began using online data collection methods, respondents were typically contacted by mail, by phone, or in face-to-face interviews and focus groups (Evans & Mathur, 2005; Schibrowsky, Peltier, & Nill, 2007). These practices were inefficient, time consuming, and costly. As a result, much like their academic counterparts, market researchers began looking at the web to streamline finding and collecting data from research participants.

Market research differs from basic research in the social and behavioral sciences in a number of critical ways. First, because market research is integrated with commerce, it is a better-funded industry. In 2015, market research generated $21 billion in revenue (Rivera, 2015). In the early days of online research, these considerable financial resources were used to develop a robust infrastructure for recruiting online participants for this industry. A second way market research differs from academic research is that market researchers are often interested in specific market segments. In the Volvo study, for example, the specific market segment was women living in California who drive regularly. In other studies the market segment might be people who shop at Walmart or people who take cruise ship vacations at least once per year. Although general population studies are also common in market research, without the ability to break the market into specific segments, much of market research would not be feasible. Therefore, in addition to the need to reach a large and diverse online participant population, which market research shared in common with research in the social and behavioral sciences, there was a need to develop the tools to sample specific groups.

To meet the tremendous demand of market research companies, dozens of sample suppliers such as Survey Sampling International (now known as Dynata) and Survey-Monkey emerged to provide participants and robust web-based solutions. Using these platforms, companies conducting market research could request a sample with a thousand participants that are matched to the U.S. Census in terms of age, gender, and ethnicity, and who have specific shopping profiles. Companies that specialize in recruiting such participants for market research studies are known as panel providers or online access panels (Baker et al., 2010; Comley & Beaumont, 2011).

Panel providers often use two approaches to reach online participants. First, there are opt-in panels, which are made up of people who have agreed to be contacted for online research studies. Once people express an interest in being part of an opt-in panel, they are profiled by being asked to provide demographic information and to answer questions about their background, interests, and preferences. Panel companies use this information to make individuals of interest available for specific market research studies. The second commonly used approach is called river sampling. In river samples, respondents are recruited as they surf the web (Baker et al., 2010). Individuals might see an advertisement to participate in a survey when they are playing a video game or shopping. In both opt-in panels and river samples, participants are given incentives to take surveys, for example, by being given the opportunity to earn cash or rewards points, and via sweepstakes, as we discuss in more detail in Chapter 10.

In addition to creating large online panels with tens of millions of participants, panel providers developed a robust infrastructure for research. Specifically, panel providers developed the technology to recruit and compensate participants, to target participants within specific geographic locations, and to protect the integrity of the data collection process.

At about the same time as the creation of online panels, there was a parallel explosion in the tools available for conducting online market research. Survey platforms such as Qualtrics and SurveyMonkey were created to make it easy to design and implement methodologically sophisticated research studies. In addition, numerous platforms emerged with specialized tools to accommodate different types of stimuli. At G2 Analytics, for example, researchers can employ technology that allows them to conduct studies where respondents watch videos such as political speeches or advertisements and respond any time they see or hear something they like or dislike. Such tools allow for real-time, in-depth assessment of video content.

By 2005, dozens of market research panel companies were providing access to millions of participants around the world. Driven by the need to reach specific market segments, hundreds of companies began specializing in recruiting specific populations. For example, some companies focused on recruiting Latino participants and others focused on recruiting participants in Asia. Eventually, companies started specializing in recruiting participants from social networks like Facebook, and through mobile technology (Poynter, Williams, & York, 2014). After 2005, many companies began to collaborate with one another in an attempt to meet the increasing demand for sampling hard-to-reach groups. Companies realized quickly that, alone, they could not meet the demand of many market research studies, especially if those studies targeted rare and difficult-to-access groups. Collectively, however, panel providers could find nearly any group of participants and, as a result, many companies either merged or developed partnerships to increase their overall reach. Currently, panel providers typically work closely with multiple industry partners. If any one sample provider cannot meet the demands of a study, it reaches out to its partners to increase the likelihood of meeting the required quota.

While the market research industry developed on its own for a time, beginning in 2010 there existed two communities that increasingly sought access to online research participants: academic researchers in the social and behavioral sciences and applied researchers in market research and related fields. At that time, online academic research was in its infancy—enough online research had been conducted to demonstrate the vast potential of web-based recruitment, but virtually no infrastructure existed to support this field. Academic researchers interested in conducting online studies had no specific platform they could use to recruit online participants. Instead, researchers had to post studies on their own websites or various online forums in hopes of attracting enough interested participants. Significant expertise was required to ensure that participants were not completing the study multiple times and that the dataset was not corrupted by unscrupulous respondents. Beyond the ability to conduct a simple one-time study, no infrastructure existed for longitudinal follow-up or for recruiting participants within specific population segments. In short, social and behavioral scientists interested in conducting online studies had virtually no resources at their disposal, had to have significant programming expertise, and had to improvise ways of recruiting participants for each study.

At the same time, the infrastructure for conducting web-based market research was at a significantly more advanced stage of development. Sophisticated technological solutions were in place to manage the recruitment process. A market researcher wanting to conduct an online study had numerous online sample suppliers to choose from to recruit general population samples, or samples based on specific targeting criteria. These platforms had built-in protections against fraud, and sophisticated technology was available to conduct methodologically complex studies.

At first glance, online market research providers would seem to be a perfect recruiting tool that academics should have turned to for meeting their participant recruitment needs. However, panel companies had little penetration into the academic research space. The primary reason for this was cost. Many academic studies are not well funded and could not afford access to online research panels. For this reason, even though significant resources were available for online recruitment of participants through online panels, little research in social and behavioral sciences was conducted using these panels.

In summary, multiple barriers prevented research in the social and behavioral sciences from being conducted online on a large scale. This set the stage for the emergence of Amazon Mechanical Turk.

AMAZON MECHANICAL TURK

Amazon's Mechanical Turk was created in 2005. With Mechanical Turk, Amazon sought to create a platform on which people could solve problems that did not have automated computer-based solutions. The term *Mechanical Turk* is based on an 18th-century chess machine that started to travel the world in 1770 and exhilarated crowds by outplaying many of the top chess players of that time. Among the more illustrious opponents of the Mechanical Turk were Benjamin Franklin and Napoleon Bonaparte, both of whom were beaten by the machine, and the world's then top chess player, Philidor, who beat the Turk though not without significant effort.

Unbeknownst to anyone at the time, inside the machine sat a chess master who used a magnet to move the pieces. The human player was concealed by an ingenious set of moving contraptions that may go down in history as the greatest magic act of all time. In almost 100 years of exhibitions around Europe, no one figured out the trick. Only after a fire tragically destroyed the machine in 1854 did its owner reveal the secret. In hindsight it is now obvious that in the 1800s no machine could have been sophisticated enough to play chess, much less to pose a challenge to great players like Philidor. Indeed, it was not until Deep Blue beat Gary Kasparov in 1997 that chess programs were able to pose a serious threat to the world's top players.

The Mechanical Turk chess machine demonstrated a principle that is at the heart of Amazon's MTurk platform: Certain tasks are better done by people than by machines. Although the ability of machines to conduct complex tasks is dramatically more advanced today than it was in 1800, the principle that people are able to do many things that computers can't is as true now as it was back then. For this reason, tasks that are conducted on Mechanical Turk are called Human Intelligence Tasks, or HITs for short. This name highlights that the problems being worked on through Mechanical Turk require the kind of human intelligence that machines do not yet possess. Often, using people is simply more efficient even when the task can be accomplished by machines. Increasingly, human input via Mechanical Turk is being used to train neural networks and is used for tasks in which humans and machines solve problems synergistically.

Workers and Requesters

The MTurk platform has two types of actors: workers and requesters. Typical tasks that workers do on Mechanical Turk are transcriptions of audio files, identification of objects in visual images, and categorization tasks. HITs may ask workers to review a website's usability and functionality, or to download an app and provide feedback about the user experience. Within a few years, Mechanical Turk reported 500,000 registered workers all over the globe on its platform. Thousands of HITs were available for these workers to choose from at any one time.

Mechanical Turk has some aspects in common with other platforms that recruit people online to perform research studies for monetary compensation, such as those run by market research panel providers. There are also fundamental differences. At its core Mechanical Turk is a platform that connects people who are willing to do work for monetary rewards with people who need that work done. The two key differences between Mechanical Turk and the market research platforms that preceded it are that monetary compensation on Mechanical Turk is set by market forces on the requester-worker exchange and that Mechanical Turk hosts a much wider range of tasks than traditional market research platforms.

Mechanical Turk as an Exchange

As an exchange, Mechanical Turk is a marketplace where wages are driven by market forces. Requesters set prices for how much they want to pay workers for any given HIT, and workers are free to choose whether to work on those HITs or not. Mechanical Turk charges the requester a standard transaction fee for each HIT when that requester agrees that the HIT was completed properly. When Mechanical Turk was launched in 2005, the transaction fee was 10%, but that fee was increased in 2015 to 20% or 40% depending on the task.

The MTurk exchange operates in stark contrast to other platforms where monetary compensation for participants is set not by the requester but by the platform itself. On Mechanical Turk it is possible to conduct a study where participants are paid $0.10 or even less for a HIT (Buhrmester et al., 2011; Litman, Robinson, & Rosenzweig, 2015). Although it is not common practice to pay participants so little, it is in principle possible to conduct a study that costs orders of magnitude less than it would on other platforms. For example, on SurveyMonkey, participants who complete a five-minute task are typically given a reimbursement of $0.50 donated to their charity of choice. SurveyMonkey typically charges the researcher $5 for each participant, thus adding a $4.50 transaction fee. A study with 500 participants could cost $2,500 on Survey-Monkey. On Mechanical Turk, by contrast, a five-minute study can be conducted paying each participant $0.10, which means that with 500 participants, the study can be completed for $50 (or 1/50th the cost). Even when participants are paid $1 for a five-minute study—a rate of $12 per hour—the price for the study would total $600 including MTurk fees. Interestingly, when conducted on Mechanical Turk, this study is not only cheaper for the researcher but also provides a higher level of compensation to the participant. (See Chapter 11 for data on compensation rates and a discussion of ethics concerning pay.) The difference in price between Mechanical Turk and its alternatives is dramatic.

Reputation Mechanism and Data Quality

Because Mechanical Turk was created to provide solutions for technically challenging tasks, it did not originally focus on profiling its workers. After all, it doesn't matter whether workers categorize images in Los Angeles or in New York City, or whether they are 20 or 50 years old. For such projects all that matters is that the images are categorized correctly. Thus, rather than creating an infrastructure for selectively targeting specific groups, Mechanical Turk focused on mechanisms for ensuring data quality. Key among these mechanisms was a reputation system that allowed requesters to select workers based on their experience and past performance. Unlike other online panel providers, MTurk's reputation system was unique and eventually became so successful that workers became hyperattentive to task demands for fear of damaging their reputation.

The Right Platform at the Right Time for Academic Research

Mechanical Turk emerged as a platform on which many thousands of workers were available to complete tasks at a high level of quality, but where the demographic characteristics and geographic locations of those workers could not be controlled (this functionality would be added in 2016). For this reason, Mechanical Turk initially had limited use for most market researchers. For researchers in the social and behavioral sciences, however, Mechanical Turk provided the solutions they were seeking. The limited ability to selectively target participants was not a major barrier because most studies in the social and behavioral sciences were being conducted using university subject pools anyway, and those pools generally lacked the ability to target specific populations. For social and behavioral scientists, general population studies were the norm.

Because the price of transactions was significantly lower on Mechanical Turk than on other platforms, accessing online participants was now affordable in the academic community. The built-in reputation mechanism helped maintain data quality, as did the built-in mechanisms for preventing duplicate workers. And, because a payment mechanism was built into the system, participants could be paid seamlessly. Mechanical Turk eliminated the need for academic researchers to develop the technological expertise to host their own websites for data collection and the time needed to search internet forums in hopes of finding enough people to participate in their studies. With Mechanical Turk, social and behavioral researchers finally had access to a platform that could be used to recruit online participants easily, quickly, and affordably.

But numerous questions needed to be answered before the platform would be adopted by the research community. The most important question was whether data collected on Mechanical Turk would meet the rigorous standards of quality required for scientific research. Many rightly wondered, is it realistic to expect high data quality from studies conducted on a platform where workers usually make less than a dollar to participate? In addition, in the early days of MTurk it was unclear what tasks researchers could realistically expect workers to perform—it is one thing to expect workers to stay attentive for 5 minutes, but it's another to expect them to carefully attend to task demands for 30 minutes or more. Was research on Mechanical Turk limited to studies that ask only survey questions, or could more sophisticated studies like reaction-time tasks also be conducted?

These questions were addressed in multiple early studies (e.g., Berinsky, Huber, & Lenz, 2012; Buhrmester et al., 2011; Goodman, Cryder, & Cheema, 2013; Horton, Rand, & Zeckhauser, 2011; Paolacci, Chandler, & Ipeirotis, 2010). In particular, Gosling and colleagues had been conducting research in personality psychology for over a decade using both online and subject pool participants (e.g., Gosling, Rentfrow, & Swann, 2003; Robins, Tracy, Trzesniewski, Potter, & Gosling, 2001). They thus had large data-sets against which the performance of MTurk workers could be compared. Their deep experience with online research in the decade preceding the launch of Mechanical Turk perfectly positioned them to explore how data quality on Mechanical Turk stacked up against other online forums and more traditional laboratory settings.

The First Explorations of Data Quality on Mechanical Turk

One of the very first questions researchers addressed when assessing the utility of Mechanical Turk for academic research was whether participants who were paid little money could be relied on to provide high-quality data for survey tasks. Buhrmester et al. (2011) used the Big Five inventory to examine whether MTurk workers attentively fill out surveys. Focusing on the unique capability of Mechanical Turk to set any price for a study, they examined how different levels of monetary compensation affected data quality. Four monetary compensation conditions were used: $0.02, $0.05, $0.10, and $0.50. Participants in all four conditions were asked to fill out the Big Five personality inventory as well as multiple other surveys. Additionally, the number of survey instruments was changed across conditions to vary the length of the survey. In some conditions the study included many surveys and on average took 30 minutes to complete. Other conditions had fewer survey instruments and took just five minutes to complete. The goal of the study was to gain insight into the relationships among survey length, monetary compensation, and data quality.

Intuitively, one might expect the data quality from lower paying HITs to be worse than HITs that pay more. One might also expect data quality to be worse in longer HITs than shorter HITs, especially when the longer HITs do not pay well.

Surprisingly, however, data quality was consistently high across all conditions and remained the same whether participants were paid $0.02 or $0.50 and whether the study took 5 minutes or 30 minutes to complete (Buhrmester et al., 2011). The alpha reliability coefficients for every one of the Big Five personality dimensions was within a few decimal points of the reliabilities that had been reported both in previous online studies and in studies using undergraduate samples. Thus, this initial study showed that the data quality of surveys on Mechanical Turk was as good as the data quality using more traditional methods, including undergraduate and online samples, and was independent of task length and payment.

At the same time that Buhrmester et al. (2011) were conducting their research, the present authors were conducting similar studies to examine the quality of data collected on Mechanical Turk, some also using the Big Five (Litman et al., 2015). We found exactly the same pattern of results but under an extended range of payment conditions. We also used multiple data-quality screens within these studies, such as the squared discrepancy procedure, which examines the consistency with which workers respond to forward and reversed questions, and multiple attention manipulation checks (see Chapter 5). Our data-quality results were consistent with Buhrmester et al.'s findings and showed that whether participants were paid $0.02 or $1 had no impact on data quality.

Initially, these results seemed counterintuitive. How could paying $0.02 for a 30-minute task result in the same level of data quality as paying $1 for a 5-minute task? The answer to this question lies in Mechanical Turk's reputation mechanism. As both Buhrmester et al.'s (2011) and our data showed, the differences between the various payment and length conditions are revealed in the speed with which participants accepted and completed HITs. The longer and lower paying tasks took many days to recruit a sufficient number of participants. The shorter and better paying tasks, by contrast, were completed within minutes. Most workers were simply not willing to take HITs that did not pay well. However, because workers were careful to protect their reputation, they did not want to click through a task quickly just to receive a small monetary reward—and risk being rejected and having their reputation suffer. As a result, the majority of workers simply refused to work on those tasks, but those who did accept the task worked on it diligently. Chapter 7 provides an in-depth examination of the effect of pay rate on sample composition.

The key findings from these early studies revealed that Mechanical Turk's reputation mechanism is extremely successful at maintaining high levels of data quality on the platform, even when pay is relatively low. That is not to say monetary compensation does not play any role in data quality on Mechanical Turk. HITs that require high levels of creativity and effort are likely to be affected by pay rate. For example, as a later study conducted by researchers at the NYU Law School revealed, tasks that require high levels of creativity are significantly affected by monetary compensation in the form of bonuses (Buccafusco, Burns, Fromer, & Sprigman, 2014). Further, monetary compensation affects retention rates in longitudinal studies (see Chapter 10). Monetary compensation thus has important implications for ethics (see Chapter 11), sample composition (see Chapter 7), and data quality for demanding tasks such as open-ended responses. But in terms of workers meeting basic task demands, the Buhrmester et al. (2011) and Litman et al. (2015) data revealed that high-quality data can be attained quickly and at low cost for many types of tasks.

Collecting Reaction-Time Data on Mechanical Turk

As interest in Mechanical Turk grew, researchers began exploring the extent to which Mechanical Turk could be used as a valid source of data in a variety of areas within the social and behavioral sciences. During the initial stages of this vetting era, researchers asked many of the same questions about Mechanical Turk that were originally asked about web-based research (see Gosling et al., 2004). One central question was whether reaction-time data could be collected reliably over the internet. The collection of reaction-time data presents several challenges that are of specific interest to cognitive scientists. First, reaction-time data are collected at the millisecond (ms) level, and small differences between groups and/or conditions often lead to important findings. Second, there is considerable heterogeneity in the computers used by online participants, including differences in processor speeds, internet connectivity, and monitor refresh rates. Finally, there is little or no control over the experimental environment in which such studies are conducted. Due to instrument heterogeneity and a lack of experimenter control, there were real concerns about whether Mechanical Turk could accommodate studies that rely on reaction-time data recorded with millisecond precision. Because the collection of reaction time affects numerous research areas in the social and behavioral sciences, this question seemed particularly important to address.

Shortly after academic researchers began running studies on Mechanical Turk, one group of researchers examined the efficacy of running reaction-time studies by attempting to replicate several classic cognitive psychology experiments (Crump, McDonnell, & Gureckis, 2013). Across multiple studies, they demonstrated that stimuli can be presented with at least 80 ms presentation speed and that effect sizes of at least 20 ms can be reliably detected. This level of precision meets the requirements of the majority of reaction-time studies. These effects are much better than may have been expected given the technical demands and lack of experimenter control over the study settings on Mechanical Turk. Later studies showed that significantly faster presentation speeds and even finer levels of reaction-time resolution are also possible when using more specialized software (Barnhoorn, Haasnoot, Bocanegra, & van Steenbergen, 2015). The Crump et al. (2013) results showed that data quality for studies that rely on extremely fine levels of reaction-time measurement can be reliably attained on MTurk, leading to increasingly widespread adoption of Mechanical Turk for studies requiring reaction-time measures (for an overview, see Stewart, Chandler, & Paolacci, 2017).

Expanding the Range of What Is Possible on Mechanical Turk

Initially, research looking at data quality on Mechanical Turk showed that it held considerable promise for collecting high-quality data with studies that used both survey instruments and reaction-time measures as outcomes. There were, however, formidable challenges to running more complex social and behavioral research studies on Mechanical Turk. Even the most rudimentary requirements of behavioral research studies were difficult to implement. For example, researchers typically did not want participants from a first study to participate in subsequent studies, since the workers were now familiar with the study's protocols. But on Mechanical Turk it was extremely difficult to prevent workers from participating in a study based on their previously taken HITs. After all, as far as Mechanical Turk was concerned, if a worker was experienced at categorizing images, why wouldn't someone want that individual to do it again? Thus there was no easy mechanism put in place to flexibly manage participant recruitment. On the flip side, it was also difficult to conduct longitudinal studies. Recruiting participants from previous studies on Mechanical Turk was complex and required the management of what are called qualifications (see Chapters 3 and 4).

Various solutions were developed by the research community to solve these problems. Eventually, specialized third-party platforms such as psiTurk (Gureckis et al., 2016), TurkServer (Mao et al., 2012), and TurkPrime (now CloudResearch; Litman, Robinson, & Abberbock, 2017) were developed to help researchers navigate various intricacies of Mechanical Turk. With the robust capabilities of Mechanical Turk now augmented by third-party solutions, the use of Mechanical Turk among scientists exploded with unprecedented speed.

The rate of adoption of Mechanical Turk was dramatic. Within a few years following the publication of Buhrmester et al.'s (2011) seminal paper in the journal *Perspectives on Psychological Science*, the paper was cited more than 5,000 times. As of 2015, 40% of all research papers published in the *Journal of Personality and Social Psychology* had at least one study with MTurk workers (Zhou & Fishbach, 2016). Researchers quickly began to explore how Mechanical Turk could accommodate research in each of their specific subfields of the social and behavioral sciences. Within a short time, researchers from more than 30 different academic disciplines were routinely using Mechanical Turk for their research studies (Bohannon, 2016).

The scientific literature is replete with research questions explored using the MTurk participant pool. Table 1.1 lists some examples of research questions that have been

TABLE 1.1 ● EXAMPLES OF RESEARCH QUESTIONS ADDRESSED USING MECHANICAL TURK	
Research Question	**Citation**
Does cognitive reappraisal ability buffer against the indirect effects of perceived stress reactivity on Type 2 diabetes?	Sagui and Levens (2016)
How can individuals be mobilized to action against voter ID laws?	Valentino and Neuner (2017)
Is there support for a general factor of well-being?	Longo, Coyne, Joseph, and Gustavsson (2016)
How might men who are depressed express themselves?	Nadeau, Balsan, and Rochlen (2016)
Is there a connection between eating pathology and risk for engaging in suicidal behavior?	Skinner, Rojas, and Veilleux (2017)
What factors predispose some individuals toward holding beliefs in God?	Wlodarski and Pearce (2016)
How does charismatic leadership affect cooperation?	Grabo and van Vugt (2016)
Are people more authentic after having vivid thoughts about their death?	Seto et al. (2016)
How does psychopathy relate to individuals' ability to discriminate trustworthy and untrustworthy faces and genuine expressions?	Sacco et al. (2016)
Does a feminine appearance for women pursuing STEM erroneously signal that they are not well suited for science?	Banchefsky et al. (2016)
Is belief in God linked to social and emotional cognition?	Jack et al. (2016)
Does pathogen-avoidance motivation lead to health protective behaviors?	Gruijters et al. (2016)
Do parenting styles affect parental feeding practices?	Kiefner-Burmeister et al. (2016)
Are there sociocultural differences in people's beliefs in the utility of preventive medicine?	Dye et al. (2016)
What factors influence customers' likelihood to join a program in the casino industry?	Quigno and Zhang (2016)
How can privacy concerns help predict mobile commerce activity?	Eastin et al. (2016)

(Continued)

Research Question	Citation
What are the characteristics of an ideal dairy farm?	Cardoso et al. (2016)
Does smiling when giving people service impact evaluations of service providers?	Andrzejewski and Mooney (2016)
Does an ad background with a warm color make people's judgments toward a company more positive?	Choi et al. (2016)
How do consumer preferences influence moral judgments of corporate misconduct?	Lewis et al. (2016)
How does the way people organize semantic information change with age?	Unger et al. (2016)
How can automatic methods for assessing credibility and relevance of social media posts be improved?	Figueira et al. (2016)
Do people update their representations when making judgments from memory, or do they maintain their representations based on the initial encoding?	Sharif and Oppenheimer (2016)
Does thinking about a limited future enhance the positivity of subsequently recalled information?	Barber et al. (2016)
How do the instructions jurors receive affect the way they consider confessional evidence?	O'Donnell and Safer (2017)
What are the characteristics of an ideal mentor/advisor?	Bailey et al. (2016)

TABLE 1.1 ● (Continued)

addressed using MTurk workers as research participants. As this table illustrates, the studies conducted on Mechanical Turk span multiple disciplines and topics.

CONCLUSION

Prior to Mechanical Turk, online research remained a niche field, existing largely outside of mainstream science. Despite interest from a growing number of researchers (Birnbaum, 2004; Fraley, 2004; Gosling & Johnson, 2010; Hewson, 2003), several factors kept online research from entering the mainstream. First, significant skepticism remained about the level of data quality of online samples (see Gosling et al.,

2010). The inability to control what participants were doing during the study raised researchers' suspicions. Perhaps most important, at the time, significant technical skills were required to conduct even the simplest study online, putting online research out of reach of most researchers who did not have the technical expertise to carry out such studies.

The emergence of Mechanical Turk has democratized online research. With Mechanical Turk, no longer does online research require significant programming expertise and high levels of research funding. Online research in general, and Mechanical Turk in particular, has moved on from being a niche field. Soon, almost every researcher will be dealing with Mechanical Turk in one form or another, either for data collection for their own studies or in reading and evaluating the research of others.

While research on Mechanical Turk is becoming increasingly more sophisticated and complex, new research tools and methodologies are increasingly becoming available. Researchers are now able to collect data via live audio (Gašić, Jurčíček, Thomson, Yu, & Young, 2011; Gašić et al., 2013; McGraw, 2013) and video chat (Miller, Mandryk, Birk, Depping, & Patel, 2017). It is becoming increasingly possible to collect physiological data during live video interviews (Muender, Miller, Birk, & Mandryk, 2016) and by accessing databases from wearable devices (Brinton et al., 2017). Clinical research is also becoming increasingly more commonplace (see Chandler & Shapiro, 2016). For example, workers grant access to their Twitter accounts, which can be used to gain clinical insights into critical areas such as suicidality and depression (Braithwaite et al., 2016). Additionally, since Mechanical Turk was originally intended as a marketplace for work, researchers are increasingly learning how to use MTurk workers as their research assistants for tasks like stimulus development and validation (see Chapter 2, where we use MTurk workers to provide feedback about parts of this book).

With exponential increases in the number of tools available for conducting research on Mechanical Turk, the amount of data available about the MTurk worker population, and the quality of the available data, it is becoming increasingly difficult for researchers to keep track of all the new advances and resources.

Getting started on Mechanical Turk requires familiarity with the basic mechanisms and concepts that make Mechanical Turk unique. MTurk workers function within a unique online culture that many researchers are not familiar with. Third-party platforms are becoming more sophisticated and provide researchers with increasingly powerful new tools to enhance Mechanical Turk's functionality. The demographic composition of MTurk workers, including the question of how many workers are available, is also generally poorly understood. Important questions about ethical concerns surrounding research on Mechanical Turk commonly arise. Finally, as researchers increasingly begin to look to the web for their data collection needs, interest in using other platforms is also beginning to increase. Although Mechanical Turk has substantial advantages over other platforms, alternative sources of data collection such as market research platforms have much to offer social and behavioral scientists. However, the relative advantages and disadvantages of Mechanical Turk versus market research platforms are often not clear.

This book aims to address these and many other issues. In the upcoming chapters we provide an overview of basic concepts that are unique to Mechanical Turk, including an overview of the MTurk culture and ecosystem. The first part of the book (Chapters 1–5) offers an introduction. Its aim is to provide an overview of stimulus development platforms, show how to set up a study on Mechanical Turk, discuss best practices for study setup, and provide a conceptual introduction to the MTurk application programming interface (API) and third-party systems such as CloudResearch. The second part of the book addresses advanced topics, including data quality on Mechanical Turk and other platforms, the demographic composition of Mechanical Turk, the activity levels of workers, best sampling practices, the representativeness of studies conducted on Mechanical Turk, best practices for conducting longitudinal research, and the ethics of conducting research on Mechanical Turk.

Finally, this book is not limited to Mechanical Turk. We aim to provide a comprehensive and up-to-date overview of the complex and quickly evolving ecosystems available for online participant recruitment. Mechanical Turk is one of many approaches for recruiting participants online. Each approach has its advantages and limitations, which are discussed in Chapter 10. We provide an overview of market research platforms, data quality and demographic differences between Mechanical Turk and online panels, and advantages and disadvantages of using Mechanical Turk relative to other platforms. Overall, we see Mechanical Turk and online panels as being complementary, with each well suited for specific research questions. This book aims to introduce readers to the many options available to help researchers complete their projects successfully using online research participants.

REFERENCES

Andrzejewski, S. A., & Mooney, E. C. (2016). Service with a smile: Does the type of smile matter? *Journal of Retailing and Consumer Services, 29*, 135–141. doi:10.1016/j.jretconser.2015.11.010

Arechar, A. A., Gächter, S., & Molleman, L. (2017). Conducting interactive experiments online. *Experimental Economics*, 1–33.

Bailey, S. F., Voyles, E. C., Finkelstein, L., & Matarazzo, K. (2016). Who is your ideal mentor? An exploratory study of mentor prototypes. *Career Development International, 21*(2), 160–175. doi:10.1108/CDI-08-2014-0116

Baker, R., Blumberg, S. J., Brick, J. M., Couper, M. P., Courtright, M., Dennis, J. M., & Kennedy, C. (2010). AAPOR report on online panels. *Public Opinion Quarterly*, *74*(4), 711–781.

Banchefsky, S., Westfall, J., Park, B., & Judd, C. M. (2016). But you don't look like a scientist! Women scientists with feminine appearance are deemed less likely to be scientists. *Sex Roles*, *75*(3–4), 95–109. doi:10.1007/s11199-016-0586-1

Barber, S. J., Opitz, P. C., Martins, B., Sakaki, M., & Mather, M. (2016). Thinking about a limited future enhances the positivity of younger and older adults' recall: Support for socioemotional selectivity theory. *Memory & Cognition*, *44*(6), 869–882. doi:10.3758/s13421-016-0612-0

Barnhoorn, J. S., Haasnoot, E., Bocanegra, B. R., & van Steenbergen, H. (2015). QRTEngine: An easy solution for running online reaction time experiments using Qualtrics. *Behavior Research Methods*, *47*(4), 918–929. doi:10.3758/s13428-014-0530-7

Berinsky, A. J., Huber, G. A., & Lenz, G. S. (2012). Evaluating online labor markets for experimental research: Amazon.com's Mechanical Turk. *Political Analysis*, *20*(3), 351–368. doi:10.1093/pan/mpr057

Birnbaum, M. H. (2004). Human research and data collection via the Internet. *Annual Review of Psychology*, *55*(1), 803–832. doi:10.1146/annurev.psych.55.090902.141601

Bohannon, J. (2016). Psychology. Mechanical Turk upends social sciences. *Science*, *352*(6291), 1263–1264. doi:10.1126/science.352.6291.1263

Boynton, M. H., & Richman, L. S. (2014). An online daily diary study of alcohol use using Amazon's Mechanical Turk. *Drug and Alcohol Review*, *33*(4), 456–461. doi:10.1111/dar.12163

Braithwaite, S. R., Giraud-Carrier, C., West, J., Barnes, M. D., & Hanson, C. L. (2016). Validating machine learning algorithms for Twitter data against established measures of suicidality. *JMIR Mental Health*, *3*(2), e21. doi:10.2196/mental.4822

Brinton, J. E., Keating, M. D., Ortiz, A. M., Evenson, K. R., & Furberg, R. D. (2017). Establishing linkages between distributed survey responses and consumer wearable device datasets: A pilot protocol. *JMIR Research Protocols*, *6*(4), e66. doi:10.2196/resprot.6513

Buccafusco, C., Burns, Z. C., Fromer, J. C., & Sprigman, C. J. (2014). Experimental tests of intellectual property laws' creativity thresholds. *Texas Law Review*, *93*, 1921–1980.

Buhrmester, M., Kwang, T., & Gosling, S. D. (2011). Amazon's Mechanical Turk: A new source of inexpensive, yet high-quality, data? *Perspectives on Psychological Science*, *6*(1), 3–5.

Cardoso, C. S., Hötzel, M. J., Weary, D. M., Robbins, J. A., & von Keyserlingk, M. A. (2016). Imagining the ideal dairy farm. *Journal of Dairy Science*, *99*(2), 1663–1671. doi:10.3168/jds.2015-9925

Chandler, J., & Shapiro, D. (2016). Conducting clinical research using crowdsourced convenience samples. *Annual Review of Clinical Psychology*, *12*, 53–81.

Choi, J., Chang, Y. K., Lee, K., & Chang, J. D. (2016). Effect of perceived warmth on positive judgment. *Journal of Consumer Marketing*, *33*(4), 235–244. doi:10.1108/JCM-02-2015-1309

Comley, P., & Beaumont, J. (2011). Online market research: Methods, benefits and issues—Part 1. *Journal of Direct, Data and Digital Marketing Practice*, *12*(4), 315–327. doi:10.1057/dddmp.2011.8

Crump, M. J. C., McDonnell, J. V., & Gureckis, T. M. (2013). Evaluating Amazon's Mechanical Turk as a tool for experimental behavioral research. *PLoS ONE*, *8*(3), e57410. doi:10.1371/journal.pone.0057410

Dye, T., Li, D., Demment, M., Groth, S., Fernandez, D., Dozier, A., & Chang, J. (2016). Sociocultural varia-tion in attitudes toward use of genetic information and participation in genetic research by race in the United States: Implications for precision medicine. *Journal of the American Medical Informatics Association*, *23*(4), 782–786. doi:10.1093/jamia/ocv214

Eastin, M. S., Brinson, N. H., Doorey, A., & Wilcox, G. (2016). Living in a big data world: Predicting mobile commerce activity through privacy concerns. *Computers in Human Behavior*, *58*, 214–220. doi:10.1016/j. chb.2015.12.050

Evans, J. R., & Mathur, A. (2005). The value of online surveys. *Internet Research*, *15*(2), 195–219. doi:10.1108/10662240510590360

Figueira, A., Sandim, M., & Fortuna, P. (2016). March). An approach to relevancy detection: Contributions to the automatic detection of relevance in social networks. *WorldCIST*, *1*, 89–99.

Fraley, R. C. (2004). *How to conduct behavioral research over the Internet: A beginner's guide to HTML and CGI/Perl*. New York: Guilford Press.

Gašić, M., Breslin, C., Henderson, M., Kim, D., Szummer, M., Thomson, B., & Young, S. (2013). On-line policy optimisation of Bayesian spoken dialogue systems via human interaction. In *2013 IEEE International Conference on Acoustics, Speech and Signal Processing (ICASSP)* (pp. 8367–8371). New York: IEEE.

Gašić, M., Jurčíček, F., Thomson, B., Yu, K., & Young, S. (2011). On-line policy optimisation of spoken dialogue systems via live interaction with human subjects. In *2011 IEEE Workshop on Automatic Speech Recognition and Understanding (ASRU)* (pp. 312–317). New York: IEEE.

Goodman, J. K., Cryder, C. E., & Cheema, A. (2013). Data collection in a flat world: The strengths and weaknesses of Mechanical Turk samples. *Journal of Behavioral Decision Making*, *26*(3), 213–224. doi:10.1002/bdm.1753

Gosling, S. D., & Johnson, J. A. (2010). *Advanced methods for conducting online behavioral research*. Wash-ington, DC: American Psychological Association.

Gosling, S. D., Rentfrow, P. J., & Swann, W. B. (2003). A very brief measure of the Big-Five personality domains. *Journal of Research in Personality*, *37*(6), 504–528. doi:10.1016/S0092-6566(03)00046-1

Gosling, S. D., Sandy, C. J., John, O. P., & Potter, J. (2010). Wired but not WEIRD: The promise of the Internet in reaching more diverse samples. *Behavioral and Brain Sciences*, *33*(2–3), 94–95. doi:10.1017/S0140525X10000300

Gosling, S. D., Vazire, S., Srivastava, S., & John, O. P. (2004). Should we trust web-based studies? A compar-ative analysis of six preconceptions about Internet questionnaires. *American Psychologist*, *59*(2), 93–104. doi:10.1037/0003-066X.59.2.93

Grabo, A., & van Vugt, M. (2016). Charismatic leadership and the evolution of cooperation. *Evolution and Human Behavior*, *37*(5), 399–406. doi:10.1016/j.evolhumbehav.2016.03.005

Gruijters, S. L. K., Tybur, J. M., Ruiter, R. A. C., & Massar, K. (2016). Sex, germs, and health: Pathogen-avoidance motives and health-protective behaviour. *Psychology & Health*, *31*(8), 959–975. doi:10.1080/08870 446.2016.1161194

Gureckis, T. M., Martin, J., McDonnell, J., Rich, A. S., Markant, D., Coenen, A., . . . Chan, P. (2016). psiTurk: An open-source framework for conducting replicable behavioral experiments online. *Behavior Research Methods*, *48*(3), 829–842. doi:10.3758/s13428-015-0642-8

Henrich, J., Heine, S. J., & Norenzayan, A. (2010). Most people are not WEIRD. *Nature, 466*(7302), 29–29. doi:10.1038/466029a

Hewson, C. (2003). *Internet research methods: A practical guide for the social and behavioural sciences.* Newbury Park, CA: Sage.

Horton, J. J., Rand, D. G., & Zeckhauser, R. J. (2011). The online laboratory: conducting experiments in a real labor market. *Experimental Economics, 14*(3), 399–425. doi:10.1007/s10683-011-9273-9

Jack, A. I., Friedman, J. P., Boyatzis, R. E., & Taylor, S. N. (2016). Why do you believe in God? Relationships between religious belief, analytic thinking, mentalizing and moral concern. *PLoS ONE, 11*(3), e0149989. doi:10.1371/journal.pone.0149989

Kiefner-Burmeister, A., Hoffmann, D., Zbur, S., & Musher-Eizenman, D. (2016). Implementation of parental feeding practices: Does parenting style matter? *Public Health Nutrition, 19*(13), 2410–2414. doi:10.1017/S1368980016000446

Kiesler, S., & Sproull, L. S. (1986). Response effects in the electronic survey. *Public Opinion Quarterly, 50*(3), 402–413.

Krantz, J. H., & Dalal, R. (2000). Validity of web-based psychological research. In *Psychological experiments on the Internet* (pp. 35–60). New York: Academic Press.

Lewis, R., Anderson, R., & Pounders, K. (2016). Morality shifting: How consumer preferences influence moral judgments of corporate misconduct. *Journal of Promotion Management, 22*(1), 1–15. doi:10.1080/1049 6491.2015.1107014

Litman, L., Robinson, J., & Abberbock, T. (2017). TurkPrime.com: A versatile crowdsourcing data acquisition platform for the behavioral sciences. *Behavior Research Methods, 49*(2), 433–442. doi:10.3758/s13428-016-0727-z

Litman, L., Robinson, J., & Rosenzweig, C. (2015). The relationship between motivation, monetary compensation, and data quality among US- and India-based workers on Mechanical Turk. *Behavior Research Methods, 47*(2), 519–528. doi:10.3758/s13428-014-0483-x

Longo, Y., Coyne, I., Joseph, S., & Gustavsson, P. (2016). Support for a general factor of well-being. *Personality and Individual Differences, 100*, 68–72. doi:10.1016/j.paid.2016.03.082

Mao, A., Chen, Y., Gajos, K. Z., Parkes, D., Procaccia, A. D., & Zhang, H. (2012). Turkserver: Enabling synchronous and longitudinal online experiments. *Proceedings of HCOMP, 12.*

Mao, A., Chen, Y., Gajos, K. Z., Parkes, D. C., Zhang, H., & Procaccia, A. D. (2012). Turkserver: Enabling synchronous and longitudinal online experiments. *In Workshops at the Twenty-Sixth AAAI Conference on Artificial Intelligence.*

McGraw, I. (2013). Collecting speech from crowds. In M. Eskenazi, G. A. Levow, H. Meng, G. Parent, & D. Suendermann (Eds.), *Crowdsourcing for speech processing: Applications to data collection, transcription and assessment* (pp. 38–71). Hoboken, NJ: John Wiley & Sons.

Miller, M. K., Mandryk, R. L., Birk, M. V., Depping, A. E., & Patel, T. (2017). Through the looking glass: The effects of feedback on self-awareness and conversational behaviour during video chat. In *Proceedings of the 2017 CHI Conference on Human Factors in Computing Systems* (pp. 5271–5283). New York, NY: Association for Computing Machinery.

Muender, T., Miller, M. K., Birk, M. V., & Mandryk, R. L. (2016). Extracting heart rate from videos of online participants. In *Proceedings of the 2016 CHI Conference on Human Factors in Computing Systems* (pp. 4562–4567). New York, NY: Association for Computing Machinery.

Nadeau, M. M., Balsan, M. J., & Rochlen, A. B. (2016). Men's depression: Endorsed experiences and expressions. *Psychology of Men & Masculinity, 17*(4), 328–335. doi:10.1037/men0000027

Nosek, B. A., Banaji, M. R., & Greenwald, A. G. (2002). Harvesting implicit group attitudes and beliefs from a demonstration web site. *Group Dynamics: Theory, Research, and Practice, 6*(1), 101–115. doi:10.1037/1089-2699.6.1.101

O'Donnell, C. M., & Safer, M. A. (2017). Jury instructions and mock-juror sensitivity to confession evidence in a simulated criminal case. *Psychology, Crime & Law*, 1–21.

Paolacci, G., Chandler, J., & Ipeirotis, P. G. (2010). Running experiments on Amazon Mechanical Turk. *Judgment and Decision Making, 5*, 411–419.

Parasuraman, A., Grewal, D., & Krishnan, R. (2006). *Marketing research.* Boston, MA: Cengage Learning.

Poynter, R., Williams, N., & York, S. (2014). *The handbook of mobile market research: Tools and techniques for market researchers.* West Sussex, United Kingdom: John Wiley & Sons.

Quigno, J., & Zhang, L. (2016). Casino customers' intention to join a loyalty rewards program: The effect of number of tiers and gender. *Cornell Hospitality Quarterly, 57*(2), 226–230.

Reips, J. M. U. D., & Musch, J. (2000). A brief history of web experimenting. In M. H. Birnbaum (Ed.), *Psychological experiments on the internet* (pp. 61–87). New York, NY: Academic Press.

Rivera, E. (2015). Market research in the US. *IBISWorld Industry Report, 54191.*

Robins, R. W., Tracy, J. L., Trzesniewski, K., Potter, J., & Gosling, S. D. (2001). Personality correlates of self-esteem. *Journal of Research in Personality, 35*(4), 463–482. doi:10.1006/jrpe.2001.2324

Sacco, D. F., Merold, S. J., Lui, J. H. L., Lustgraaf, C. J. N., & Barry, C. T. (2016). Social and emotional intelligence moderate the relationship between psychopathy traits and social perception. *Personality and Individual Differences, 95*, 95–104. doi:10.1016/j.paid.2016.02.031

Sagui, S. J., & Levens, S. M. (2016). Cognitive reappraisal ability buffers against the indirect effects of perceived stress reactivity on type 2 diabetes. *Health Psychology, 35*(10), 1154–1158. doi:10.1037/hea0000359

Schibrowsky, J. A., Peltier, J. W., & Nill, A. (2007). The state of Internet marketing research: A review of the literature and future research directions. *European Journal of Marketing, 41*(7/8), 722–733.

Schnur, J. B., Dillon, M. J., Goldsmith, R. E., & Montgomery, G. H. (2018). Cancer treatment experiences among survivors of childhood sexual abuse: A qualitative investigation of triggers and reactions to cumulative trauma. *Palliative & Supportive Care, 16*(6), 767–776.

Seto, E., Hicks, J. A., Vess, M., & Geraci, L. (2016). The association between vivid thoughts of death and authenticity. *Motivation and Emotion, 40*(4), 520–540. doi:10.1007/s11031-016-9556-8

Sharif, M. A., & Oppenheimer, D. M. (2016). The effect of relative encoding on memory-based judgments. *Psychological Science, 27*(8), 1136–1145. doi:10.1177/0956797616651973

Skinner, K. D., Rojas, S. M., & Veilleux, J. C. (2017). Connecting eating pathology with risk for engaging in suicidal behavior: The mediating role of experiential avoidance. *Suicide and Life-Threatening Behavior, 47*(1), 3–13. doi:10.1111/sltb.12249

Smith, M. A., & Leigh, B. (1997). Virtual subjects: Using the Internet as an alternative source of subjects and research environment. *Behavior Research Methods, 29*(4), 496–505.

Stewart, N., Chandler, J., & Paolacci, G. (2017). Crowdsourcing samples in cognitive science. *Trends in Cognitive Sciences, 21*(10), 736–748. doi:10.1016/j.tics.2017.06.007

Tran, M., Cabral, L., Patel, R., & Cusack, R. (2017). Online recruitment and testing of infants with Mechanical Turk. *Journal of Experimental Child Psychology, 156*, 168–178. doi:10.1016/j.jecp.2016.12.003

Unger, L., Fisher, A. V., Nugent, R., Ventura, S. L., & MacLellan, C. J. (2016). Developmental changes in semantic knowledge organization. *Journal of Experimental Child Psychology, 146*, 202–222. doi:10.1016/j.jecp.2016.01.005

Valentino, N. A., & Neuner, F. G. (2017). Why the sky didn't fall: Mobilizing anger in reaction to voter ID laws. *Political Psychology, 38*(2), 331–350. doi:10.1111/pops.12332

Welch, N., & Krantz, J. H. (1996). The world-wide web as a medium for psychoacoustical demonstrations and experiments: Experience and results. *Behavior Research Methods, Instruments, & Computers, 28*(2), 192–196.

Wlodarski, R., & Pearce, E. (2016). The God allusion. *Human Nature, 27*(2), 160–172. doi:10.1007/s12110-016-9256-9

Zhou, H., & Fishbach, A. (2016). The pitfall of experimenting on the web: How unattended selective attrition leads to surprising (yet false) research conclusions. *Journal of Personality and Social Psychology, 111*(4), 493–504. doi:10.1037/pspa0000056

THE MECHANICAL TURK ECOSYSTEM

Jonathan Robinson, Cheskie Rosenzweig, and Leib Litman

INTRODUCTION

Mechanical Turk is a unique ecosystem in which interactions between workers and requesters take place within a specific culture. In this chapter, we describe that culture and discuss how data quality is maintained by Mechanical Turk's reputation mechanism, the approval and rejection process, and the options available to requesters for choosing specific workers. We also outline features the MTurk ecosystem has developed that protect requesters from fraud and help workers and requesters get the most out of their MTurk experience.

In the second part of the chapter, we describe Mechanical Turk from the perspective of workers, with the aim of helping requesters better understand what happens to a study once it is launched. We describe online worker communities and discuss how they contribute to the MTurk workers' culture. We also let MTurk workers lend their own voices to this chapter. As part of a Human Intelligence Task (HIT), workers read parts of this chapter and gave us their feedback. Their responses are provided later in the chapter. We gathered responses from workers to demonstrate the power of Mechanical Turk as a platform for quickly aggregating high-quality feedback. We hope that reading their responses in their own words will help readers better appreciate MTurk workers as people who are smart, thoughtful, insightful, and helpful.

Throughout this chapter we use workers' conversations on various popular forums as anecdotal evidence to supplement our own experience with MTurk workers. This chapter is not a how-to guide. Rather, we describe the ecosystem of Mechanical Turk at a conceptual level. Chapter 3 will provide a detailed guide for how to set up and launch MTurk studies and Chapter 4 will explain how third-party platforms can enhance Mechanical Turk through the use of MTurk's API. Readers who are experienced with Mechanical Turk might be able to skip portions of this chapter, Chapter 3, and Chapter 4 as we describe some of the more basic and technical details of the platform. Although we believe there is useful information in each of these chapters for even experienced readers and provide a summary of best practices at the end of Chapters 3 and 4, the goal of the next several chapters is to lay the foundation for the information presented throughout the rest of the book.

Workers and Requesters

Mechanical Turk allows one group of users, called requesters, to interact with another group of users, called workers. When requesters want to connect to workers, they *launch* a task, which Mechanical Turk refers to as a HIT (Human Intelligence Task). The task becomes visible on the workers' dashboard. Figure 2.1 shows an example of the workers' dashboard with a number of HITs that ask workers to link company names to stock market symbols, get contact details for pharmaceutical companies, look up fashion products, and classify whether a lesion is malignant.

When a worker submits a HIT, payment for that work is not automatically remitted to the worker. Instead, the requester has the ability to review the work and to decide whether or not to pay for it. If the requester decides the work meets their standards of quality, they can accept the HIT, which releases funds to the worker. If, by contrast, the requester decides the work does not meet their standards of quality, they can reject the work, in which case the worker does not get paid.

Requesters on Mechanical Turk have complete control over the approval process. When a requester rejects a HIT, there is little the worker can do about it. Even if a HIT is rejected for no reason, Mechanical Turk does not have an appeal process and often the only option for workers is to ask the requester about the rejection. Although this level of control can seem unfair, Mechanical Turk gives requesters complete control in order to protect them from fraud. In practice, requesters rarely reject submitted work (see Chapter 11). Additionally, workers have developed a few systems of their

---

FIGURE 2.1 ● THE WORKERS' HIT DASHBOARD

own which help them avoid requesters who have mistreated them in the past, which we discuss later in this chapter.

At its core, Mechanical Turk is a system for transferring funds to people in exchange for work done over the internet. As such, it is a system that is vulnerable to fraud. Fraud can occur when workers do not take the work seriously, or when people game the system in hopes of collecting payment. An electronic system for transferring funds can also be susceptible to money laundering. For these reasons, Mechanical Turk spends significant resources on maintaining an infrastructure that prevents fraud. Many of Mechanical Turk's rules are intended to prevent such misuses of the system, and they need to be understood in that context.

Particularly because requesters have so much of the systemic power on Mechanical Turk, they have a heightened responsibility to act ethically and to have clearly defined reasons for rejecting work (this issue is discussed in more detail in Chapter 11, which deals with the ethics of conducting research on Mechanical Turk). Ethical behavior on the part of requesters is particularly important because rejecting a HIT not only prevents the worker from getting paid, but it also harms the worker's overall *reputation*.

HOW QUALITY IS MAINTAINED

Data quality on Mechanical Turk is maintained by a set of rules that govern the behavior of workers and requesters. These rules apply to actions that requesters and workers can take with respect to launched and completed tasks (see Box 2.1).

BOX 2.1 ACTIONS AVAILABLE FOR A LAUNCHED HIT

REQUESTER ACTIONS

launch - Makes a HIT live.

accept - Approves the work and pays the worker. Positively affects the worker's approval rating.

reject - Does not approve the work. Does not pay the worker. Negatively affects the worker's approval rating.

unreject - Reverses a rejection.

block - Prevents the worker from ever taking a HIT with the requester.

WORKER ACTIONS

preview - Selects the HIT from a dashboard to view the HIT's details.

accept - Makes the worker obligated to complete the HIT in the time allotted.

skip - Worker decides not to work on a HIT after previewing it.

submit - Marks the HIT as complete and hands the HIT over to the requester for review.

return - Marks the HIT as not complete. Makes room available for another worker to work on the HIT. Does not affect the approval rating. Does become part of the worker's visible record.

When workers view their dashboard, there are a limited number of actions they can take with regard to any specific HIT. Workers can sort the HITs visible on their dashboard so that they see HITs posted most recently, or those that pay the largest sum. They can also see the requesters' overall *HIT approval rate* and *Average payment review time*, by hovering over the HIT with their mouse. One action workers can take is to *preview* a HIT. Previewing allows workers to find out more specific information such as how long the task might take and whether there are any task-specific instructions. After previewing a HIT, workers can either *accept* the HIT or *skip* the HIT, which returns the worker to the dashboard. After accepting a HIT, workers can either *submit* the HIT when they are finished or *return* the HIT if they choose not to finish it. If a worker abandons the HIT, the HIT will be returned automatically after the *maximum allowable time* is reached. Once a worker submits a HIT, a requester can take one of two actions: *accept* the HIT or *reject* it (see Box 2.1).

REPUTATION MECHANISM

When a worker accepts a HIT, the outcome of that HIT becomes part of that worker's permanent record—referred to as that worker's *approval rating*. For example, if a worker submitted 100 HITs and 10 of them were rejected, that worker's approval rating would be 90%. Mechanical Turk also keeps track of the number of HITs successfully submitted by each worker, referred to as the *number of HITs approved*. Requesters can selectively open the HIT to workers based on the number of HITs they have completed and based on their overall approval rating (see Chapters 3 and 4).

Blocking Workers

In addition to being able to reject a HIT and not pay the worker, requesters can also *block* a worker. Blocking workers prevents them from working for the requester in the

FIGURE 2.2 ● DISCUSSION ON REDDIT ABOUT THE CONSEQUENCES OF BLOCKING A WORKER

Rejection/Block Discussion Blocked a worker, a little surprised (self.mturk)
submitted 2 years ago by

One of the workers sent a pretty rude e-mail to my staff. We didn't respond and approved his HIT, but thought we'd block him so that they can do no further HITs for us.

From the requester's perspective all we had to do was click the "Block" button.

However, after having blocked him I read through some forums that apparently this notifies Amazon and gives him some kind of warning threatening to suspend him, which is certainly not as far as we wanted to take it (just wanted him to not do our HITs or contact us anymore).

Is this true? And if so, is it salvageable? I don't want him working on our HITs but I don't want to jeopardize what could be his primary source of income! Amazon does a terrible job at telling you this, by the way.

15 comments share report

future. Critically, when a worker is blocked by multiple separate requesters, the worker's account may become permanently disabled. This would prevent the worker from using Mechanical Turk to make money, unless the block is reversed. For this reason, workers should be blocked only when a requester is certain fraud has been committed.

Worker forums make it clear that many requesters are not aware of the difference between rejecting a HIT and blocking a worker (see Figure 2.2 for an example from a Reddit forum). Requesters sometimes block workers, not realizing the dramatic effect this can have on the status of the worker's account. Rather than blocking workers, requesters should use what are called *qualifications* to prevent specific workers from participating in their studies (see Chapter 3 and Chapter 5).

Returned HITs

In addition to a worker's approval rating, MTurk tracks other aspects of a worker's history, including how many HITs the worker has *returned*. Workers can return a HIT if, after having accepted it, they decide not to work on the HIT for some reason. Mechanical Turk also marks a HIT as returned if a worker runs out of time. Each HIT needs to be submitted within the time frame indicated by the requester. If a worker does not complete a HIT on time, the status of the HIT will be set to *returned*.

Tracking Dropout Rates With Returned HITs

Although the primary purpose of reputation indicators is to track workers' performance history, these indicators also have methodological uses. Because Mechanical Turk keeps track of returned HITs, requesters can examine how many workers returned a HIT to determine the rate of dropout from their study. The ratio of workers who skipped a HIT after previewing it can also be a useful indicator of dropout, referred to as the *bounce rate*. While Mechanical Turk does not offer information about the dropout and bounce rates on the point-and-click graphical user interface, these metrics can be accessed through the API and through third-party apps (see Chapter 4).

Workers' Reputation Metrics

Together, the approval rating and the number of HITs completed make up each worker's *reputation*. The mechanism by which workers establish their reputations is key for understanding what motivates workers to take each HIT seriously. Requesters on Mechanical Turk commonly recruit only workers with a good reputation (i.e., high number of HITs completed and high approval rating) (Peer, Vosgerau, & Acquisti, 2014). In Chapter 7 we provide a critique of this practice and suggest that researchers should reduce their use of worker reputation metrics to select participants. However, because using reputation qualifications is currently the norm, a worker's reputation affects his or her likelihood of qualifying for high-paying HIT opportunities. For this reason, workers are careful to protect their reputation. Workers are often even more concerned about their reputation than about payment for any one HIT.

More than any other aspect of the platform, Mechanical Turk's reputation mechanism is responsible for its culture. Each worker's desire to maintain a good reputation increases attentiveness and data quality to levels that often far surpass those of other platforms (Berinsky, Huber, & Lenz, 2012) and undergraduate subject pools (Hauser & Schwarz, 2016).

SELECTIVELY RECRUITING SPECIFIC WORKERS

One limitation of Mechanical Turk relative to market research platforms is the limited ability to selectively recruit and directly screen specific participants. On market research platforms, it is common practice to have participants fill out screening questionnaires as part of a survey. Respondents who do not meet the study's target criteria are prevented from participating. This screening process makes market research platforms much more effective than Mechanical Turk at finding rare populations and sampling specific demographic segments (see Chapter 10 for an in-depth comparison of MTurk and online panels).

Selectively screening participants on Mechanical Turk is more difficult than on market research platforms because, as a general rule, MTurk workers do not like to accept HITs unless they know in advance they will be able to complete them. Telling workers about a study's targeting criteria before they accept the HIT, such as in the HIT's title or description, can lead to unscrupulous behavior (Chandler & Paolacci, 2017). Instead, two-wave studies and *qualifications* should be used to selectively recruit participants on Mechanical Turk (see next section and Chapter 4).

Qualifications Issued by Mechanical Turk

When Mechanical Turk first launched, there were few criteria that requesters could use to selectively recruit workers. Requesters had the option to recruit workers by their approval rating, number of completed HITs, and location such as country and state. By the end of 2016, however, Mechanical Turk started to expand the range of targeting criteria. Currently, requesters can choose from multiple demographic

FIGURE 2.3 ● STANDING INVITATION ON EACH WORKER'S DASHBOARD TO COMPLETE PROFILE HITS

Complete Profile Tasks to qualify for more HITs
Click here to add or update your profile information. By providing this information, you may qualify for HITs from Requesters looking for Workers like you.

characteristics including age, gender, house and car ownership, income, employment status, and many others.

To make workers with various demographic characteristics available for different HITs, MTurk uses a qualification system. Qualifications are values assigned to workers and used to qualify them for various HITs. To assign qualifications, Mechanical Turk profiles workers by allowing them to participate in optional screener HITs (Figure 2.3). These screener HITs are always available for workers to complete and are visible on their dashboard (Figure 2.4).

While some MTurk screener HITs ask workers for their background information, others profile workers' skills. For example, a profile HIT designed to establish language proficiency may include an audio file in Spanish. Workers may be asked to answer a number of in-depth questions about what they heard in order to establish their fluency. Requesters are then able to create HITs requiring translation services that are open only to workers with Spanish language proficiency qualifications.

Premium qualifications, such as those just described, incur additional costs. Typically, the harder it is to find a group of participants, the more expensive the sample is. For example, less common population segments, such as fluent German

FIGURE 2.4 ● SAMPLE PROFILING HITS USED BY MECHANICAL TURK TO CREATE BUILT-IN QUALIFICATIONS

Requester	Title
Amazon Mechanical Turk Team	Profile Information - German Fluency Evaluation
Amazon Mechanical Turk Team	Profile Information - Brazilian Portuguese Fluency Evaluation
Amazon Mechanical Turk Team	Profile Information - French Fluency Evaluation
Amazon Mechanical Turk Team	Profile Information - Chinese Mandarin (Simplified) Fluency Evaluation
Amazon Mechanical Turk Team	Profile Information - Spanish Fluency Evaluation
Amazon Mechanical Turk Team	Profile Information - Skills and Specialization
Amazon Mechanical Turk Team	Profile Information - Lifestyle
Amazon Mechanical Turk Team	Profile Information - Personal Finance
Amazon Mechanical Turk Team	Profile Information - Employment and Home
Amazon Mechanical Turk Team	Profile Information - Marriage and Family
Amazon Mechanical Turk Team	Profile Information - Basic Demographics
Amazon Mechanical Turk Team	Profile Information - Online Activity and Social Profile HIT

speakers, cost more than broader categories of participants such as men or women. This is true both on Mechanical Turk and on market research platforms. On Mechanical Turk, however, researchers have the ability to selectively target participants with two-wave studies using their own qualifications. Two-wave studies are required when a specific qualification is not available on Mechanical Turk. At times, recruiting participants via two-wave studies can be more cost effective than using premium qualifications, although not always. Additionally, as discussed in Chapter 4, third-party apps provide access to some additional qualifications that Mechanical Turk does not have.

Qualifications Issued by Requesters

Although the range of qualifications that Mechanical Turk makes available is increasing constantly, many characteristics that a requester may want to target are not likely to be available. Requesters who want to selectively recruit workers based on characteristics that are not available on Mechanical Turk, such as race or ethnicity, can create their own qualifications by conducting two-wave studies.

For example, a requester may be interested in conducting a study with 100 male college students. This can be accomplished by conducting a two-wave study. In the first wave, a requester can open a short demographic HIT for 1,000 workers. This HIT may include as few as 10 demographic questions. When running these studies, it is good practice to include some questions that are not relevant to the targeting criteria so that workers will not know in advance what the qualification criteria are. Based on workers' responses to the first wave of the study, the requester can grant qualifications (more details on this in Chapter 3) to those who meet the criteria. Then, the qualification can be used to target only eligible participants in a future HIT. Requester-issued qualifications make it possible to follow up with specific groups of workers based on the profiles the requester has collected.

Technical note

In order for a requester to issue qualifications to a worker, the worker must have already completed at least one HIT for that requester. When a worker completes a HIT for a requester it establishes a relationship between them. Prior to this, a requester cannot assign a qualification to a worker, communicate with them, or issue bonuses. Importantly, a returned HIT does not establish a requester/worker relationship.

Although creating two-wave studies can be effective for recruiting some workers, it is not an efficient way to find rare populations. For example, because the base rate of multiraciality is around 3% in the United States, a researcher interested in recruiting multiracial workers may have to screen more than 10,000 workers in a first-wave study to find roughly 300 qualified workers. Due to the limits of the size of the MTurk population (discussed further in Chapters 6 and 7), it is rarely possible to recruit that many workers in a short span of time. Further, even at $0.10 per screener, it would cost $1,000 just to identify 300 participants, assuming that all 300 would participate in the second wave. In practice the second wave is likely to have substantial dropout, increasing the number of people who need to be screened.

Overall, the qualification mechanism is an effective tool that allows requesters to selectively recruit specific groups of workers, but with significant limitations. Third-party apps have been created to improve the ability to selectively recruit rare groups on Mechanical Turk (see Chapter 4). However, due to their ability to freely screen participants before a study begins, market research platforms remain a more versatile choice for studies that focus on recruiting specific, hard-to-sample groups (see Chapter 10).

PROTECTIONS FOR WORKERS

The preceding section described the mechanisms Mechanical Turk put in place to protect requesters from fraudulent workers. Similarly, Mechanical Turk put other mechanisms in place to protect workers from unscrupulous requesters. Specific rules govern the behavior of requesters and dictate what requesters are allowed to ask workers to do as part of a HIT. For example, requesters are not allowed to use HITs for advertising purposes. And, generally speaking, requesters are not allowed to ask workers to download apps for fear that they may include viruses or malicious software. Requesters are also not allowed to ask workers for any type of personally identifying information. This includes names, phone numbers, or email addresses. Similarly, requesters are not allowed to require workers to provide email addresses of their friends. This puts limitations on the ability of researchers to conduct group studies. Researchers interested in conducting studies with groups of workers such as coworkers or multiple family members need to be mindful that asking workers to provide email addresses of others violates Mechanical Turk's terms of service. Many workers take these rules seriously, as can be seen in the feedback that workers leave on Turkopticon (Figure 2.5), a forum for workers to leave feedback about requesters and HITs. Requesters who require workers to provide information that is against Mechanical Turk's terms of service are often reported to other workers and to Mechanical Turk. The potential consequences of violating MTurk's rules are that the requester's account may be suspended.

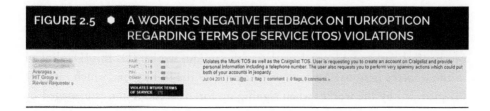

FIGURE 2.5 ● A WORKER'S NEGATIVE FEEDBACK ON TURKOPTICON REGARDING TERMS OF SERVICE (TOS) VIOLATIONS

Practically speaking, there are many exceptions to the rules that govern requesters. Starting in 2015, Mechanical Turk began allowing requesters to run studies that required workers to download certain apps, especially those commonly used for research in the social and behavioral sciences. For example, Inquisit software is commonly used to collect millisecond-precision reaction-time data over the internet, and requesters can feel safe asking workers to download the Inquisit app. It is important, however, for requesters to let workers know about requirements to download software as part of the instructions that are visible in the HIT preview window rather than after workers accept the HIT.

Mechanical Turk does not provide a clear definition of what it considers to be personally identifiable information (PII). Names, addresses, and emails are clear examples of PII, but determining what qualifies as PII is less clear in many other cases. For example, a person's voice can be used to uniquely identify the individual and may thus be considered PII for some purposes. It is also unclear whether video interviews on Mechanical Turk are considered PII. It is likewise not uncommon for requesters to ask workers to give them access to their personal databases such as their Twitter accounts or Fitbit databases (Braithwaite, Giraud-Carrier, West, Barnes, & Hanson, 2016; Brinton, Keating, Ortiz, Evenson, & Furberg, 2017), which may provide identifying information.

On a practical level, the most important consideration for a requester should be the workers' comfort level in providing such information. Requesters need to be careful not to create HITs where workers will be surprised by what they are required to do after accepting the HIT. When workers find out they have to download an app or provide personal information after they have accepted a HIT, their only options are to do something they are uncomfortable with or return the HIT. However, if workers are able to understand a HIT's requirements in the HIT preview window, they can skip the HIT without any consequences for their reputation. For this reason, requesters should strive to carefully and clearly describe their HIT's requirements in the HIT preview window.

Anonymity and Worker IDs

Because Mechanical Turk does not allow requesters to collect personally identifiable information such as email addresses, it includes a mechanism that allows requesters to interact with workers through what are referred to as *worker IDs*. Worker IDs preserve workers' anonymity while allowing requesters to contact and interact with specific workers.

Mechanical Turk provides each worker with a unique worker ID. This ID is linked to the worker's personal Amazon worker profile. The full profile, which includes PII provided by the worker when signing up for an account and is managed by

Amazon, is not available to the requester. When workers initially join Mechanical Turk, they have to provide Amazon with personal information including their name, address, email, banking information, and Social Security number, for fraud prevention and to facilitate monetary payments. All this information is hidden from requesters. This allows requesters to keep track of which workers submit their HITs without collecting personal information about those workers. (Worker IDs are not perfectly anonymous and are considered PII by some institutional review boards. This problem and potential solutions are discussed further in Chapter 11.)

COMMUNICATING WITH WORKERS

Through the MTurk interface, requesters can use MTurk worker ID's to invite workers to future studies by setting up qualifications based on previously completed studies. This mechanism allows requesters to conduct studies anonymously. Requesters can send a message when they bonus a worker for a completed study. Without third-party applications such as CloudResearch, requesters have no other way of messaging workers unless workers contact them first. Workers can email requesters about any particular HIT by clicking on "Contact This Requester" under HIT details. If a worker decides to email a requester via MTurk's communication system, the worker's email account and associated name will automatically be visible to the researcher in the email that the researcher receives. Researchers are then able to reply.

A WORKER'S PERSPECTIVE

Creating a Worker Account

At this point, we recommend that you create a Mechanical Turk worker account if you do not already have one (https://www.mturk.com/mturk/welcome). Completing a few HITs as a worker can help requesters understand the user experience from the workers' perspective. Posting a HIT on Mechanical Turk can be thought of as putting an advertisement on the Mechanical Turk workers' dashboard. To do so effectively, requesters should become familiar with the dashboard, including factors that affect the visibility of HITs.

The Dashboard

When workers log in, they are immediately brought to the dashboard, where they can view the HITs that requesters post (see Figure 2.1). The dashboard contains a worker-specific list of all HITs that are available to a specific worker on Mechanical Turk. Other

HITs that exist but that the worker is not eligible to take will not appear on that worker's dashboard. Workers are ineligible for a particular HIT if they do not have the required approval rating or if it requires specific qualifications the worker does not have. For example, in Figure 2.1, the dashboard indicates that there are 448 available HITs. These are the only HITs that this specific worker can view. The actual number of HITs being conducted on Mechanical Turk at that time is likely significantly higher.

How Workers View and Choose Their HITs

The dashboard has six columns: the name of the requester, the title of the HIT, the number of assignments available for that HIT, how much the HIT pays, the date on which the HIT was created, and an *actions* column. In the actions column, the worker can preview the HIT and/or choose to accept it. The requester inputs the title, description, time allotted, expiration date, payment, and number of assignments of the HIT when creating the HIT (see Chapter 3 for more details).

Sorting and Finding HITs

The list of HITs on the dashboard can be sorted based on the reward and date created columns. Studies show that workers commonly sort HITs based on these columns, increasing the likelihood of certain HITs being more visible (Chilton, Horton, Miller, & Azenkot, 2010). Workers tend to sort HITs based on whatever options are available. For example, in the past it was possible to sort HITs based on the title. This made HITs whose title started with the letters *a* and *z* more likely to be previewed and accepted by workers (Chilton et al., 2010). Workers look to the title of a HIT for other information that they use to decide whether to accept a particular HIT (see Chapter 3 for best practices).

The most common way that workers sort HITs is based on reward. This allows workers to quickly identify the highest paying opportunities. As such, high-paying HITs are likely to be seen first and fill up the fastest. In addition, highly experienced workers have other tools with which to find high-paying HITs, including extensions developed for workers and forums where good HITs are shared (see "Worker Communities," later in this chapter). For example, a Reddit group called "HITs Worth Turking For" (www.reddit.com/r/HITsWorthTurkingFor) posts many of the available high-paying HITs. Experienced workers who keep track of HITs on Reddit are likely to find high-paying HITs first, before they reach the targeted number of workers. As a result, HITs that pay more are more likely to be taken by fairly experienced workers, thus potentially biasing the sample toward those workers (see Chapter 7 for a full discussion).

Workers also sort HITs based on the launch date. The dashboard contains a list of all HITs that are available on Mechanical Turk. Workers can choose to filter the HITs visible on their dashboard so that HITs they are not eligible to take do not appear. Requesters who need many participants to take their HITs should stop the HIT after one or two days, copy it, and resubmit it to bring it to the top of the queue. This will make the HIT more visible to workers (see Chapter 4 for more on this).

Previewing a HIT

The last column on the dashboard is the *actions* column. In this column a worker can *preview* or *accept and work* on the HIT. Clicking on the preview button will take the worker to a HIT preview window. Accessing the preview window does not mean that the worker has accepted the HIT. Here, the worker will see a more detailed description of the HIT. In order for the worker to officially start working on the HIT, he or she will have to accept it by clicking on the accept button.

Mechanical Turk contains two kinds of HITs: internal HITs and external HITs. Internal HITs are HITs that are hosted entirely on Mechanical Turk itself. Such HITs are designed with one of several Mechanical Turk templates that are available to requesters (see Figure 3.9). These HITs will be visible in their entirety in the preview window and can be worked on directly on Mechanical Turk. External HITs are housed on third-party software platforms such as Qualtrics or SurveyMonkey. For external HITs, the preview window will contain a link that will take the worker out of Mechanical Turk to the platform hosting the survey.

The information reviewed above is all the information that workers can get about HITs on Mechanical Turk. However, over the past several years, worker communities have developed where workers share information about HITs, requesters, and how to optimize the worker experience on Mechanical Turk. Extensions have also been created that give workers more flexibility in navigating the process of finding and accepting HITs. These extensions are highly popular among workers, and the way they are used impacts the composition of samples (see Chapter 7).

WORKER COMMUNITIES

The MTurk community consists of a diverse group of people (see Chapter 6) who work on HITs for a variety of reasons. These reasons range from earning a primary income, to making some extra money on the side after a long day at work, to the enjoyment some people receive from completing surveys that help them learn more about themselves (Paolacci, Chandler, & Ipeirotis, 2010; Ross, Irani, Silberman, Zaldivar, & Tomlinson, 2010; Staffelbach et al., 2014). Some workers gravitate to forums where they post about many topics relating to work on Mechanical Turk. These worker forums act as a community center of sorts, allowing workers to talk about issues they find important. Common topics include worker rights, advice about which HITs to take and which to avoid, and guidance on how to interact with requesters. There is no single website with which all workers affiliate. Rather, a variety of websites host messaging forums, and workers choose which of these they visit and are active on. Each of these forums has a unique flavor, and they have different balances of what workers post about. The review that follows here focuses on the different worker communities that gather and a few main purposes these communities serve. The discussions on these forums provide insight into several important topics, such as the way workers find and accept new HITs and the importance of requesters' reputations in this selection process.

Forums

Multiple websites host forums that are used by MTurk workers. Most of these websites are created specifically for MTurk users (e.g., http://www.mturkcrowd.com/, https://turkerhub.com/, http://www.mturkforum.com/, http://turkernation.com/, and https://turkopticon.ucsd.edu/), while others are popular websites, such as Reddit, that have developed forums for the "turking community" (https://www.reddit.com/r/mturk/). Some of these forums are also used by requesters, but here we focus primarily on the ways that workers use these spaces.

Like most forums, worker forums contain many *threads*, or pages for people to post on and read information about specific topics. Most of these forums have threads dedicated to topics such as worker help, how-to's, daily available HITs, and worker scripts/extensions. Additionally, users can be found commenting on current events, sharing inspirational memes with each other, or wishing other forum members "good

turker
Angry Loner, possibly Unemployable

Contributor	
Joined:	Jan 23, 2016
Messages:	8,273
Likes:	15,001

hunting" on Mechanical Turk. Workers usually *do not* post information revealing details of the content of a HIT, but they may do so for various reasons if they feel they want to share something. It is difficult to estimate the number of workers who read or post on forums, and some forums are much more active than others. One of the most popular forums is hosted on http://www.mturkcrowd.com/, which often has more than 30,000 views and 1,000 posts on a given day, on a single thread. These forums are used by a wide range of workers, some of whom are new to the world of Mechanical Turk and are looking for advice, and others of whom have taken thousands of HITs and give lots of advice. Users on these forums have profiles, with avatars (an icon or figure representing them as part of their profile) and some information about their turking activities (number of HITs taken, total earnings on Mechanical Turk) and contributions to the forum (number of posts, popularity of posts, etc.). As in other online forums and communities, individuals are unique, creative, and often quite expressive.

Workers' Opinions About Forums: A Demonstration of Data Collection on Mechanical Turk

As our first demonstration of data collection on Mechanical Turk, we created a HIT in which we asked workers to read this chapter's section about worker forums and to provide feedback, as mentioned earlier in the chapter. Box 2.2 shows several of the open-ended responses. As can be seen, worker responses were intelligent, thoughtful, and helpful. In many cases they disagreed with us or qualified our descriptions. In other cases they agreed. As always, open-ended responses will lead to a range of diverse opinions, and interpretation requires a sound data-analytic approach. At a high level, however, these results demonstrate how easy it is to get fast and high-quality open-ended opinions on Mechanical Turk. Such open-ended responses can be harnessed for questionnaire development, as in, for example, one of our recent studies about the experiences of sexual abuse survivors (Schnur et al., 2017). We encourage researchers to post their own questions to workers as a way to get answers to questions they may have about workers' experiences and, more broadly, to explore the power of Mechanical Turk for open-ended research.

Worker Help/How-To's

Among both workers and requesters, there is a wide range of expertise in how to use Mechanical Turk. Most of the time, creating an MTurk account is easy, but understanding the platform and using all its available resources is much more challenging. Workers use forums to learn how to use Mechanical Turk more efficiently and to discuss topics of concern. Here is a sample of the kinds of issues that are addressed on multiple forums:

- New user questions

- Guidelines for your first 1,000 HITs

- What are the best scripts/extensions I can use to find good HITs faster?

- Scripts/extensions help

- Masters qualification information—all you need to know

- Who are some requesters that post great HITs?

- How do I contact a requester?

- What can I do if a requester rejected me for no reason?

- How do I report my income for tax purposes?

- What other websites can I earn good money on?

BOX 2.2 WORKERS' COMMENTS AFTER HAVING READ PARTS OF THIS CHAPTER

Reviews of our descriptions of online worker communities:

- "This is a pretty accurate description of the forums. I visit mturkcrowd.com and view the daily thread constantly throughout the day while I'm working. It helps me find hits that I might have missed and it's nice to read what others are chatting about."

- "The paragraph defines PII to include e-mail addresses, but I do not view an e-mail address as necessarily personally identifiable. For example, I created a random e-mail address for MTurk purposes that is in no way connected to me. I also disagree with some of the editing of the paragraph, like cut-off words or other small grammar issues, as it detracts from the statements being made. As to creating HITs that clearly indicate what might be required of a worker, I agree with that point. If a worker fully previews a HIT before accepting it, chances are the HIT will no longer be available by the time the person tries to accept it. Accepting a lot of HITs with acceptable pay often involves an 'accept first, return later' policy."

- "I do think requesters should detail things clearly so workers can see before they accept hits. I've run into several hits that I didn't realize required microphone or webcam and I just return them. It's a minor annoyance since it wastes a couple seconds but nothing too bad. Returning a hit doesn't really affect me since I never cap out at 3800 hits per day (returns count as one of those 3800 I believe), and return rate is an unused metric by requesters."

- "Although these websites have thousands of views a day, it is still important to remember that the number of unique views would be a lot lower. Workers on these websites tend to visit many times a day throughout the day, looking for hits and chatting with other workers."

We asked workers to write their own paragraph on the topic:

- "Any personal identifying information pertaining to the worker should be guaranteed private unless if the worker has beforehand agreed and clearly understood what information they're giving away in the task. The requester needs to clearly explain in the task title and description what information they'll be asking for."

- "It is important to know that the mTurk community is very divided on this. Some want a nanny workplace, where everything is followed to the tee. Where there are tons of things considered as PII and those things are not posted ever! If they are, then ALL workers must report them as soon as they see it. On the other hand, there are many workers who feel that it is not Amazon's right to tell a worker what they can do and not do in this area. It seems to be more reasonable, though, to allow workers to decide. That way there is choice in the matter. If you don't like it, don't do it."

- "While these [forums] are useful and at times fun resources of information about MTurk it is important to not just believe everything that you read. Many people will suggest the wrong thing to do in any given situation or bad-mouth a requester who's good leaving out the things that they did wrong and are at fault for. You should always make sure to form your own conclusions."

- "It is important to respect workers' rights while creating these HITs. One of the most important ways to respect workers is to take their time into consideration. If a worker is ten minutes into a twenty-minute survey and find out that they

(Continued)

BOX 2.2 (CONTINUED)

have to download software that they are uncomfortable downloading, they would be forced to return the HIT and thus lose the compensation that they would have acquired up until that point. Not only is that unfair to the worker, but they are likely to complain about the HIT and the requester on one of the numerous Mechanical Turk forums and review sites, which could have detrimental results for the requester."

- "Workers rarely have interaction with others, with the rare exception of 'group HITs' where they will occasionally work with another worker to complete a task. Most of the time, they are completely on their own. These forums can help amend the isolation that comes with working from home."

- "A worker is much more likely to complete a HIT with accurate and good data if they are both compensated fairly and feel they haven't been taken advantage of. There are far too many requesters on Mechanical Turk that want to get information for absolutely no money."

- "Forums are also great learning tools for new workers as most people there are willing to give some guidance. It's also a nice relaxing place to chat or just read things when work is slow."

- "These websites can help new workers feel more comfortable with using Mechanical Turk. Here they can get advice about what requesters they should avoid and the best kind of surveys they can do. Additionally, it is a place for some workers to let off steam after being 'burned' by a bad HIT or requester. Although these workers talk about the general experience of a HIT, it's important to note that they never release confidential information about the HIT itself in these forums."

We asked workers to tell us more about scripts and apps they use:

- "Scripts are absolutely essential for working on mTurk as they speed up your overall rate of work considerably. I did not see scripts for specific (often recurring) hits that do things like pre-select radio buttons or assign hotkeys to select things. These will allow you to do HITs faster, boosting your income rate. Often times they reduce strain on your hands as well by reducing the amount of clicks or keystrokes you need to make."

- "It is very important to assure that workers are not taken advantage of by requesters. If a requester gives an unfair rejection or unfair pay level, it's important that other workers know that information."

- "These extensions are very important. If you do not utilize at the very least an extension to filter HITs more efficiently and to use the PANDA feature you will be at a large disadvantage since there is so much competition for the work and you will miss out on most of the good work in my opinion."

- "There are certain scripts or extensions that aid workers to find HITs with more ease and convenience compared to looking manually for HITs. There are different kinds of scripts to choose from that generally do the same thing, but they still have their nuances that sets them apart from one another."

- "There are also add-ons for established scripts. For example there's Panda Crazy Helper that allows you to create a panda with one click on a separate page. Also, there's scripts that store every HIT you've ever done and give the worker projected earnings for the hour, day, week, or even month."

(Continued)

- "These scripts can help create a competitive environment for workers to obtain work, although it does make it hard for newcomers to come in. Because requesters are able to set qualifications for workers, it can be difficult for newcomers to be able to achieve a strong starting wage, especially when they are capped at a certain limit of HITs that they can do per day."

Workers seek advice on these forums from current workers about their practices and behaviors, and these threads also shape the behaviors of workers to come who will refer to guidelines laid out in these how-to sections.

Daily Available HITs

Figure 2.6 shows a post made by a worker who wanted to share a HIT that other workers might want to take. This post shares information about the HIT, including the worker's previous experience with this requester, the description of the HIT on MTurk, as well as the time the requester reported the HIT will take, the number of HITs available, payment, and qualifications required to take the HIT. Posts also commonly have live links to the actual HIT, the requester's MTurk profile including a list of HITs currently available to a worker, and the requester's Turkopticon (TO) profile, which has more detailed information on the requester provided by workers who had taken their HITs in the past.

A worker will typically share HITs with others if the HIT has one of several characteristics: the HIT was enjoyable or interesting, relatively easy, paid well for the time it took, had great opportunity for bonuses, or was posted by a requester who has a

FIGURE 2.6 ● A TYPICAL HIT SHARED BY A WORKER ON THE DAILY AVAILABLE HITS THREAD

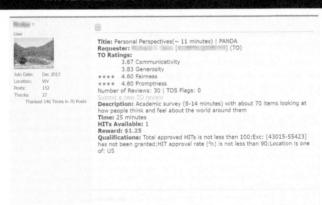

good reputation for treating workers well and posting good HITs. Importantly, when workers share HITs in this fashion, they do not need to manually enter all of this information into their post. The information is generated for them by the same apps they are using to find and accept HITs. Often, workers add their own descriptions of the HIT, letting users know how long the HIT actually took them or how much writing the HIT involved. These descriptions give other workers even more information to decide whether or not they would like to take the HIT themselves.

Worker Scripts/Extensions

Although the worker dashboard provides the basic features necessary to find and accept HITs, a number of additional features are made available to workers through scripts or extensions that take advantage of Mechanical Turk's powerful API. Using these scripts is similar to the way that requesters use the API and third-party platforms to increase Mechanical Turk's effectiveness (see Chapter 4). Scripts and extensions provide many features for workers that broadly fall into the following categories: (a) information about a requester's HIT history, (b) automatic HIT finding and accepting, and (c) a more detailed worker interface for tracking HITs and daily progress.

Information about requesters is collected through the reviews workers leave using the Turkopticon extension. This information includes ratings of each requester's *communicativity*, *generosity*, *fairness*, and *promptness*, as well as more detailed, written reviews posted by workers in the past. Turkopticon is one of the most widely used extensions and is connected to many other extensions that automatically import requester ratings into HIT previews workers see while looking for HITs to accept. This detailed HIT description can be seen in Figure 2.6 and is also available for export from workers' advanced HIT preview screens, allowing workers to share great HITs with others on forums.

Scripts and popular extensions such as MTurk Suite, HIT Catcher, and PandaCrazy help automate elements of previewing and accepting HITs, making this process easier for workers (see Kaplan, Saito, Hara, & Bigham, 2018). The most popular use of these scripts appears to be for grabbing HITs that are returned by workers who did not complete them. If a user sees a HIT that she wants that is no longer available, she can create a preview and accept (PANDA) script for this HIT, or rely on an extension to do this for her. This is particularly useful for grabbing HITs the instant they are returned by someone who accepted but did not complete it, and for HITs that requesters update to gather more responses to. Some PANDA scripts report the capability to grab HITs before they ever appear on the search page. Extensions also can automatically refresh HITs, allowing a worker to grab a HIT the instant it becomes available. Additionally, extensions can automatically search for HITs that have certain characteristics a worker can select for, including based on reward, number of HITs available, Turkopticon scores, and qualifications, making HIT finding fast and precise. For $10 a month, there is even a desktop application called Turkernator, which some workers use to grab the HITs they want quickly and simplify their workflow.

These scripts and extensions likely play an important role in some of the effects researchers are finding relating to differences in what kinds of workers accept their HITs. For example, some research has found that the kinds of workers who take HITs right after they are published are different in some ways from workers who find HITs later (Casey, Chandler, Levine, Proctor, & Strolovitch, 2017). This is likely related to the fact that "superworkers" use these scripts to find high-paying HITs shortly after they are published (see Chapter 7).

CONCLUSION

The need to maintain standards of high data quality and to prevent fraud has led Mechanical Turk to create a system in which requesters have disproportionately more control over approving submitted HITs. This power imbalance may be expected to lead to abuse. However, requesters who engage in such practices will find themselves blacklisted on worker forums, which means their HITs will be less likely to attract high-quality workers. Researchers in the social and behavioral sciences are motivated to engage in practices that maximize the likelihood of collecting high-quality data. Requesters recognize that fair payment practices are likely to motivate more workers to participate in their studies, likely leading to increased external validity. These factors exert market pressure on requesters to treat workers fairly, leading to a more balanced requester-worker power relationship.

Empirical data support the view that most requesters act responsibly toward MTurk workers. For example, the rate at which academic requesters reject HITs is just under 0.03% (see Chapter 11). There is thus no evidence that requesters are taking advantage of their ability to reject work. Indeed, evidence suggests that the wages on Mechanical Turk have been increasing steadily over the past two years, as discussed in more detail in Chapter 11. Thus, although an unregulated marketplace that favors the employer has the potential to result in unfair practices, it appears that some of the aforementioned forces have largely buffered Mechanical Turk from this kind of abuse.

Overall, Mechanical Turk is a unique economic ecosystem with characteristics that are of considerable scientific interest in and of themselves. The dynamics of the requester-worker relationship should be monitored closely in the future, both for its scientific value and for the practical insights that requesters can glean about conducting their research on Mechanical Turk.

REFERENCES

Berinsky, A. J., Huber, G. A., & Lenz, G. S. (2012). Evaluating online labor markets for experimental research: Amazon.com's Mechanical Turk. *Political Analysis, 20*(3), 351–368. doi:10.1093/pan/mpr057

Braithwaite, S. R., Giraud-Carrier, C., West, J., Barnes, M. D., & Hanson, C. L. (2016). Validating machine learning algorithms for Twitter data against established measures of suicidality. *JMIR Mental Health, 3*(2), e21. doi:10.2196/mental.4822

Brinton, J. E., Keating, M. D., Ortiz, A. M., Evenson, K. R., & Furberg, R. D. (2017). Establishing linkages between distributed survey responses and consumer wearable device datasets: A pilot protocol. *JMIR Research Protocols, 6*(4), e66. doi:10.2196/resprot.6513

Casey, L. S., Chandler, J., Levine, A. S., Proctor, A., & Strolovitch, D. Z. (2017). Intertemporal differences among MTurk workers: Time-based sample variations and implications for online data collection. *SAGE Open, 7*(2), 215824401771277. doi:10.1177/2158244017712774

Chandler, J. J., & Paolacci, G. (2017). Lie for a dime: When most prescreening responses are honest but most study participants are impostors. *Social Psychological and Personality Science, 8*(5), 500–508. doi:10.1177/1948550617698203

Chilton, L. B., Horton, J. J., Miller, R. C., & Azenkot, S. (2010, July). Task search in a human computation market. In *Proceedings of the ACM SIGKDD workshop on human computation* (pp. 1–9). New York, NY: Association for Computing Machinery.

Hauser, D. J., & Schwarz, N. (2016). Attentive Turkers: MTurk participants perform better on online attention checks than do subject pool participants. *Behavior Research Methods, 48*(1), 400–407. doi:10.3758/s13428-015-0578-z

Kaplan, T., Saito, S., Hara, K., & Bigham, J. P. (2018). Striving to earn more: A survey of work strategies and tool use among crowd workers. *Sixth AAAI Conference on Human Computation and Crowdsourcing.*

Litman, L., Robinson, J., Rosen Z., Rosenzweig, C., Waxman, J., & Bates, L. M. (2019). The persistence of pay inequality: The gender wage gap in an anonymous online labor market. *PsychArxiv.*

Paolacci, G., Chandler, J., & Ipeirotis, P. G. (2010). Running experiments on Amazon Mechanical Turk. *Judgment and Decision Making, 5*, 411–419.

Peer, E., Vosgerau, J., & Acquisti, A. (2014). Reputation as a sufficient condition for data quality on Amazon Mechanical Turk. *Behavior Research Methods, 46*(4), 1023–1031. doi:10.3758/s13428-013-0434-y

Ross, J., Irani, L., Silberman, M., Zaldivar, A., & Tomlinson, B. (2010, April). Who are the crowd workers? Shifting demographics in Mechanical Turk. In *CHI '10 extended abstracts on human factors in computing systems* (pp. 2863–2872). New York, NY: Association for Computing Machinery.

Schnur, J. B., Chaplin, W. F., Khurshid, K., Mogavero, J. N., Goldsmith, R. E., Lee, Y. -S., . . .Montgomery, G. H. (2017). Development of the healthcare triggering questionnaire in adult sexual abuse survivors. *Psychological Trauma: Theory, Research, Practice, and Policy, 9*(6), 714–722. doi:10.1037/tra0000273

Staffelbach, M., Sempolinski, P., Hachen, D., Kareem, A., Kijewski-Correa, T., Thain, D., . . .Madey, G. (2014). Lessons learned from an experiment in crowdsourcing complex citizen engineering tasks with Amazon Mechanical Turk. *Paper presented at the Collective Intelligence Conference*, Cambridge, MA.

CONDUCTING A STUDY ON MECHANICAL TURK

Leib Litman and Jonathan Robinson

INTRODUCTION

This chapter uses a project-oriented approach to describe the process of conducting social and behavioral research on Mechanical Turk. One of the goals of this chapter is to demonstrate what a typical research project on Mechanical Turk might look like and to describe the advantages of conducting this kind of study on Mechanical Turk compared to using other data sources. To this end, we begin by describing a sample study, including its methodology, validated survey instruments, study design, study objectives, and expected results. The results of the study are briefly reported at the end of the chapter.

In the first part of the chapter we discuss how to set up the study on a survey platform and generate a study link. We describe the basic functionality of different study development platforms and the specific steps that are necessary to integrate a study that was created on an external survey platform with Mechanical Turk. Although a comprehensive guide for using study development platforms is outside the scope of this book, we provide a detailed online tutorial for setting up a basic survey study using Qualtrics.

In the second part of the chapter we provide a step-by-step guide for setting up a study (i.e., a HIT) on Mechanical Turk using the sample study as a reference. We focus on best practices for completing study-specific fields such as the study name, description, payment, and qualifications, and for setting the HIT's visibility. Best practices for setting up a Mechanical Turk HIT are summarized in the chapter's Appendix.

Graphic interfaces change all the time. Because Mechanical Turk is likely to update its interface at some point, some of the screenshots in this chapter will eventually become out of date. For this reason, this chapter has an accompanying online version that is updated regularly. The updated version of this and the next chapter can be found on the book's website at https://www.cloudresearch.com/resources/book/.

Finally, readers who are familiar with the Mechanical Turk interface and with setting up studies on MTurk may be able to skip to Chapter 4 where we discuss how third-party platforms can enhance MTurk's functionality with the use of MTurk's API.

SAMPLE PROJECT

In this chapter we illustrate the typical workflow involved in conducting a Mechanical Turk HIT by describing a sample study. Our sample study aims to replicate the well-established relationship between the concept of thin-ideal internalization and disordered eating pathology (DEP). These constructs span various disciplines including clinical, health, and social psychology as well as sociology, psychiatry, and epidemiology. As a result of our study's interdisciplinary nature, the general methodology of this study is representative of many HITs that are posted on Mechanical Turk by social and behavioral scientists. The study uses validated survey instruments to measure the internalization of sociocultural messages of beauty and thinness (referred to as the thin-ideal), DEP, a number of relevant covariates, and to record responses to demographic questions.

Study Background

Eating disorders, such as anorexia nervosa, bulimia nervosa, and binge-eating disorder, are life-threatening illnesses whose prevalence continues to increase. It is well established that the etiology of these conditions is complex and multifaceted; therefore, understanding risk factors for these conditions is critical for effective prevention and treatment efforts. Large-scale prospective studies have demonstrated that among the most proximal risk factors for the development of eating disorders are body dissatisfaction and internalization of sociocultural ideals related to beauty and thinness (Rohde et al., 20152015; Stice, Gau, Rohde, & Shaw, 2017). There exists a spectrum of eating behaviors ranging from normal on the one hand to full-blown eating disorders on the other. This continuum includes a variety of behaviors that can be labeled as disordered eating or DEP (e.g., chronic dieting), which are also highly associated with the development of eating disorders. Thus our sample study examines key concepts in the understanding of risk factors for the development of these conditions, which affect a significant proportion of young women and, increasingly, young men as well (see Rogers Wood et al., 20102019; Stice & Shaw, 2002; and Striegel-Moore & Bulik, 2007, for reviews of the literature).

Thin-ideal internalization is a well-established psychosocial risk factor for DEP and body dissatisfaction (Brown & Dittmar, 2005; Dittmar, Halliwell, & Stirling, 2009; Stice, Marti, Rohde, & Shaw, 2011; Thompson & Stice, 2001). It refers to the extent to which one internalizes and is aware of cultural and media messages surrounding thinness (Stice et al., 2011; Thompson & Stice, 2001). Although cultural messages about thinness and beauty are ubiquitous, the internalization of these messages influences their level of impact with regard to DEP.

Therefore, in this study we aim to replicate the established association between thin-ideal internalization, as measured by the Sociocultural Attitudes Towards Appearance Scale (SATAQ-3), and DEP, as measured by the Eating Attitudes Test (EAT-26).

Why Conduct This Study on Mechanical Turk?

Conducting the present study on Mechanical Turk provides both methodological and practical advantages, including speed and price. This study will selectively target women because women are differentially affected by media messages of thinness and are significantly more likely than men to exhibit DEP. Mechanical Turk is a convenient and easily accessible source of participants and can be used to selectively recruit specific populations, such as women. Once launched, data collection is expected to complete within three hours. The cost is expected to be less than $200. The stimuli used in the study can be easily developed online using survey platforms and then be linked seamlessly to Mechanical Turk. Once data are collected, a labeled CSV or SPSS file will be available for download immediately, saving time over traditional pencil-and-paper approaches.

Methodological advantages include a more representative sample compared to typical samples collected from the undergraduate subject pool. The sample is expected to be more diverse in terms of age, race, and geographic location compared to other common sources of convenience samples. Additional methodological advantages include the ability to follow up with the sample longitudinally with relatively low dropout over time (see Chapter 9). There are also ample opportunities to follow up on the results of this study with more research to examine how the relationship between thin-ideal internalization and disordered eating may interact with (be moderated by) factors such as age, U.S. region, culture (e.g., U.S. vs. India), religious background, and many others. As such, Mechanical Turk is not just a platform for conducting a single study but, rather, is an environment on which a phenomenon of scientific interest can be explored systematically, across a series of studies and using a wide range of research methodologies.

Stimulus Development

Mechanical Turk's Survey Tool

Mechanical Turk is almost exclusively a platform for connecting workers (participants) and requesters (researchers). It is not a platform for creating complex surveys. Mechanical Turk does provide a rudimentary survey tool, which is called the *survey template* (see Figure 3.1). Using this template, you can create internal HITs that include a variety of question types, including multiple-choice, fill-in-the-blank, and drop-down questions. Using this template, you can collect data completely within Mechanical Turk without the need to link to an external survey platform. A further advantage of using Mechanical Turk's survey template is that it is free.

However, for most researchers, Mechanical Turk's survey template does not provide a wide enough range of features to accommodate their study designs. Some of the limitations of Mechanical Turk's survey platform include the lack

FIGURE 3.1 ● SURVEY QUESTION OPTIONS AVAILABLE ON MECHANICAL TURK'S BUILT-IN SURVEY CREATOR

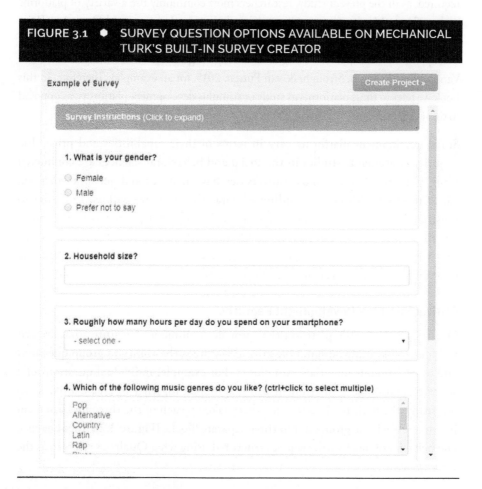

of question logic capability, the inability to group items into blocks, the inability to randomize the order of stimulus presentation or to randomize stimuli across subjects, and a limited ability to embed stimuli other than text, including audio and video stimuli. For these reasons the actual study materials are typically created on a separate platform.

Stimulus Development Platforms

When it comes to stimulus development platforms in the social and behavioral sciences, there are many options to choose from. The choice of platform depends on the type of study, study design, and budget. For example, when designing a cognitive psychology study where precision in the measurement of reaction time is an important factor, Inquisit software is usually the option of choice. Inquisit makes it possible to collect reaction time with millisecond precision over the internet and to flexibly program a wide range of experimental designs. When the collection of precision reaction time is not required, as in the present study, researchers most commonly use a variety of platforms such as SurveyMonkey, SurveyGizmo, Google Forms, Red Cap, and Qualtrics. These platforms are often referred to as "survey platforms," but this is a misnomer. Some of these platforms are capable of being used to design highly sophisticated experiments (see Van Emden, de Bruin, Strough, & van Putten, 2015, for an example). Therefore, in this book we refer to these platforms as study or stimulus development platforms, as opposed to survey platforms.

Study development platforms vary in terms of their capabilities and price. The majority of academic studies in the social and behavioral sciences are conducted using Qualtrics because most universities have institutional accounts through which researchers can collect unlimited data. Therefore, we will use Qualtrics to illustrate how to create studies using study development platforms in this book. For those who do not have access to Qualtrics through their institution, a free Qualtrics trial account (limited to 100 participants) is available, and it has the functionality needed to create our sample study.

Critical Stimulus Development Features

Qualtrics is a versatile platform that provides a number of features that are critical for flexible study design. One critical feature is the ability to group questions and other stimulus materials into blocks. For example, individual questions of a specific questionnaire instrument can be grouped together to create a block. In our study, the multiple Likert items that make up each of the three measurement instruments will be grouped into three separate blocks (Figure 3.2). The sequence and behavior of blocks will then be structured using what Qualtrics refers to as the *survey flow*.

FIGURE 3.2 ● LIKERT ITEMS GROUPED INTO FIVE STUDY BLOCKS IN A QUALTRICS SURVEY

Within the survey flow it is possible to randomize the order of blocks and thereby control for potential priming and carryover effects. It is also possible to randomly assign blocks to participants, thereby creating experiments. For example, three blocks with videos featuring models that differ in their levels of thinness can be randomly assigned across three conditions in a between-subjects experiment. This would allow researchers to examine how each video causes a change in outcomes of disordered eating, thin-ideal internalization, and depression, and how exposure to thin models may cause changes in the associations between these variables.

Design considerations of many studies require a stimulus platform that allows for flexible control over the order and behavior of blocks. When it comes to such advanced features, researchers will usually find that there is a trade-off between price and flexibility. For example, Google Forms is free, but, like the Mechanical Turk survey template, it lacks the ability to group items into blocks. Similarly, SurveyMonkey does not provide the ability to group items into blocks. For this reason, it is not possible to randomly assign participants to different conditions of a study or to control priming and carryover effects when using these platforms. Thus, although Google Forms has the advantage of being free, it has the disadvantage of not offering the flexibility that is typically needed to conduct many research studies.

Figure 3.2 shows the five block structure of the current study. The first is a welcome block that consists of a consent form, a welcome message, and instructions to participants. The next three blocks consist of groups of Likert items drawn from each of the three scales. Block 2 consists of 31 Likert items from the Social Attitudes Toward Appearance Questionnaire (SATAQ). Block 3 consists of 27 questions from the Eating Attitudes Test (EAT). Block 4 consists of 21 questions from the Beck Depression Inventory (BDI) (Beck, Steer, & Garbin, 1988). The last block consists of 20 demographic questions.

Figure 3.3 shows the survey flow for this study. For the present study, the welcome and demographics blocks are presented first and last, respectively, for all participants. The order of the three middle blocks is randomized across participants.

As stated earlier, Qualtrics is the platform most commonly accessible to researchers through their institutional accounts, and it also has the advantage of being perhaps the most versatile platform for the design of social and behavioral research studies. In addition to having the ability to group items into blocks, Qualtrics has multiple other features, such as the ability to time responses (although not with the same precision as Inquisit) and a wide range of stimulus presentation options.

A full overview of Qualtrics or any other stimulus development platform is beyond the scope of this book. For those who are less familiar with online stimulus development

FIGURE 3.3 ● SURVEY FLOW IN WHICH THE ORDER OF THE FIRST AND FIFTH BLOCKS REMAINS CONSTANT, AND BLOCKS 2–4 ARE RANDOMIZED

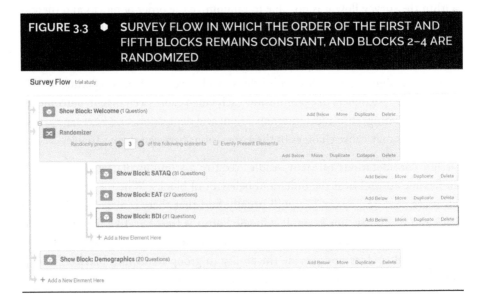

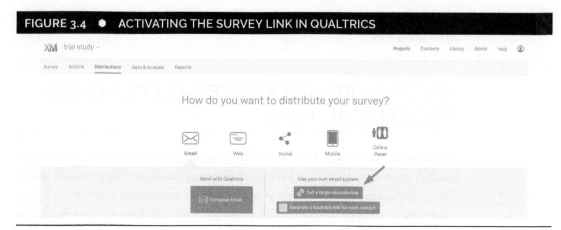

FIGURE 3.4 ● ACTIVATING THE SURVEY LINK IN QUALTRICS

software, we provide a Qualtrics tutorial that can be downloaded from this book's website at https://www.cloudresearch.com/resources/book/. Once the study is set up on a stimulus development platform, a study link needs to be generated and added to the Mechanical Turk HIT.

Generating the Survey Link for Distributing the Study

All stimulus development platforms have the ability to generate a survey link. Once a survey link is generated, clicking on the link takes participants directly to the survey. The survey link can be distributed to participants in many different ways. It can be emailed or distributed through platforms such as Facebook. After clicking on the link, the participant is taken directly to the survey and can begin participating in the study. On Mechanical Turk, this link is made available to workers once they accept a HIT. To generate a survey link in Qualtrics, click the *Distributions* tab on the dashboard and choose *Get a single reusable link* (Figure 3.4). This will generate the survey link (Figure 3.5) that can be copied and pasted to Mechanical Turk. Once a survey link has been generated on a

FIGURE 3.5 ● THE SURVEY LINK THAT CAN BE DISTRIBUTED TO PARTICIPANTS

stimulus development platform, the researcher is ready to begin setting up the HIT on Mechanical Turk.

SETTING UP A REQUESTER ACCOUNT ON MECHANICAL TURK

To set up a Mechanical Turk requester account, go to https://www.mturk.com/mturk/welcome, and sign in as a requester (Figure 3.6). You will be prompted to sign in to your Amazon account. Users who already have an Amazon account can sign in using their existing Amazon email and password. Users can also create a new account using a new email address. We recommend that users create a new Amazon account due to potential privacy and security issues that we discuss later. Once signed in to Amazon, you will be taken to a page for creating a Mechanical Turk account and asked to enter basic contact information. The most important part of this page is what Mechanical Turk refers to as the *company name*. The company name is the requester name by which you will be known to workers. Once logged in, a requester will see their requester name as it will appear to workers in the upper right of the screen. The name of our account is "psychlab" (Figure 3.7). This is the *company name* that had been entered when the requester account was first created.

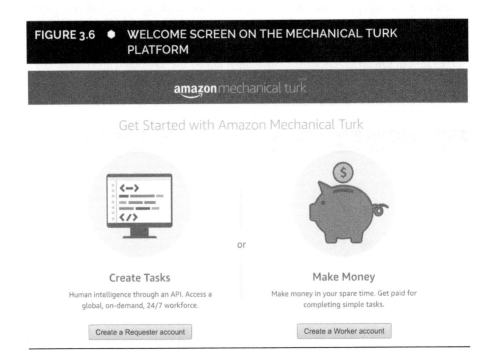

FIGURE 3.6 ● WELCOME SCREEN ON THE MECHANICAL TURK PLATFORM

amazon mechanical turk

Get Started with Amazon Mechanical Turk

or

Create Tasks

Human intelligence through an API. Access a global, on-demand, 24/7 workforce.

Create a Requester account

Make Money

Make money in your spare time. Get paid for completing simple tasks.

Create a Worker account

FIGURE 3.7 ● THE MECHANICAL TURK REQUESTER ACCOUNT

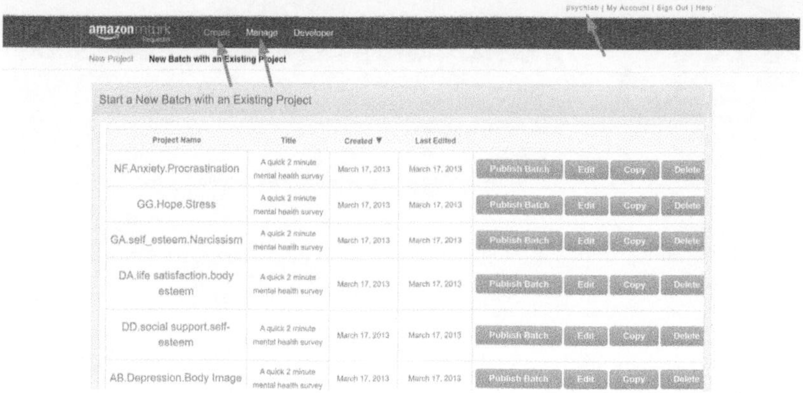

CREATING A HIT

The *Create* and *Manage* tabs are used for launching and monitoring HITs. To create a study, go to the *Create* tab. We will come back to the *Manage* tab once the study has been created. In the future, under the *Create* tab you will find a list of all previously created HITs, with options to edit, copy, or delete them (Figure 3.7). Copying and editing an existing HIT is much easier than creating a HIT from scratch, so once you create your first study, make use of the ability to copy this study in the future.

To begin creating a new HIT, click on *New Project* (Figure 3.8). Under the *Create* tab, on the left side you will find a series of template options for launching different types of HITs (Figure 3.9). Most of the HIT templates listed here, such as sentiment

FIGURE 3.8 ● THE CREATE PROJECT ENVIRONMENT

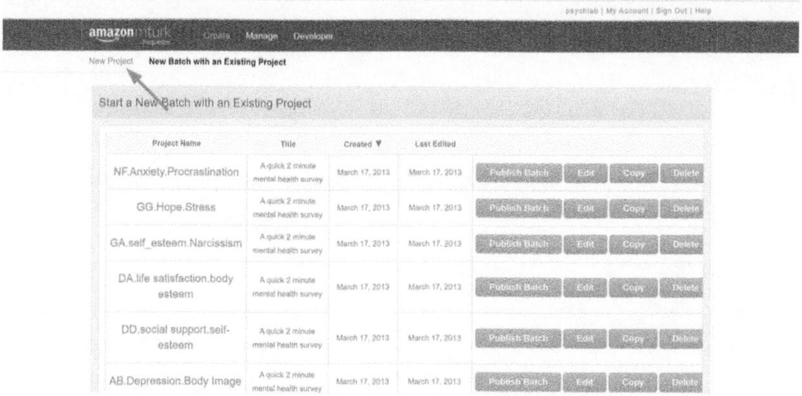

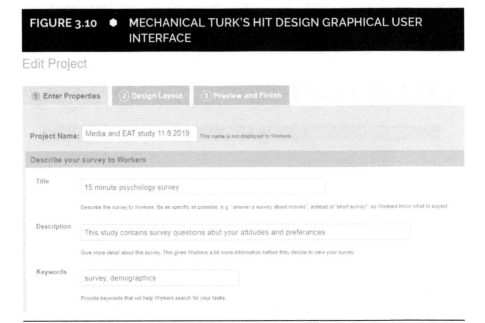

FIGURE 3.9 ● MECHANICAL TURK'S BUILT-IN TEMPLATE OPTIONS

Survey
Survey Link
Survey
Vision
Image Classification
Bounding Box
Semantic Segmentation
Instance Segmentation
Polygon
Keypoint
Image Contains
Video Classification
Moderation of an Image
Image Tagging
Image Summarization
Language
Sentiment Analysis
Intent Detection
Collect Utterance
Emotion Detection
Semantic Similarity
Audio Transcription
Conversation Relevance
Document Classification
Survey Link Instructions (Click to expand)
Survey link:
http://example.com/survey345.html
Provide the survey code here:
123456
You must ACCEPT the HIT before you can submit the results.
Create Project

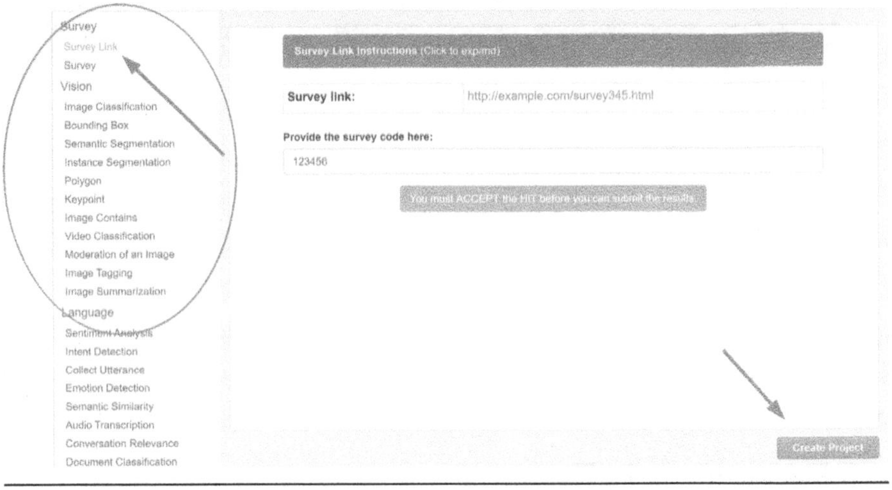

and categorization, are not commonly used in research in the social and behavioral sciences. The *Survey Link* option allows a requester to paste a URL link (see Figure 3.5) to a study hosted on another platform, such as Qualtrics. Click *Survey Link* and then *Create Project* (see Figure 3.9).

You are now in the design environment (see Figure 3.10). Designing a study requires sequentially filling fields within three tabs: the *Enter Properties* tab, the *Design Layout*

FIGURE 3.10 ● MECHANICAL TURK'S HIT DESIGN GRAPHICAL USER INTERFACE

Edit Project
1 Enter Properties
2 Design Layout
3 Preview and Finish
Project Name: Media and EAT study 11.6.2019
This name is not displayed to Workers.
Describe your survey to Workers
Title
15 minute psychology survey
Describe the survey to Workers. Be as specific as possible, e.g. "answer a survey about movies", instead of "short survey", so Workers know what to expect.
Description
This study contains survey questions abut your attitudes and preferances
Give more detail about this survey. This gives Workers a bit more information before they decide to view your survey.
Keywords
survey, demographics
Provide keywords that will help Workers search for your tasks.

tab, and the *Preview and Finish* tab. In the *Enter Properties* tab under *Describe your HIT to Workers*, fill out basic information about the study's specifications, starting with the study's title.

The *project name* is not visible to workers. It is for the requester's internal use. The project name can be anything that makes the study easy to track in the future. The *title* is visible to workers on both the workers' dashboard (see Figure 2.1) and the HIT preview window.

Communicating Time Expectations to Workers

It is good practice to include the expected length of the study as part of the title. This allows workers to know not only how much a study pays, which is presented automatically on the Mechanical Turk dashboard, but also how long the study is expected to take. This will make it easier for workers to calculate the study's approximate hourly wage.

The design template does not include a field for how long a study is expected to take. Instead, the design template has a field for the maximum time allotted to a worker before the HIT expires. This is likely because, prior to Mechanical Turk becoming popular for scientific studies, most tasks were expected to be short. There was thus no reason to specifically indicate the expected completion time. Because the lengths of scientific studies can vary widely, providing the expected completion time can aid workers' decisions as to whether or not a HIT is worth working on (see Figure 2.7 for an example of a HIT title that includes a time estimate).

Estimating a Study's Completion Time

A useful rule of thumb is that it takes 10 seconds to answer one survey question and 5 seconds for a demographic question. Because our sample study has 80 survey questions and 20 demographic questions, it is likely to be completed in 900 seconds, or 15 minutes on average. It is a good idea to pilot a study to get a more accurate time estimate before launching the full data collection. Doing so helps researchers pay workers appropriately for the time a study takes.

Naming the HIT

It is generally good practice for the study title to be generic so as not to introduce self-selection bias. For example, a name such as "A Survey Study Examining the Relationship between Body Image and Eating Disorders" provides a clear description of the study's aims. However, this may attract workers who may be particularly interested in this topic, perhaps because they have a history of eating disorders. At the same time, other workers may not wish to participate in the study knowing that it is examining eating disorders. This can introduce selection bias in the sample.

Rather than using a descriptive study name, we recommend using a title that is general, such as "Psychology Survey" or "Public Health Study." The title we will use for the current study is "15 Minute Psychology Survey." This title lets workers know that they will be asked to fill out questionnaires and that the task will take approximately 15 minutes. As such, their expectation will be that they are being asked to participate in a typical Mechanical Turk psychology study.

The *Description* field is also visible to workers. However, it is only visible on the dashboard and not in the HIT preview window. For this reason, most details about the study's procedure should be included in the *Instructions* field and not as part of the study's description. Like the title, the description should be generic so as not to introduce self-selection bias. Our study description will be "This study contains survey questions about your attitudes and preferences."

Filling in the *Keywords* field is optional. Data suggest that workers search studies mostly based on price and recency.

Setting the Reward

The *reward per response* (see Figure 3.11) is the amount workers will be paid for completing the HIT. Academic requesters pay upwards of $6.00 per hour on average (see Chapter 11). The pay rate suggested by Mechanical Turk is $6.00 per hour, which would set the reward at $1.50 for our sample study, although we recommend paying more as discussed in more detail in Chapter 11. Workers do not get paid based on how much time they spend on a HIT. A worker who spends

FIGURE 3.11 ● BASIC FIELDS OF THE DESIGN INTERFACE

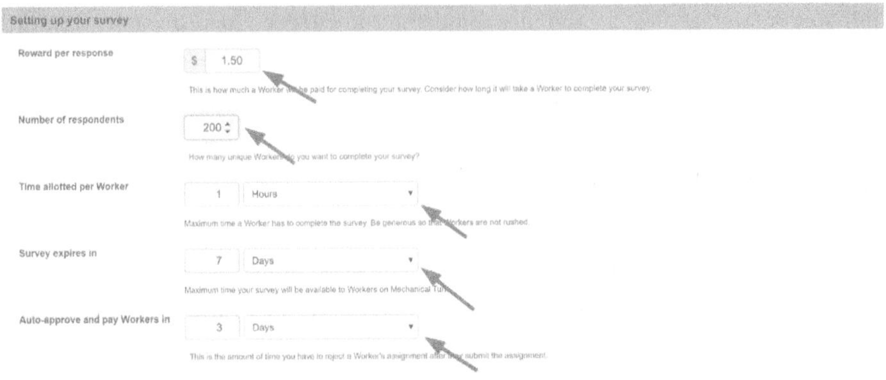

Setting up your survey

Reward per response
$ 1.50
This is how much a Worker will be paid for completing your survey. Consider how long it will take a Worker to complete your survey.

Number of respondents
200
How many unique Workers do you want to complete your survey?

Time allotted per Worker
1 Hours
Maximum time a Worker has to complete the survey. Be generous as Workers are not rushed.

Survey expires in
7 Days
Maximum time your survey will be available to Workers on Mechanical Turk.

Auto-approve and pay Workers in
3 Days
This is the amount of time you have to reject a Worker's assignment after they submit the assignment.

20 minutes on a HIT gets paid exactly the same as a worker who spends 2 minutes. Instead, requesters should set the reward based on what they expect the average completion time to be.

Number of Assignments per HIT

The *number of assignments per HIT* is the total number of workers who can participate in a HIT. It is also the maximum number of workers who can be taking a HIT at any one time. Most HITs have at least some dropout, where workers do not complete the task in the allotted time. Mechanical Turk does not anticipate how many workers will drop out. Instead, it waits either for a worker to return the HIT or for the worker's time to run out before allowing another worker to begin the HIT. This mechanism places constraints on the time allowed for the assignment, which the next field on the template addresses.

Time Allotted per Assignment

The *time allotted per assignment* is the maximum time that a participant has to complete the HIT. Workers who do not submit a HIT within the time allotted will be locked out of the HIT. Those workers also will not be able to get paid as a result (see the section "When a Worker Runs Out of Time" for what to do when this happens). For this reason, requesters should make sure to give workers enough time to complete the study. At the same time, giving workers too much time can be problematic. About 5% of workers will always take the maximum time to complete a HIT in order to maximize their earnings—a practice we refer to as *HIT sniping*. HIT sniping involves accepting multiple HITs at once and then completing them at the worker's convenience. This allows workers to maximize their earnings by grabbing high-paying HITs as soon as they become available and then completing them at a later time.

Additionally, some workers who choose not to complete a HIT will simply abandon it, rather than return it. This prevents the full study from completing until the time allotted per assignment runs out, giving other workers the opportunity to start the returned HIT. Some requesters set the *Time allotted per assignment* field to 48 hours or more, thinking that this will be helpful to workers. Instead, this practice often leads to HITs that do not complete for many days.

To prevent HIT sniping and very long completion times, the *Time allotted per assignment* field should not be set to more than four times the expected completion time. For our study we will set that field to one hour, since the time to complete the HIT is expected to be 15 minutes.

HIT Expires In

The *HIT expires in* field is the maximum time that a HIT will remain active and visible on the dashboard. Keep in mind that just because the study is active does not mean that workers are able to see it. Over time, HITs move down on the dashboard queue and after a few days a worker may need to scroll through many pages before seeing a HIT. Chapter 4 describes the available tools for keeping a long-running HIT visible to workers.

Auto-Approve

The *Auto-approve and pay Workers in* field indicates the maximum time before all workers are paid. Workers are not automatically paid when they complete a HIT. The requester has to approve the assignment first. In the event that a requester forgets to approve or reject a HIT, or does not approve or reject it for some other reason, an automatic approval will be granted after the auto-approve time is reached.

Qualifications

As discussed previously, Mechanical Turk has a qualifications system by which specific workers can be selected to participate in a HIT, or by which specific workers can be restricted from participating in a HIT. There are two types of qualifications: those assigned by Mechanical Turk and those assigned by the requester.

Worker Requirements

Masters (Figure 3.12) are workers who were given the Master qualification by Mechanical Turk based on their high performance. It is not known exactly how Mechanical Turk determines high performance, and there is no evidence that there is any benefit in using masters for most survey studies (Rogers Wood et al., 20102019). In addition, there are few published academic studies that report using master workers.

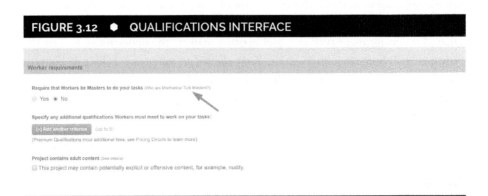

FIGURE 3.12 ● QUALIFICATIONS INTERFACE

FIGURE 3.13 ● WORKER REQUIREMENTS FIELDS

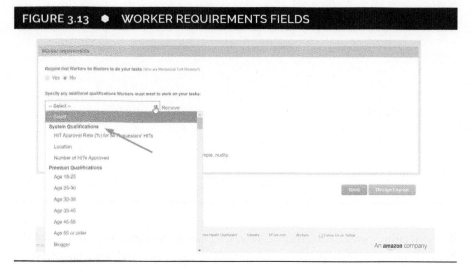

Mechanical Turk System Qualifications

Click on *(+) Add another criterion* (see Figure 3.12) to see a list of Mechanical Turk qualifications (Figure 3.13). The drop-down menu lists Mechanical Turk system qualifications, Mechanical Turk premium qualifications, and qualifications that the requester has created.

The first system qualification, the *Location* qualification, allows requesters to specify which country workers are from. Practically speaking, workers are likely to be in the United States, Canada, and India. Most other countries are highly limited in terms of how many workers can be recruited.

Data quality can vary significantly by country, particularly in India (see Litman, Robinson, & Rosenzweig, 2015). For research in the social and behavioral sciences, using workers from countries where English is not the primary language is not recommended, unless the study's research question specifically requires the use of participants from other countries. Litman et al. (2015) found that one reason for the lower rate of data quality in India is the lack of English proficiency among India-based workers. When using workers from countries where English is not the primary language, including English proficiency checks in the study is a highly effective way to increase data quality (see Chapter 5).

Selecting Workers Based on Approval Rating and Number of HITs Completed

The second system qualification, the *HIT approval rate,* is based on the ratio of approved to rejected HITs for each worker. The third system qualification is the HIT completion history. Studies show that restricting a HIT to workers who have a 95% or above

FIGURE 3.14 ● PREMIUM QUALIFICATIONS INTERFACE

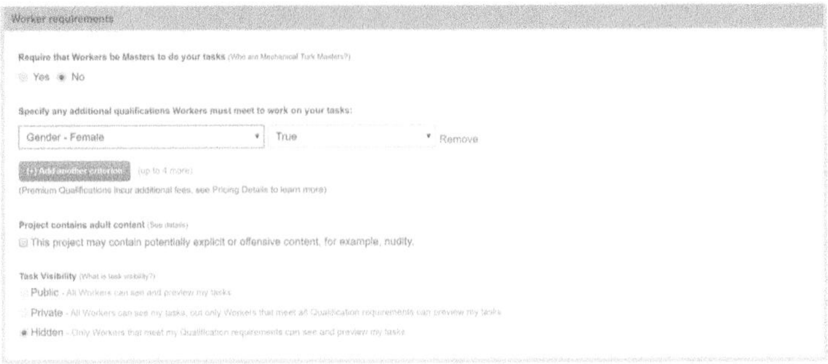

approval rating increases data quality (Peer, Vosgerau, & Acquisti, 2014). It is therefore a common practice to let only workers with a 95% or higher approval rating take the study.

Critically, the default approval rating for workers is 100% at the time when they create their worker accounts. A worker needs to have completed at least 100 HITs in order to be assigned an actual approval rating. Thus, when using approval ratings, researchers need to set the number of completed HITs to 100 if they want every worker to have a verified approval rating.

Researchers wishing to follow commonly accepted practice should use the 95% approval rating and a 100 HIT completion minimum as participation requirements. However, this recruitment practice introduces selection biases by increasing the proportion of highly experienced workers. More recent research casts doubt on whether this practice actually increases data quality (Robinson, Rosenzweig, Moss, & Litman, 2019). These issues are discussed in more detail in Chapter 7.

Our sample study specifically targets women, so *Gender-Female* will be set to *True* as a *premium qualification* in the *Worker requirements* field (see Figure 3.14). Note that the HIT will not be open to all female workers on Mechanical Turk. Instead the HIT will be open to only those workers who filled out Mechanical Turk's qualification survey and indicated their gender is female. This is a subset of the Mechanical Turk worker population. It is currently not known what percentage of workers take qualification HITs.

HIT Visibility

The *HIT Visibility* selection (see Figure 3.14) determines which workers are able to see the HIT on their dashboard and in the HIT preview window. Selecting the incorrect *HIT Visibility* option will prevent the requester from correctly calculating the dropout rate and may prevent the requester from being able to view their own HIT on the workers' dashboard.

Selecting the *Public* visibility option will make the HIT visible to all workers on the dashboard and will allow all workers to preview the HIT, even if they do not have the qualifications required to accept the HIT. Setting the HIT visibility to *Public* will prevent the proper calculation of the bounce rate. Workers may preview the HIT only to find out they cannot accept it because they do not have the necessary qualifications. When this happens the bounce rate will be inflated because the bounce rate is calculated independent of whether or not the worker is qualified to accept the HIT. For example, in our study, setting the visibility to *Public* will allow men to preview the HIT, even though they will not be able to accept and work on it. All the men who previewed and returned the HIT will be included in the bounce rate calculation. If a large number of men preview the HIT, a requester may incorrectly conclude that many workers are not interested in the HIT due to unrelated reasons such as the pay rate.

Setting the HIT visibility to *Private* will allow workers to see the HIT on the dashboard but prevent them from previewing it without the necessary qualifications. Additionally, it will enable requesters who want to preview their HITs as workers to do so on the workers' dashboard even when they do not have the qualifications to take those HITs. It is common for requesters to want to view their HITs on their dashboard. This can sometimes cause confusion as requesters have been surprised that they cannot see their own HIT when logged in as workers. This will happen if the requester had specified the HIT visibility as *Hidden*, which will only allow workers who meet the qualification requirements to see the HIT on the dashboard (unless their worker profile also meets the appropriate qualifications). On the requester account, selecting *Private* will allow the requester to preview their HIT, while not interfering with the bounce rate calculation.

This completes the *Enter Properties* tab. Click *Save* and *Create* to create the project. The project will now be visible under the *Create* tab (Figure 3.15). Click *Edit* to continue to the *Design Layout* tab.

FIGURE 3.15 ● NEWLY CREATED STUDY VISIBLE UNDER THE *CREATE* TAB

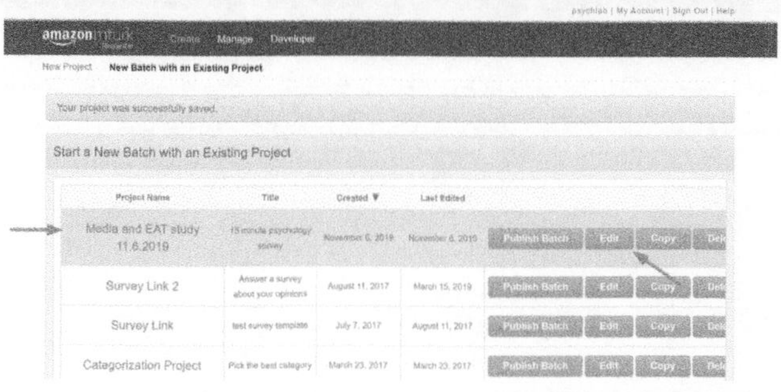

THE *DESIGN LAYOUT* TAB

Instructions

The information presented in the *Survey Link Instructions* field (Figure 3.16) is what the worker will see in the HIT preview window after selecting the HIT from the workers' dashboard. This is the most important information that workers use to decide whether or not to accept the HIT. Describing the HIT correctly both in terms of time requirements and procedure has a significant impact on whether or not a worker will accept the HIT.

If a study requires extra effort or anything out of the ordinary, it is important to include a description of what the participants will be expected to do. For example, Inquisit studies require workers to download a file and install it on their computers. When a study requires workers to download software or apps, that information should be included in the description. Cognitive battery studies, or any study that requires more effort than the average HIT, should also be described here. At the same time, one should not include too much complicated information. It is best to present instructions simply, and in bullet point form, if possible. For survey studies that use stimulus development platforms, the instructions should also indicate that workers need to enter a code in the secret code window.

Secret Code

The *secret code* is a way of verifying that a participant finished the survey. When creating an external-linked HIT that is housed on a platform such as Qualtrics or

FIGURE 3.16 ● THE *DESIGN LAYOUT* PAGE

FIGURE 3.17 ● SECRET CODE PRESENTED AT THE END OF A QUALTRICS STUDY

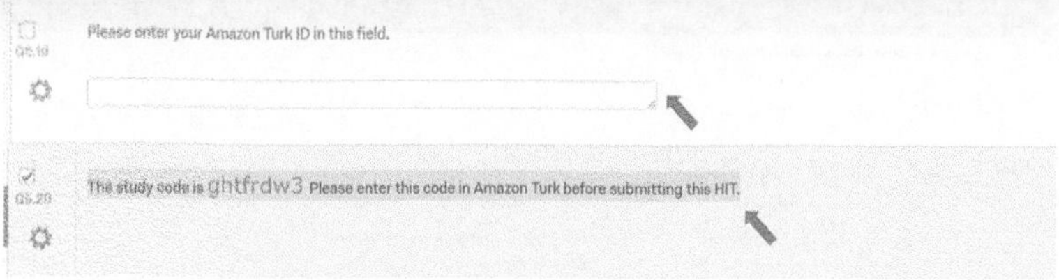

Please enter your Amazon Turk ID in this field.

The study code is ghtfrdw3 Please enter this code in Amazon Turk before submitting this HIT.

SurveyMonkey, Mechanical Turk does not provide a way for a requester to know whether the worker actually completed the study. Once a worker accepts the HIT on the preview page, nothing stops that worker from submitting the HIT without even having looked at the external survey. For this reason, secret codes are used to inform the requester that the worker made it to the end of the survey before submitting the HIT. To add a secret code at the end of a survey, a requester should add an additional question to the survey with a random alphanumeric code. This should be accompanied by a request for the worker to enter that code on the Mechanical Turk HIT window before submitting the HIT. When a worker enters the correct code, requesters know that the worker made it to the end of the survey. The standard way of doing this on Qualtrics is shown in Figure 3.17.

Additionally, workers should be asked to provide their worker IDs using an open-ended survey item (Figure 3.17). If the dataset does not have accompanying worker IDs, it is impossible to match the data to each worker. In the event that specific workers are not attentive or do not properly follow the instructions, having the worker ID in the data file will allow requesters to match the data to those specific workers.

FIGURE 3.18 ● PREVIEW SCREEN TO REVIEW THE STUDY SETTINGS

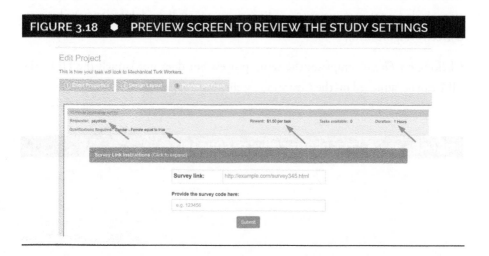

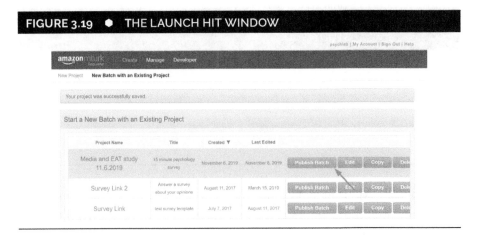

FIGURE 3.19 ● THE LAUNCH HIT WINDOW

These workers can then be excluded from participating in future studies, or in cases of clear negligence their work can be rejected.

Having worker IDs in a data file is even more critical for longitudinal research, where data cannot be analyzed without matching worker IDs across the longitudinal datasets. In the next chapter we describe how to add worker IDs to the data file automatically, without having to ask workers to provide them.

Importantly, adding worker IDs to the data file introduces potential confidentiality concerns that are explored further in Chapter 11.

Once the instructions are completed, the URL created previously on Qualtrics (see Figure 3.5) should be added to the *Survey link* field (see Figure 3.16). The study should be reviewed on the *Preview and Finish* tab to make sure that all the specifications, including the study name, qualifications, payment, and duration have been set correctly (Figure 3.18).

Clicking on *Finish* completes the setup process but does not launch the HIT. The HIT can be launched on the *Create* tab by clicking *Publish Batch* (Figure 3.19).

FIGURE 3.20 ● THE REQUESTER'S DASHBOARD

App excercise study 2   Review Results   Delete

Created:	March 21, 2014	Assignments Completed:	700 / 500
Time Elapsed:	7 days	Estimated Completion Time:	COMPLETE
Batch Progress:	100% submitted	100% published	

MONITORING PROGRESS ON THE REQUESTER'S DASHBOARD

Studies are monitored on the dashboard under the *Manage* tab. When monitoring the study on the dashboard, a requester is able to see the study's progress and average completion time (Figure 3.20). Once the progress bar indicates that the study has completed, the requester will need to approve or reject the workers. To approve workers, click on *Results* under the *Manage* tab. There, the requester can approve or reject workers and download a CSV file with information about each worker's assignment.

WHEN A WORKER RUNS OUT OF TIME

Because workers differ from one another in terms of how fast they complete HITs, some workers may legitimately run out of time. Workers may also run out of time because of network outages or other technical problems. After having put in time and effort working on a HIT, workers will sometimes find that the time to complete the HIT had expired and they are no longer able to submit it. Without submitting a HIT, a requester is not able to issue a payment for that HIT, even if the requester wants to pay the worker. The payment mechanism on Mechanical Turk is enabled only for HITs that were submitted. This issue introduces a common problem, where workers will email requesters asking to be paid for their work, but the requester is unable to do so even if they wish to through the standard Mechanical Turk payment mechanisms.

In such cases, requesters can do one of two things. If the requester has a prior established relationship with a worker, they can issue a payment in the form of a bonus for a previous HIT. If, by contrast, the requester does not have an established relationship with a worker, the requester can create a qualification for that worker and open a new HIT where only that worker is eligible to participate. The requester should notify the worker to expect to see that HIT on his or her dashboard. The HIT should not involve any additional work and the worker can simply accept and submit the HIT. Once that HIT is submitted, the requester will have an established relationship with the worker and then can pay the worker either through the standard payment mechanism or by issuing a bonus.

In the future, Mechanical Turk is likely to allow giving bonuses for HITs that were started but not submitted, even if there is no prior relationship between that worker and the requester. Check the updates to the online version of this chapter and the Mechanical Turk documentation to see if this feature has been implemented.

TABLE 3.1 ● CORRELATIONS AMONG DISORDERED EATING, DEPRESSION, AND BODY DISSATISFACTION VARIABLES			
Measure	1	2	3
1. EAT	–	.42**	.55**
2. SATAQ-Gen		–	.38**
3. BDI			–

Note: EAT = Eating Attitudes Test–Total Score; SATAQ–GEN = Sociocultural Attitudes Towards Appearance Questionnaire–General Internalization Subscale; BDI = Beck Depression Inventory.

**$p < .01$.

SAMPLE STUDY RESULTS

By setting up the study on Mechanical Turk, the full dataset was collected within three hours. Once the study was complete, an SPSS dataset was downloaded from Qualtrics. Examining the data revealed a pattern of results that was consistent with previously published findings. Our findings show that Mechanical Turk was an effective way of selectively recruiting a sample of women whose results closely resemble those of previously reported findings. As expected, disordered eating, thin-ideal internalization, and depressive symptoms were strongly correlated with each other (see Table 3.1). The Cronbach's alpha reliabilities for the EAT, SATAQ, and BDI were .75, .89, and .95, respectively, and are all well within acceptable norms, suggesting that within a matter of hours we were able to reliably replicate well-established findings.

We have so far reviewed the procedure for setting up a basic study using Qualtrics and launching the study on Mechanical Turk. Best practices for setting up a study on Mechanical Turk are summarized in Appendix A. In the next section we describe the process of creating requester-specific qualifications in order to design follow-up studies.

CONDUCTING FOLLOW-UP STUDIES USING REQUESTER-SPECIFIED QUALIFICATIONS

In the previous section we described how to conduct a study that included 100 female Mechanical Turk participants. Researchers often need to conduct multiple follow-up studies to further investigate the phenomenon in question. We now show how to set up a follow-up study that will sample 200 more female workers. It is critical that the 100 workers from the original study be prevented from participating in the follow-up HIT. To accomplish this goal, all workers from the first HIT will be

FIGURE 3.21 ● LIST OF WORKERS WHO COMPLETED HITS FOR A REQUESTER UNDER THE *MANAGE* TAB

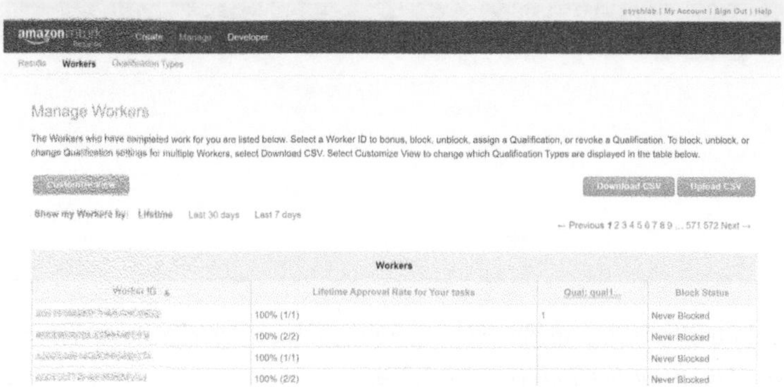

issued a qualification and this qualification will be used to prevent those workers from accepting the current HIT. Below, we provide a detailed description of how to create and use requester-specified qualifications using the Mechanical Turk interface.

When a study is completed, all the workers who complete that HIT become visible on the *Manage Workers* page under the *Manage* tab, in the *Worker ID* column (Figure 3.21).

Clicking on any worker ID in this list takes you to the corresponding *Manage Individual Worker* page (Figure 3.22). From this page, the worker can be assigned qualifications, which can then be used to manage the worker's participation in subsequent HITs.

FIGURE 3.22 ● THE *MANAGE INDIVIDUAL WORKER* PAGE THAT APPEARS WHEN A REQUESTER CLICKS ON A WORKER ID FROM THE LIST OF WORKERS WHO COMPLETED HITS

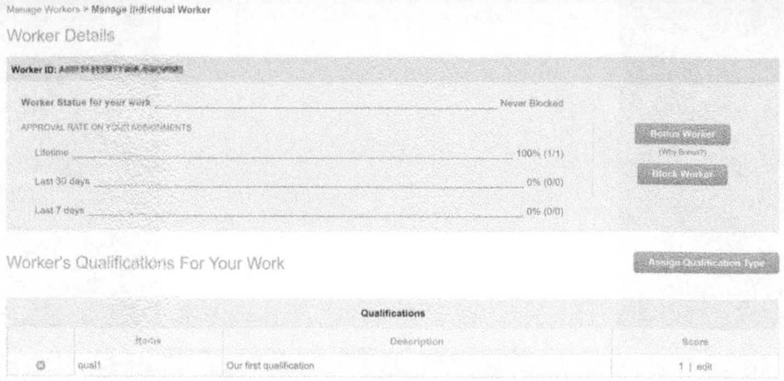

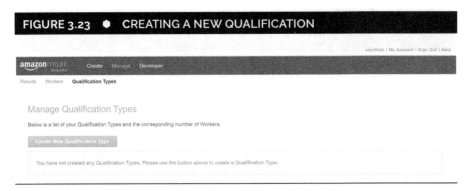

FIGURE 3.23 ● CREATING A NEW QUALIFICATION

To create a qualification, on the *Manage* tab, click on *Qualification Types* and select *Create New Qualification Type* (Figure 3.23).

In the *Friendly Name* field (Figure 3.24), enter the name of the qualification. Note that this qualification name is visible to workers when they preview a HIT on the workers' dashboard. For this reason, the name of the qualification should not be meaningful, unless the requester wants workers to know why they are being selected for a study. For example, if a requester is creating a qualification for workers who have been identified as being depressed, they should not title the qualification "Depressed workers," unless the intention is for the workers to know they are being selected because they are thought to be depressed. We generally recommend using random strings as qualification names.

Because most qualifications will consist of random digits, it is a good practice to create a separate file to keep track of qualification names and their definitions. Over time, requesters are likely to create dozens or even hundreds of qualifications. Many

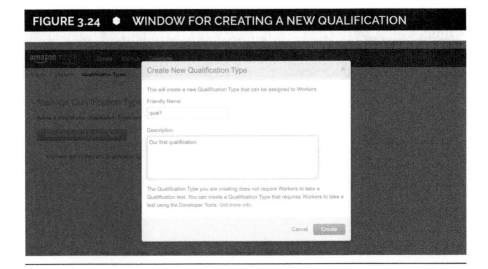

FIGURE 3.24 ● WINDOW FOR CREATING A NEW QUALIFICATION

of these qualifications will need to be updated frequently. For example, the list of workers with depression will grow as a requester collects information on more workers. For this reason, requesters should create a way to manage these qualifications as early as possible.

Adding Qualifications to a HIT

We are going to give our qualification the name "qual1" with "Our first qualification" as the description (see Figure 3.24). After the qualification is created, the *Manage Workers* page will show a new *Qual: qual1* qualification column. There are two ways to assign qualifications to workers: one at a time, and by uploading a CSV file with worker IDs. First, let's assign a qualification to a single worker. Click on the name of the first worker in the worker ID column (Figure 3.21). Click on *Assign Qualification Type*. Select *qual1* and give it a score of *1* (Figure 3.25).

Scores are used to differentiate between different groups of workers under the same qualification. You will now see that the worker's page lists *qual1* on the bottom of the page as having been assigned to this worker. You can also see on the worker's page that the *Qual: qual1* column now lists a *1* for the first worker.

Because repeating this process would be extremely time consuming for multiple workers, uploading a CSV file provides a way to assign qualifications to many workers at once. To assign qualifications to multiple workers, create a CSV file with a "WorkerID" column and a column titled "UPDATE-qual1" (Figure 3.26). If you

FIGURE 3.25 ● CREATING A QUALIFICATION

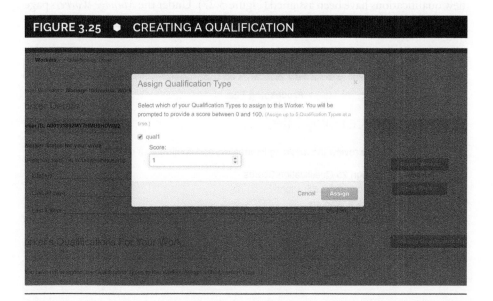

FIGURE 3.26 ● CSV FILE FOR WORKER QUALIFICATIONS

	A	B	C
1	WorkerId	UPDATE-qual1	
2	A00191882MY7HMU9HDWM2	1	
3	A00236363DL2ZN8A4FD78	1	
4	A002544014QZD5R95DO75	1	
5	A0073377ZHUE9505MVC4	1	
6	A014570429HSF84C0QZCF	1	
7	A0217417E4SVFYPETQH9	1	
8	A02285231KBH33XIG7PVQ	1	
9	A02712401N4WIWZDIH35P	1	
10	A03201681XQ17X5BS2KZZ	1	
11	A034420738QHAX9TNO9BA	1	
12	A04612451X3K1REKZJHOT	1	
13	A050383932MZW4XOYPJAY	1	
14	A05062513MWBSOJW7FC52	1	
15	A0533430WOF7V9XR82TB	1	

created this file in Excel, make sure that it is saved as a CSV file. Add all the worker IDs for the first sample project HIT to this CSV file.

On the *Manage Workers* page, select *Upload CSV File* and then locate and upload your file. When the file uploads successfully you will see a progress message indicating that new qualifications have been assigned (Figure 3.27). Under the *Manage Workers* page in the *qual1* column all the uploaded worker IDs should now have a 1.

FIGURE 3.27 ● SUCCESSFUL CREATION OF A QUALIFICATION

Manage Workers > **Processing File**

Processing File

Please review the following information and confirm your choices:

- Assign **25** Qualification Scores
- Revoke **0** Qualifications
- Block **0** Workers
- Unblock **0** Workers

Would you like to continue?

 Yes   Cancel

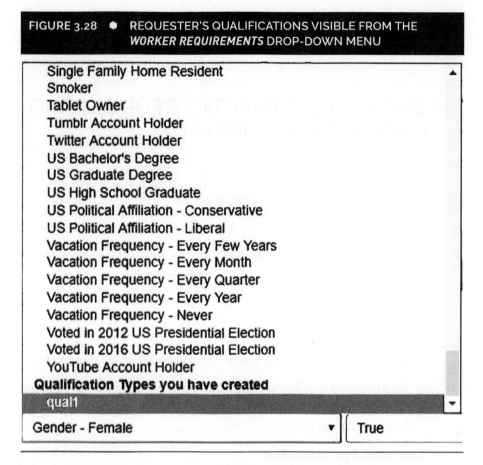

FIGURE 3.28 ● REQUESTER'S QUALIFICATIONS VISIBLE FROM THE *WORKER REQUIREMENTS* DROP-DOWN MENU

Single Family Home Resident
Smoker
Tablet Owner
Tumblr Account Holder
Twitter Account Holder
US Bachelor's Degree
US Graduate Degree
US High School Graduate
US Political Affiliation - Conservative
US Political Affiliation - Liberal
Vacation Frequency - Every Few Years
Vacation Frequency - Every Month
Vacation Frequency - Every Quarter
Vacation Frequency - Every Year
Vacation Frequency - Never
Voted in 2012 US Presidential Election
Voted in 2016 US Presidential Election
YouTube Account Holder
Qualification Types you have created
qual1

Gender - Female ▼   True

These qualifications can now be assigned in the *Worker requirements* section of the *HIT Properties* tab (Figure 3.28). Under the *additional qualifications* drop-down menu, the qualification types that have been created by the requester are listed on the bottom. There are several options for how workers can be added to the HIT. To make sure that workers with a specific qualification cannot participate in this HIT, select *Has Not Been Granted*. Using qualifications in this way will prevent workers who participated in previous HITs from participating in the current study. For longitudinal studies where a requester wants only workers with a specific qualification to participate, select *Has Been Granted*.

Once created, this qualification will always be available from the *additional qualifications* drop-down menu to exclude or include workers from the first sample project in future HITs. The most common uses for requester-specified qualifications are (a) to exclude workers from previous HITs, (b) to conduct longitudinal studies, and (c) to create two-wave studies for targeted recruitment. Longitudinal studies and targeted recruitment are discussed further in Chapter 9. In the next chapter we discuss how the Mechanical Turk API and third-party apps make the process of assigning qualifications significantly easier to manage and the additional functionality that these tools provide.

APPENDIX A: BEST PRACTICES FOR SETTING UP A MECHANICAL TURK HIT

1. **Title**

   a. Include expected completion time in the title.

   b. Use generic title so as not to introduce self-selection bias.

   c. Do not include qualifying criteria in the title, instructions, or description. For example, the title should not say "for women only."

2. **Description**

   a. The description should be a few sentences.

   b. The description should be generic so as not to introduce self-selection bias.

   c. The description is visible only on the dashboard and not in the HIT preview window. The detailed description of the HIT should be added to the *Instructions* under the *Design Layout* tab.

3. **Time allotted per assignment**

   a. Should not be more than three or four times longer than the expected completion time. This will help to prevent HIT sniping.

4. **HIT visibility**

   a. HIT visibility should be set to *Private* or *Hidden* to allow for accurate calculation of bounce rate.

   b. Setting HIT visibility to *Private*, rather than *Hidden*, will allow requesters to view their own HITs even if they do not have the required qualifications.

5. **Instructions**

   a. The instructions should be generic so as not to introduce self-selection bias.

   b. The instructions should describe anything out of the ordinary, such as a requirement to download an app, or tasks that require extra effort or creative work.

   c. The instructions should mention anything that can disqualify a worker, such as a requirement to take a screener.

   d. The description should be as short and succinct as possible. Use bullet points whenever possible.

   e. The instructions should tell the worker to enter the survey code in the HIT preview window before submitting the HIT.

6. **Approval rating**

   a. The standard practice is to set the approval ratings to ≥ 95%. However, see Chapter 7.

   b. Researchers may want to set the number of HITs completed to > 100 (otherwise, the approval rating will be 100% for all workers who have completed fewer than 100 HITs). However, see Chapter 7.

7. **Worker IDs**

   a. Workers should be asked to provide their worker IDs using an open-ended survey item. Tools for doing this automatically are available.

REFERENCES

Beck, A. T., Steer, R. A., & Garbin, M. G. (1988). Psychometric properties of the Beck Depression Inventory: Twenty-five years of evaluation. *Clinical Psychology Review, 8*(1), 77–100. doi:10.1016/0272-7358(88)90050-5

Brown, A., & Dittmar, H. (2005). Think "thin" and feel bad: The role of appearance schema activation, attention level, and thin-ideal internalization for young women's responses to ultra-thin media ideals. *Journal of Social and Clinical Psychology, 24*(8), 1088–1113.

Dittmar, H., Halliwell, E., & Stirling, E. (2009). Understanding the impact of thin media models on women's body-focused affect: The roles of thin-ideal internalization and weight-related self-discrepancy activation in experimental exposure effects. *Journal of Social and Clinical Psychology, 28*(1), 43–72. doi:10.1521/jscp.2009.28.1.43

Litman, L., Robinson, J., & Rosenzweig, C. (2015). The relationship between motivation, monetary compensation, and data quality among US- and India-based workers on Mechanical Turk. *Behavior Research Methods, 47*(2), 519–528. doi:10.3758/s13428-014-0483-x

Peer, E., Vosgerau, J., & Acquisti, A. (2014). Reputation as a sufficient condition for data quality on Amazon Mechanical Turk. *Behavior Research Methods, 46*(4), 1023–1031. doi:10.3758/s13428-013-0434-y

Robinson, J., Rosenzweig, C., Moss, A. J., & Litman, L. (2019). Tapped out or barely tapped? Recommendations for how to harness the vast and largely unused potential of the Mechanical Turk participant pool. *PLoS One, 14*(12), e0226394. doi:10.1371/journal.pone.0226394

Rogers Wood, N. A., & Petrie, T. A. (2010). Body dissatisfaction, ethnic identity, and disordered eating among African American women. *Journal of Counseling Psychology, 57*(2), 141–153.

Rohde, P., Stice, E., & Marti, C. N. (2015). Development and predictive effects of eating disorder risk factors during adolescence: Implications for prevention efforts. *International Journal of Eating Disorders, 48*(2), 187–198. doi:10.1002/eat.22270

Rouse, S. V. (2019). Reliability of MTurk data from masters and workers. *Journal of Individual Differences,* 1–7.

Stice, E., Gau, J. M., Rohde, P., & Shaw, H. (2017). Risk factors that predict future onset of each DSM-5 eating disorder: Predictive specificity in high-risk adolescent females. *Journal of Abnormal Psychology, 126*(1), 38–51. doi:10.1037/abn0000219

Stice, E., Marti, C. N., Rohde, P., & Shaw, H. (2011). Testing mediators hypothesized to account for the effects of a dissonance-based eating disorder prevention program over longer term follow-up. *Journal of Consulting and Clinical Psychology, 79*(3), 398–405. doi:10.1037/a0023321

Stice, E., & Shaw, H. E. (2002). Role of body dissatisfaction in the onset and maintenance of eating pathology: A synthesis of research findings. *Journal of Psychosomatic Research, 53*(5), 985–993. doi:10.1016/s0022-3999(02)00488-9

Striegel-Moore, R. H., & Bulik, C. M. (2007). Risk factors for eating disorders. *American Psychologist, 62*(3), 181–198. doi:10.1037/0003-066X.62.3.181

Thompson, J. K., & Stice, E. (2001). Thin-ideal internalization: Mounting evidence for a new risk factor for body-image disturbance and eating pathology. *Current Directions in Psychological Science, 10*(5), 181–183. doi:10.1111/1467-8721.00144

Van Emden, R., de Bruin, W. B., Strough, J., & van Putten, M. (2015). Exploratory TurkPrime study: Windfall bias—young versus old. Retrieved from https://pavlov.tech/2015/07/15/the-effects-of-age-on-the-windfall-bias/

API AND THIRD-PARTY APPS

Leib Litman and Jonathan Robinson

INTRODUCTION

In this chapter we describe how researchers can employ Mechanical Turk's advanced functionality using third-party apps. First, we introduce Mechanical Turk's application programming interface (API) and describe the significant advantages it offers. We then discuss third-party applications that are built on top of Mechanical Turk's API. Third-party platforms provide researchers with powerful tools that can be used together with Mechanical Turk. After reviewing a number of third-party platforms and their functionalities, we describe CloudResearch (formerly Turk-Prime) and its interface in detail. We show how to set up a CloudResearch account, link it to Mechanical Turk, and set up a project on the CloudResearch platform.

As with the previous chapter, it is likely that some of the screenshots in this chapter will become dated over time. Visit the book's website at https://www.cloudresearch.com/resources/book/ to keep up with the latest changes.

THIRD-PARTY API-BASED PLATFORMS

Mechanical Turk was designed to provide basic functionality through its graphical user interface (GUI). Its API was designed to provide significantly greater functionality. Behavioral scientists typically find that the range of actions available through Mechanical Turk's GUI, described in the previous chapter, puts significant constraints on their ability to flexibly conduct research. For example, through the GUI a requester can send one email to one worker at a time. Through the API, however, multiple emails can be sent to several workers at the same time. Similarly, using the API, requesters can send bonuses to multiple workers at once, as opposed to doing it one at a time through the GUI. Multiple other tools are available that give requesters significantly greater control over HITs.

As Mechanical Turk became more popular among scientists, various API-based solutions became available. Multiple platforms now provide add-on tools that facilitate the research process. Among them are psiTurk (Gureckis et al., 2016), TurkServer (Mao et al., 2012), CloudResearch (Litman, Robinson, & Abberbock, 2017), RTurk, MmmTurkey (Dang, Hutson, & Lease, 2016), Longii, and TurkGate (Goldin & Darlow, 2013).

PsiTurk (Gureckis et al., 2016) is an open-access platform that provides significant control over running HITs, including the ability to exclude participants, offer batch bonuses, and make automatic payments, as well as many other features. PsiTurk is a Unix-based command line system. It runs on Unix-based platforms such as Linux and has a command line interface rather than a GUI. Many of the API-based platforms specialize in specific research designs. For example, TurkServer facilitates synchronous experiments involving real-time interactions between workers. Longii facilitates longitudinal research. The next section describes some of the most common functions these platforms provide and that give them an advantage over the MTurk interface.

COMMON USES FOR API SCRIPTS AND THIRD-PARTY API-BASED APPS

Enhanced Sampling

The power of Mechanical Turk lies in the speed with which a study can be completed. But this might also be one of its limitations. Most studies are completed within a few hours after they are launched. When studies are launched on a weekday morning, for example, they will be biased toward workers who are available to take studies at that time. Multiple studies show that the demographic composition and psychological profile of workers differ depending on what time of the day they choose to participate in online studies (Arechar, Kraft-Todd, & Rand, 2017; Chilton, Horton, Miller, & Azenkot, 2010; Fordsham et al., 2019). Thus, sampling at any one particular point in time may introduce various types of bias. Third-party platforms offer tools for sampling across different times of the day and days of the week. These tools allow a requester to set the pace of data collection so that, say, only 5% of the data are collected during any one-hour period. Such tools are an important way of enhancing sampling representativeness when collecting data on Mechanical Turk.

Communication Tools

Increasingly, researchers are conducting studies involving the participation of multiple workers in interactive social science studies (Mao et al., 2012). Researchers are also increasingly engaging with participants in more in-depth ways. For example, researchers conduct audio interviews with participants, and they may observe participants in their natural environment using video studies. Researchers may collect heart rate, eye tracking, and other types of biophysical data through video. Mechanical Turk does not provide the tools for interacting with workers in these ways. However, third-party platforms are increasingly making such interactions possible.

Controlling a Running HIT

Very few things can be changed on Mechanical Turk after a HIT has been launched. However, editing a HIT can often be important. For instance, a researcher who is under the impression that a HIT can be completed in 10 minutes may describe the HIT as being 10 minutes long and assign a payment of $1.00, at a $6.00 per hour pay rate. After the HIT is launched, the requester may realize that it actually takes 20 minutes for workers to complete the HIT. This may result in a poor user experience for the workers, leading them to leave negative feedback on worker forums such as Turkopticon.

Studies can be edited using the GUI to some extent. But this involves stopping a study, copying it, and excluding workers from the pilot by using their worker IDs and assigning qualifications for the full study. Third-party apps offer the ability to edit almost all aspects of a HIT after it is launched. By using third-party tools, researchers can pause a study, change the description of the study, change the pay rate, and relaunch the study when ready. We recommend always running a small pilot study for 20 participants, reviewing study indicators and data quality, and attending to dropout rates, prior to launching the full study. If the researcher finds technical or other problems after running the pilot study, the full study can be modified and relaunched.

Controlling Who Participates in a Study

Issuing qualifications by uploading CSV files can be a time-consuming process. It also becomes cumbersome to keep track of worker IDs and study IDs for labs that run dozens or hundreds of different studies. Third-party platforms make the process of excluding workers from previous studies much easier to manage. Some aspects of excluding workers cannot be done at all through the GUI. For example, researchers often want to run multiple studies at once. It is not possible to exclude workers from HITs that are running simultaneously through the GUI. However, third-party apps make excluding workers from HITs running in parallel simple. Additionally, third-party apps can exclude workers who started a HIT even if they did not complete it.

Longitudinal Studies

Managing longitudinal studies through the GUI is fairly complicated on Mechanical Turk. For this reason, third-party platforms such as Longii have been created specifically to assist requesters with managing longitudinal studies. For example, when launching a follow-up study, it is necessary to notify workers from the first wave that the study is available for them. Many workers may not be looking at the dashboard at the time that the follow-up HIT is launched, and without a notification they may not become aware that the study is available. The same problem arises in two-wave studies, where a researcher may want to follow up with workers who have been identified through a screening process. API scripts and third-party platforms simplify the process of notifying workers.

Automated Payment

After a worker completes a HIT, the requester has to review that HIT and either approve it or reject it. Third-party tools can automate this process. Once the worker adds the correct secret code, the payment is issued automatically, reducing payment delays to workers.

Advanced HIT Dashboard

After a HIT is launched, it is monitored on the MTurk dashboard. The MTurk dashboard provides a progress bar displaying the number of HITs that have already been completed. In addition to this information, third-party platforms provide data on how long it takes workers to complete a study and how many workers drop out of the study. The time to complete a study can be measured with the mean or the median. The median is typically more accurate because the mean is skewed toward workers who take the maximum allowable time to complete the HIT. This can have an impact on the estimation of how much to pay participants. The median completion time is a more accurate metric on which to base hourly wages. It is also important to know what percentage of workers drop out of a study. Dropout can occur at two points. Workers can choose not to accept the study when they are previewing it in the HIT preview window. Workers can also return the study after accepting it. Both of these metrics can have an effect on the study's external validity. These and other metrics are available via third-party apps.

CLOUDRESEARCH

In this section we describe CloudResearch, a third-party API-based app that has many of the features described in the previous section (see Litman et al., 2017). CloudResearch has a point-and-click interface, and many features are free for academic use. CloudResearch provides enhanced controls in seven general areas: tools for communicating with workers such as chat, audio, and video portals for live interviewing; tools for running longitudinal studies; control over who participates in a study; control over launching and running HITs; batched functionality for communication; payment tools for enhanced sampling; and advanced dashboard indicators. CloudResearch has been used in numerous scientific studies (e.g., Goodman & Paolacci, 2017; Stewart, Chandler, & Paolacci, 2017). Here we provide a general overview of the capabilities that CloudResearch offers.

Getting Started With CloudResearch

To set up a CloudResearch account, first create an account on the CloudResearch home page (www.cloudresearch.com). Once logged on, this guide (https://www.cloudresearch. com/resources/book/) describes the step-by-step process of linking an MTurk account to CloudResearch. Once a CloudResearch account has been linked to Mechanical Turk, all aspects of launching and monitoring HITs are handled on the CloudResearch platform. Requesters can set up, launch, and monitor the progress of HITs on the CloudResearch *Study Design* page and dashboard. When a HIT is launched on CloudResearch, it will also be launched on the requester's MTurk account.

Creating and Launching a HIT on CloudResearch

To begin creating a HIT on CloudResearch, select *MTurk Toolkit* from the *Create a Study* drop-down menu on the home page. The *MTurk Toolkit* page has several sequential tabs that need to be filled out when creating a HIT (Figure 4.1).

On Tab 1 (*Panel Options*) of the CloudResearch interface, a requester can specify the target sample for their study (Figure 4.2). CloudResearch has many demographic, behavioral, and psychological variables to choose from. Some variables, such as gender, are the same as on Mechanical Turk. Other variables are unique to CloudResearch. There is no limitation on the number of qualifications that can be assigned. CloudResearch calculates the feasibility of completing a HIT based on

FIGURE 4.1 ● TAB SEQUENCE FOR DESIGNING A HIT ON CLOUDRESEARCH

CloudResearch MTurk Toolkit

Workers Payments and MTurk Fees funded with your MTurk Requester account. CloudResearch Lab Fees are funded through your CloudResearch Lab account.

1. Panel Options (Optional)   2. Basic Info   3. Describe HIT   4. Setup HIT and Payment

5. How Workers are Approved   6. Worker Requirements   7. MicroBatch (Pro Feature)   8. Pro Features

9. Save

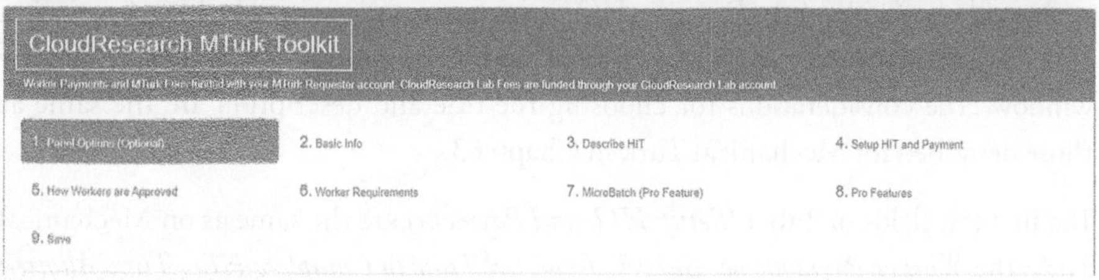

FIGURE 4.2 ● SELECTIVELY RECRUITING SPECIFIC MTURK WORKERS ON CLOUDRESEARCH

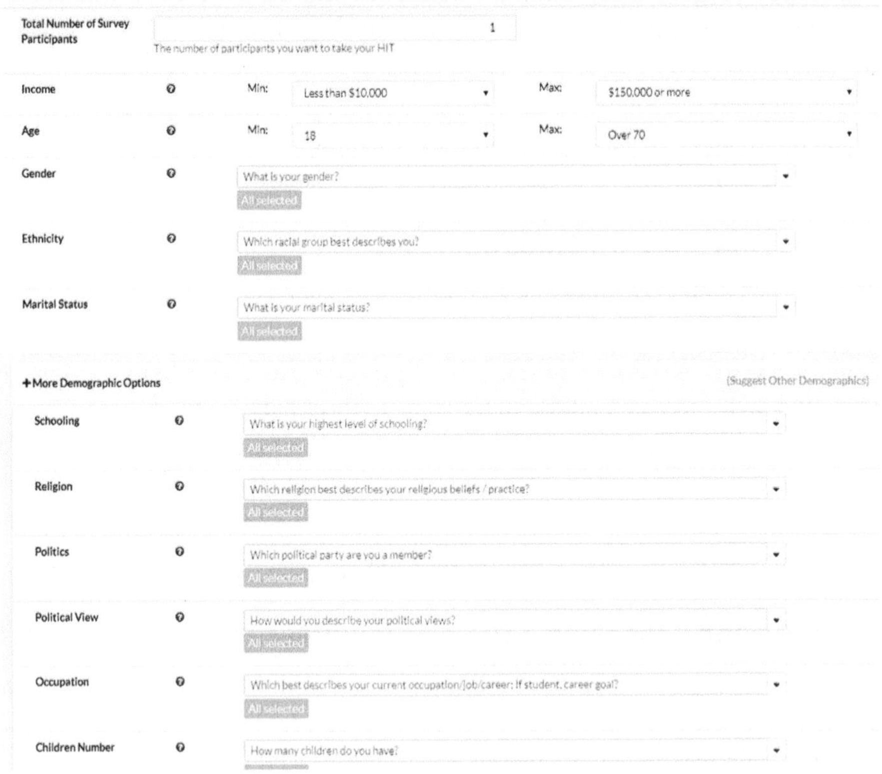

how many MTurk workers in its database meet the targeting criteria. For example, if a requester selects a target sample of 1,000 divorced 20-year-old men, CloudResearch will display a message indicating that there are not enough MTurk workers to complete that study. Like on Mechanical Turk, HIT qualification increases the price of the HIT. The price is calculated based on the number of MTurk workers who meet the targeting requirements.

On Tab 2 (*Basic Info*), requesters provide the project name, which is not displayed to workers, and the email address that the requester wants to use for communicating with workers. On Tab 3 (*Describe HIT*), the requester enters the title, description, and custom instructions, all of which are visible to workers in the HIT preview window. The considerations for choosing the title and description are the same as those described for Mechanical Turk in Chapter 3.

The first few fields of Tab 4 (*Setup HIT and Payment*) are the same as on Mechanical Turk: the *Worker Payment per Survey, Expected Time to Complete HIT, Time Allotted*

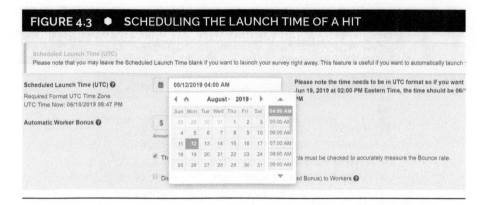

FIGURE 4.3 ● SCHEDULING THE LAUNCH TIME OF A HIT

per Assignment, *HIT Expires In*, and *Survey Hyperlink* fields should be filled out in the same way as described in Chapter 3.

This page also has a number of fields that are unique to CloudResearch. *Scheduling Launch Time* (Figure 4.3) allows a requester to schedule a specific time for launching a study. The HIT scheduler is useful for requesters who may not be available to launch the study at their preferred time. It is also useful for diary studies. Conducting diary studies often involves launching a HIT at a specific time each day. If a diary study runs over a 30-day period, a researcher can set up and launch all 30 studies at once. The CloudResearch calendar is based on Coordinated Universal Time (UTC), the same time that Mechanical Turk uses. Requesters need to check how UTC time is offset relative to their specific time zone in order to set the launch time correctly.

Below the calendar there is an option to add an automatic worker bonus. This field is typically used by requesters who prefer to pay by bonuses rather than direct payments. The option to make the HIT visible only to workers who qualify prevents workers from previewing a HIT if they are not qualified to take it. This is equivalent to setting the privacy mode to *Private* on the MTurk interface.

Requesters who want to advertise how much their HIT pays to workers can select to display the median hourly rate (Figure 4.4). This will display the hourly wages, which are calculated in real time, to workers on the HIT preview page. Requesters

FIGURE 4.4 ● OPTIONS FOR DISPLAYING THE HIT

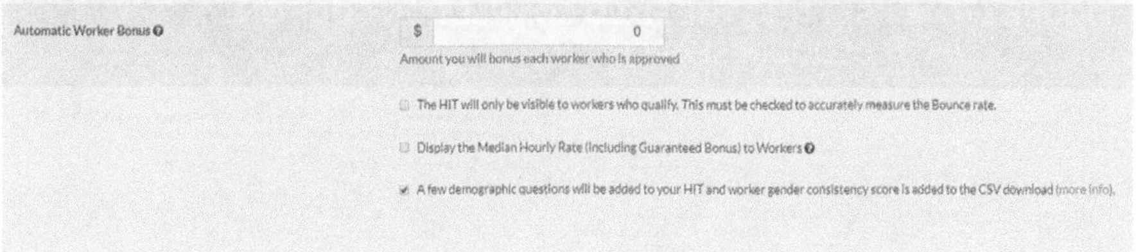

Automatic Worker Bonus ●

$ [0]

Amount you will bonus each worker who is approved

☐ The HIT will only be visible to workers who qualify. This must be checked to accurately measure the Bounce rate.

☐ Display the Median Hourly Rate (Including Guaranteed Bonus) to Workers ●

☑ A few demographic questions will be added to your HIT and worker gender consistency score is added to the CSV download (more info).

FIGURE 4.5 ● SPSS DATA FILE WITH WORKER, ASSIGNMENT, AND HIT IDs THAT WERE ADDED AUTOMATICALLY BY PASSING URL PARAMETERS

RJL

workerId	assignmentId	hitId	C
A1JUAIMXS...	3RANCT1ZVFHPB5F...	39TX062QX1OA...	
AI7YTRYN64...	3Q5C1WP23M17DS...	39TX062QX1OA...	
A14BVDD0J...	3OXV7EAXLEQZ6ZL...	39TX062QX1OA...	
A1HH2KZIFL...	3AWETUDC92SGK...	39TX062QX1OA...	
AMYURTQIM...	3E7TUJ2EGCMK6A...	39TX062QX1OA...	
A3I1W58P6S...	3ERMJ6L4DYSJWL...	39TX062QX1OA...	
A38VMTKS3...	31QOU3WYDPFM0...	3PMR2DOWOO...	
A2R9VWNA...	3RRCEFRB7MCQU7...	3PMR2DOWOO...	
A2541C8MY...	3GA6AFUKOOOF3O...	3PMR2DOWOO...	
A1TH0PTGD...	3KKG4CDWKIY76E...	3PMR2DOWOO...	
A150GMV1Y...	317HQ483I7SM3N9B...	3PMR2DOWOO...	

---

commonly underestimate how long their HITs take to complete and thus overestimate the hourly pay rate. With this feature, requesters can provide an accurate pay rate, calculated based on how long it actually takes workers to complete the HIT.

Tab 4 also provides instructions for how to automatically send the worker IDs to SPSS or other data files. To automatically embed worker IDs in Qualtrics, go to the *Survey Flow* and click on *Add a New Element Here* (Figure 3.3). In the fields provided, add the worker ID, assignment ID, and HIT ID (Figure 4.5). This feature is important for matching worker IDs across different data files of a longitudinal study, and for creating qualifications for selective targeting in two-wave studies.

Tab 5 (*How Workers are Approved*) provides three options for secret codes: fixed, custom, and dynamic. The first option is referred to as a fixed completion code. This is similar to the secret code on Mechanical Turk. Entering a completion code in the *Fixed Completion*

FIGURE 4.6 ● SETTING THE FIXED COMPLETION CODE ON CLOUDRESEARCH

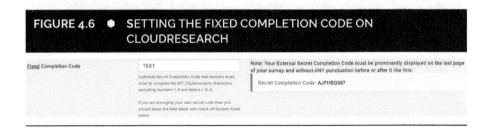

FIGURE 4.7 ● SETTING CLOUDRESEARCH TO AUTOMATICALLY APPROVE AND PAY WORKERS BASED ON A CORRECT SECRET CODE

Manual Assignment Management	☐ You will manually approve the HIT assignments and it will NOT be auto-approved based on the secret key.	
Auto pay workers in	30	Days ▼
	The time before workers are automatically approved for work (Useful only if no Secret Code is specified and HIT is manually approved)	

Code field will require every worker to enter that same code before submitting a HIT. To use this option a requester needs to present this code at the end of the study and ask workers to enter it in the HIT preview field before submitting the HIT (see Figure 3.16).

When selecting a fixed completion code (Figure 4.6), a requester has the option of letting CloudResearch automatically approve submitted HITs when workers enter this code correctly. Should the worker not enter the code correctly, the HIT will not be rejected. Rather, the assignment will be listed as *pending* and the requester will then have to approve or reject this assignment manually.

Requesters who do not want to approve workers automatically based on the correct fixed completion code should select the *manual approval* option (Figure 4.7). When this option is selected workers will not be approved automatically when entering a correct code. Instead, they will enter a pending status and will not be paid until either the HIT is approved or the maximum allowable time passes. When the maximum time passes, workers who have not been approved or rejected will be paid regardless of whether they entered a correct code or not.

The second option is to use a *custom completion code*. This code is not integrated with CloudResearch, and CloudResearch has no way of checking whether a worker entered the custom code correctly. When the custom completion code is used, the codes must be approved manually.

The third option is the *dynamic completion code*, used together with Qualtrics. When this option is selected, Qualtrics generates a unique completion code for every worker.

FIGURE 4.8 ● SETTING QUALTRICS TO DISPLAY A UNIQUE COMPLETION CODE FOR EACH WORKER

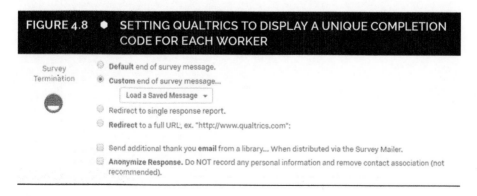

Survey Termination

○ **Default** end of survey message.
◉ **Custom** end of survey message...
　　Load a Saved Message ▼
○ **Redirect** to single response report.
○ **Redirect** to a full URL; ex. "http://www.qualtrics.com":

☐ Send additional thank you **email** from a library... When distributed via the Survey Mailer.
☐ **Anonymize Response.** Do NOT record any personal information and remove contact association (not recommended).

This option can be used with both automated and manual CloudResearch approval. Manually checking hundreds of unique codes is a time-consuming process. This is where the automated approval is most useful. When automated approval is selected, CloudResearch will check whether the unique code that was generated by Qualtrics for each worker was entered correctly by that worker. If the code was entered correctly, the worker will be approved automatically. Similarly to other completion code options, requesters also have the option to manually approve dynamic completion codes.

To set up a dynamic completion code in Qualtrics, select *Custom end of survey message* in the *Survey Termination* field (Figure 4.8).

From the custom options, select *New Message*, enter *Secret code* in the description field, and then click the source code button. Once the source code box is open, enter the following text into the box: <iframe src='https://www.CloudResearch.com/Take-LaunchedSurvey/DynamicKey' width='100%' height='200'></iframe> (Figure 4.9).

Tab 6 (*Worker Requirements*) provides a variety of options for excluding workers and running longitudinal studies. These options simplify the process of selecting qualifications and managing multiple studies. To exclude and include workers, requesters

FIGURE 4.9 ● SETTING UP A SECRET CODE SO THAT QUALTRICS DISPLAYS A UNIQUE COMPLETION CODE FOR EACH WORKER

FIGURE 4.10 ● MANAGEMENT OF INCLUSION AND EXCLUSION BY THE USE OF DROP-DOWN MENUS AND WINDOWS ON CLOUDRESEARCH

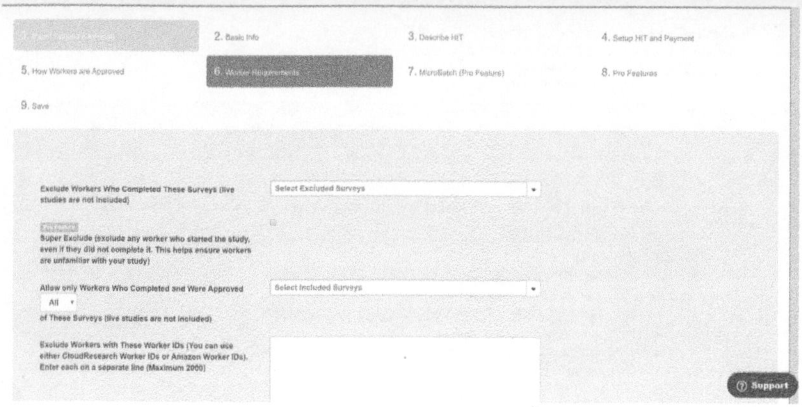

can use drop-down menus (Figure 4.10). The drop-down menus contain a list of all previous HITs that were run on the requester's CloudResearch account. A requester can select one or multiple studies at once from the drop-down list. When workers are excluded, any worker who had participated in the selected HITs will be prevented from participating. Similarly, when a longitudinal study is designed, only the workers who participated in the HITs selected from the *Include* drop-down menu will be allowed to participate in the study. The *Include* and *Exclude* windows provide further flexibility in selecting workers. If a requester wants to include or exclude specific workers, the IDs of those workers can be pasted in the *Include* and *Exclude* windows.

An additional way of flexibly managing workers across studies is to use worker groups (Figures 4.11 and 4.12). Worker groups can be accessed by selecting *Worker Groups*

FIGURE 4.11 ● ADDING WORKERS TO A GROUP IN CLOUDRESEARCH

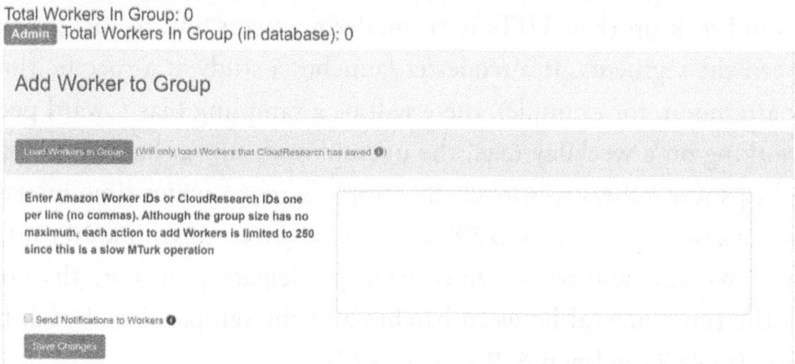

FIGURE 4.12 ● CREATING WORKER GROUPS ON CLOUDRESEARCH

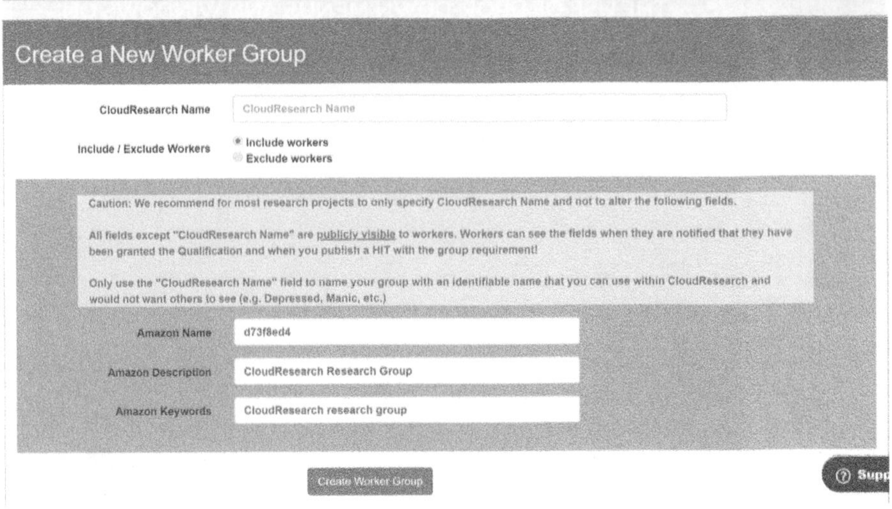

in the *Manage Workers* drop-down menu. Worker groups are created either as *exclude* or *include* groups. When creating a worker group of Republicans, for example, the Republican *include* group can be used to follow up with Republican workers, and the Republican *exclude* group can be used to exclude Republicans from future HITs.

After a worker group is created, the group can then be selected from the *Group Requirements* drop-down menu on Tab 6. Worker groups are a flexible and dynamic way of managing large groups of workers that are changing constantly. This is particularly useful for creating panels (Goodman & Paolacci, 2017). A common way to use worker groups is to keep track of workers who are consistently providing bad-quality data (e.g., not passing attention checks). Their worker IDs can be added to this group and excluded from future studies. Requesters can also maintain their own panel groups, such as groups of Republicans and Democrats, to recruit in follow-up studies.

Under Tab 7, *MicroBatch* provides greater control over sampling. This feature allows requesters to break up their HITs into smaller segments and to include time intervals between the segments. If a requester launches a study at a specific time of day (Monday afternoon, for example), there will be a sampling bias toward people who are not working on a weekday (e.g., the unemployed, stay-at-home parents). Micro-batching helps researchers to spread the sample across a wider time interval. With this feature, a study that is open to 200 workers can be set to sample 10 workers every three hours. Workers will be prevented from participating in more than one study segment. The time interval between batches and the sample size of each batch are fully customizable (Goodman & Paolacci, 2017).

FIGURE 4.13   ●   ADVANCED FEATURES ON CLOUDRESEARCH

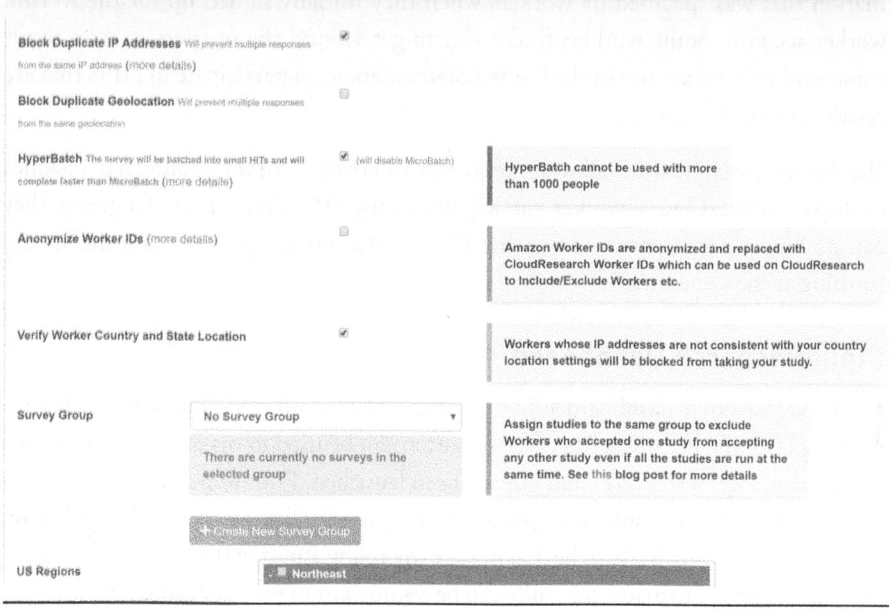

Tab 8 (*Pro Features*) provides tools for enhanced data quality and anonymity, as well as tools to exclude workers from parallel studies (Figure 4.13). The *Block Duplicate IP Address* feature prevents workers from the same IP address from participating in the same HIT. The *Block Suspicious Geolocations* feature prevents workers whose IP is linked with server farms from taking studies. Server farms are locations that have previously been shown to be associated with bad data quality (see Moss & Litman, 2018, Sept. 18). Even though Mechanical Turk blocks workers from participating in a study more than once, workers find ways to get around this restriction. One drawback of restricting an IP address to a single worker is that there are some groups of workers who are legitimately using the same computer. Typically these are workers from the same family or who live together in the same residence. Additionally, large institutions sometimes have a single IP address that is shared by multiple users.

The *Anonymize Worker ID* feature protects workers' identities by replacing Amazon MTurk worker IDs with CloudResearch-issued IDs. MTurk worker IDs can often be traced to the workers' Amazon shopping profiles (Lease et al., 2013). This is because in the past, Mechanical Turk used the same ID for workers as for their general Amazon shopping profiles. Adding MTurk worker IDs to a data file can render that data file as no longer anonymous. This is discussed further in Chapters 9 and 11.

The *Verify Worker Country and State Location* feature uses IP addresses to verify that workers are indeed in the country in which they are claiming to be. The MTurk country locator is not based on real-time data. Rather, Mechanical Turk uses information that was specified by workers when they initially signed up for the MTurk worker account. Some workers find a way to get around the restriction. As a result, some workers who are not in the United States manage to participate in HITs that are restricted to U.S. workers.

The *Survey Group* feature allows a requester to create a survey group that includes multiple studies. Once a worker participates in any HIT that is part of a group, they can no longer participate in any other HIT in that group, even if those studies are running at the same time.

CloudResearch Dashboard

The CloudResearch dashboard offers a variety of controls and information about a running HIT (Figure 4.14). The *Change* button can be used to make changes to a HIT at any time, even if that HIT has already been launched. Prior to making changes to a running HIT, the HIT should be paused. Once paused, clicking on the *Change* button will take the requester back to the design page where any aspect of the study can be edited. Once the changes are made, the study can be resumed from where it left off.

The dashboard also allows the HIT to be easily copied. When a requester copies a HIT, the newly created HIT will automatically exclude all workers who had completed the copied HIT. All workers from the copied HIT are excluded by default. The copied study is added automatically to the *Group Exclude* drop-down menu.

The dashboard also contains enhanced indicators that allow requesters to monitor the health of a HIT. For example, in addition to the average completion time, the dashboard displays the median completion time, which is often a more accurate metric of completion time. *Completion Rate* shows the percentage of workers who submitted a HIT after

FIGURE 4.14 ● CLOUDRESEARCH'S DASHBOARD

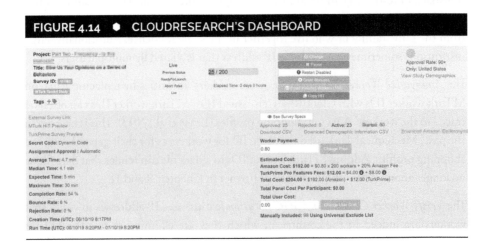

having accepted it. The *Bounce Rate* displays the percentage of workers who chose not to accept a HIT after having previewed it. The dashboard extended view also provides a number of links. The *External Survey Link* shows the survey as it appears to the workers. The *MTurk HIT Preview* shows a HIT from within the MTurk dashboard, and the *CloudResearch Preview* shows a preview of the CloudResearch HIT as it appears in the MTurk HIT preview page.

Requesters who want to collect more than a few thousand workers will need to restart their HIT about every one or two days to increase the speed of data collection by moving the HIT to the top of the dashboard. When a study requires many thousands of workers, it may not be possible to complete the HIT without relaunching it.

The dashboard contains a *Restart HIT* button that facilitates this process. When CloudResearch restarts a HIT, the HIT is moved to the top of the MTurk dashboard to increase its visibility. To do this, CloudResearch stops the HIT, which is then copied and relaunched with identical study name, description, and other parameters. From a worker's perspective there is no way to tell the difference between the original and a copied HIT. When the HIT is relaunched on the MTurk dashboard, it automatically appears at the top of Mechanical Turk's list of HITs.

CONCLUSION

The last two chapters provided a detailed guide for how to set up and monitor studies on Mechanical Turk. Mechanical Turk offers a graphical user interface for setting up studies. It also provides an API through which it is possible to conduct research more flexibly. A variety of API-basedtools are available for researchers to choose from. With these tools, researchers can use the MTurk platform to explore areas of scientific research in rich and diverse ways, flexibly, and across a wide range of demographic groups. The chapters that follow will explore Mechanical Turk more closely and will describe best practices for conducting high-qualityresearch.

REFERENCES

Arechar, A. A., Kraft-Todd, G. T., & Rand, D. G. (2017). Turking overtime: How participant characteristics and behavior vary over time and day on Amazon Mechanical Turk. *Journal of the Economic Science Association*, *3*(1), 1–11. doi:10.1007/s40881-017-0035-0

Chilton, L. B., Horton, J. J., Miller, R. C., & Azenkot, S. (2010). Task search in a human computation market. In *Proceedings of the ACM SIGKDD workshop on human computation* (pp. 1–9). New York, NY: Association for Computing Machinery.

Dang, B., Hutson, M., & Lease, M. (2016). MmmTurkey: A crowdsourcing framework for deploying tasks and recording worker behavior on Amazon mechanical Turk. *arXiv preprint arXiv:1609.00945*.

Fordsham, N., Moss, A. J., Krumholtz, S., Roggina, T., Robinson, J., & Litman, L. (2019). Variation among mechanical turk workers across time of day presents an opportunity and a challenge for research. doi:10.31234/osf.io/p8bns

Goldin, G., & Darlow, A. (2013). TurkGate (Version 0.4. 0) [Software]. Retrieved from http://gideongoldin. github.io/TurkGate

Goodman, J. K., & Paolacci, G. (2017). Crowdsourcing consumer research. *Journal of Consumer Research*, *44*(1), 196–210. doi:10.1093/jcr/ucx047

Gureckis, T. M., Martin, J., McDonnell, J., Rich, A. S., Markant, D., Coenen, A., . . .Chan, P. (2016). psiTurk: An open-source framework for conducting replicable behavioral experiments online. *Behavior Research Methods*, *48*(3), 829–842. doi:10.3758/s13428-015-0642-8

Lease, M., Hullman, J., Bigham, J. P., Bernstein, M. S., Kim, J., Lasecki, W., . . .Miller, R. C. (2013). Mechanical turk is not anonymous. *SSRN Electronic Journal*. doi:10.2139/ssrn.2228728

Litman, L., Robinson, J., & Abberbock, T. (2017). TurkPrime.com: A versatile crowdsourcing data acquisition platform for the behavioral sciences. *Behavior Research Methods*, *49*(2), 433–442. doi:10.3758/s13428-016-0727-z

Mao, A., Chen, Y., Gajos, K. Z., Parkes, D. C., Procaccia, A. D., & Zhang, H. (2012). Turkserver: Enabling synchronous and longitudinal online experiments. *Proceedings of HCOMP*.

Moss, A. J., & Litman, L. (2018, Sept. 18). After the bot scare: Understanding what's been happening with data collection on MTurk and how to stop it [blog post]. Retrieved from https://www.cloudresearch.com/resources/blog/after-the-bot-scare-understanding-whats-been-happening-with-data-collection-on-mturk-and-how-to-stop-it/

Stewart, N., Chandler, J., & Paolacci, G. (2017). Crowdsourcing samples in cognitive science. *Trends in Cognitive Sciences*, *21*(10), 736–748. doi:10.1016/j.tics.2017.06.007

DATA QUALITY ISSUES ON MECHANICAL TURK

Jesse Chandler, Gabriele Paolacci, and David J. Hauser

INTRODUCTION

In *Anna Karenina,* Tolstoy observed that all happy families are alike, but each unhappy family is unhappy in its own way. Likewise, all high-quality data sets share common features, but each poor-quality data set is flawed in its own way. Measures can be of inherently poor quality, or good measures can be poorly administered. Measures can be administered to the "wrong" people including those who are deceptive, lazy, or low ability; or measures can be administered to the "right" people at the wrong time such as when they are tired, bored, or distracted. Complicating matters further, data quality may not be uniform: different variables, subgroups, or experimental conditions within a data set may differ in quality.

As Mechanical Turk has become more popular as a source of research participants, researchers have wondered about the quality of data from MTurk samples. Although the quality of data obtained from Mechanical Turk is generally high, these are legitimate concerns because data quality constrains the interpretation of research findings. Poor data quality can introduce additional variance (noise) that attenuates true relationships between variables, making effects shrink or even disappear entirely. Poor data quality can also introduce bias, leading measurements to be falsely inflated, deflated, or associated with each other. Thus, both individual investigators and the research community must ensure that they draw conclusions only from data of adequate quality.

This chapter provides a broad overview of factors that can affect data quality, with an emphasis on Mechanical Turk–specific challenges to data quality, together with operational solutions to address these challenges. We first provide a taxonomy of data attributes that impact quality and how they can be assessed for data sets and individual responses. We then discuss five causes of problematic data that are particularly relevant to MTurk: attentiveness, language comprehension, attrition and selection effects, deceptiveness, and nonnaïveté. We highlight the unique elements of these concerns for Mechanical Turk, the available evidence of substantive consequences, and strategies to address each problem.

This chapter does not provide a step-by-step guide to obtain high-quality survey data, nor does it exhaustively summarize the extensive literature on the topic. Rather, we encourage researchers who use MTurk to complement the insights of this chapter with a thorough understanding of how measure development and web survey design can influence data quality (see Robins, Fraley, & Krueger, 2009, and Tourangeau, Conrad, & Couper, 2013, respectively, for overviews).

DEFINING AND MEASURING DATA QUALITY

Here we define high-quality data as having four attributes: consistency, correctness, completeness, and credibility (adapted from International Organization for Standardization/International Electrotechnical Commission, 2008).

- **Consistency.** Consistent data are free from internal contradiction. Similar questions should produce similar responses (referred to as reliability) and responses to the same question at different time points should be similar (referred to as test-retest reliability). For example, people should report an age that corresponds to their year of birth, and the same year of birth across different studies.

- **Correctness.** Correct data measure what they intend to measure. Correctness can be inferred if measures are correlated with variables that the underlying measure is correlated with (convergent validity), and uncorrelated with variables that the underlying measure is not correlated with (discriminant validity; for a detailed discussion, see Campbell & Fiske, 1959). For example, depression and anxiety are correlated with each other, and so this relationship should be expected in high-quality samples. But depression and visual hallucinations are not correlated and so there should be no association between measures of these two constructs. A lack of discriminant validity is particularly important because it can diagnose data-quality problems that spuriously increase apparent data quality on measures of reliability or convergent validity.

- **Completeness.** Complete data include all required information. The overall completeness of a data set can be measured by calculating the number of missing responses to individual items (item missingness), the number of people who start but fail to complete a set of measurements (attrition), or the number of people who see the study but decide not to complete any measurements (self-selection).

- **Credibility.** Credible responses represent a good faith effort by participants to provide a truthful response.

The satisfaction of any one of these criteria does not guarantee high-quality data. For example, people may provide responses that are incomplete or uncredible but consistent. Data may also fail to meet one or more of these criteria but still be fit for a specific purpose. For example, incorrect responses may be more tolerable in cases where the goal is merely to estimate the direction of an effect rather than its precise size. Importantly, this definition does not include the issue of sample representativeness, which is addressed in Chapter 8.

Assessing the Quality of Different Data Sources

Some measures provide information about the overall quality of a data set, such as whether patterns of responses observed in a sample correspond to patterns of responses typically observed in other samples. Many of these measures are typically used to evaluate the quality of specific instruments. However, these measures are also useful for deciding between various sources of participants, evaluating the quality of a newly obtained sample against existing samples, or deciding whether a particular measure or study is appropriate in a given context or with a particular sample.

Consistent Responses

MTurk samples achieve levels of consistency (measured by Cronbach's alpha or similar statistics) that are similar to traditional student samples and above conventionally recommended minimums, on measures of personality (Behrend, Sharek, Meade, & Wiebe, 2011; Buhrmester, Kwang, & Gosling, 2011), attitudes (Behrend et al., 2011; Tylka & Wood-Barcalow, 2015), behavior (Jahnke, Imhoff, & Hoyer, 2015; Kim & Hodgins, 2017), and feelings (Schleider & Weisz, 2015; Shapiro, Chandler, & Mueller, 2013). MTurk samples also achieve high levels of test-retest reliability (Buhrmester et al., 2011; Holden, Dennie, & Hicks, 2013; Kim & Hodgins, 2017; Schleider & Weisz, 2015; Shapiro et al., 2013), though these analyses do not directly compare test-retest reliabilities obtained from U.S. worker samples and student samples.

Correct Responses

MTurk samples often achieve levels of convergent validity similar to those observed in more traditional samples (Jones & Paulhus, 2014; McCredie & Morey, 2019; Miller et al., 2013). Of particular note, a large-scale comparison of variables of interest to political scientists found that 33 of 36 measured correlations did not differ across MTurk and a nationally representative sample (Clifford, Jewell, & Waggoner, 2015).

Comparisons of discriminant validity across samples reveal some reason for concern. Hamby and Taylor (2016) found that correlations between variables were inflated on MTurk relative to student samples, and they attributed this finding to a minority of MTurk workers who tended to select the same response on all items (known as "straightlining"). Measures of associations between worker experience and their responses to survey questions represent a special case of discriminant validity that we address in detail in the section on nonnaïveté later in this chapter.

Complete Responses

Item missingness is not much of a problem in web studies, where participants can be warned or even forced to provide a response if they try to skip an item. Attrition is more of a concern. Although it is negligible when data are collected from student samples in person (Cronk & West, 2002), it may average around 30% in web studies (Vehovar, Batagelj, Lozar Manfreda, & Zalatel, 2002). Mechanical Turk may fall somewhere in between these extremes: one informal estimate places attrition rates at around 15% (Harms & DeSimone, 2015; see also Paolacci, Chandler, & Ipeirotis, 2010). The presence of selection bias is generally unknowable for non-probability studies.

Credible Responses

It is difficult to measure whether participants provide good-faith responses to questions. In surveys of participant behavior, MTurk workers report relatively high levels of multitasking while participating in research studies (Goodman, Cryder, & Cheema, 2013; Necka, Cacioppo, Norman, & Cacioppo, 2016), suggesting that they may be less than fully engaged with the studies they complete. Research does suggest that MTurk workers do complete surveys faster than other participant pools (Kees, Berry, Burton, & Sheehan, 2017; Kennedy, Clifford, Burleigh, Jewell, & Waggoner, 2018); MTurkers completed one study 12% faster than a student sample, 23% faster than a Qualtrics sample, and 27% faster than a Prime Panels sample (Chapter 10), but it is unclear whether this is because MTurk workers are less engaged, or just more efficient at completing surveys.

Self-reports are unlikely to be effective as a measure of honesty because people who are not honest are probably also willing to lie about their honesty (see, e.g., Chandler

& Paolacci, 2017). However, truthfulness can be estimated based on scores of self-report scales designed to detect deceptive responses, such as presenting oneself in an overly positive (socially desirable or "faking good") light (Crowne & Marlowe, 1960; for an overview, see Paulhus, 2002) or negative (malingering, or "faking bad") light. These measures consist of questions that have nearly unanimous responses (e.g., "I have never intensely disliked anyone"), so people who provide unusual answers are unlikely to be telling the truth. There is some evidence that MTurk workers score higher on measures of malingering (Arch & Carr, 2017; McCredie & Morey, 2019; Shapiro et al., 2013). Similarly, one study found higher levels of social desirability among MTurk workers than among a student sample (Behrend et al., 2011, but also see McCredie & Morey, 2019).

Experiment Effect Sizes as Aggregate Measures of Quality

The strength of effect sizes observed in survey experiments can also serve as an index of overall data quality. Sensitivity to independent variables requires attentiveness, conscientious responding, and honesty. On this measure, the quality of MTurk data is quite good. Two large replications of survey experiment studies found that effect sizes observed on Mechanical Turk are similar to effect sizes observed in other samples. In one, 32 of 39 observed effects and null effects were consistent across samples (Mullinix, Leeper, Druckman, & Freese, 2015); in the other, 25 of 37 effects were consistent across samples (Coppock, 2019). High replication rates have also been observed within batteries of cognitive psychology experiments, which use response latencies as dependent measures and are thus presumably quite sensitive to participant attentiveness (Crump, McDonnell, & Gureckis, 2013; Zwaan et al., 2018).

Identifying Individuals Who Provide Poor-Quality Data

Within any particular sample, the quality of individual responses will vary. It is important to identify poor-quality responses, as doing so might reduce false-negative and false-positive results. However, the potential for these measures to falsely identify workers as low-effort participants is unknown, so researchers should carefully consider whether these measures should be used to determine whether participants should be paid or not.

Consistent Responses

The reliability of individual participant responses cannot be measured, but there are other ways to assess the consistency of responses. For example, if participants are asked pairs of similar questions, consistency can be assessed by correlating sets of pairs (Johnson, 2005; Meade & Craig, 2012). A major weakness of this method is that a large number of pairings are required to obtain a precise estimate of consistency (Schönbrodt & Perugini, 2013). A more complex approach is to aggregate absolute discrepancies across items, either by summing them or by squaring them and then summing the squares to penalize larger differences (Litman et al., 2015). Specific questions can also be asked more than once or in different ways (e.g., age and year of birth) to enable a direct check of consistency (e.g., Shapiro et al., 2013).

Correct Responses

Convergent and discriminant validity cannot be calculated for individual participants. However, correctness can be approximated by examining demographic details and reported life experiences that should not be contradictory. For example, people who identify as male and report being in a heterosexual relationship are unlikely to report that their partner is also male.

Complete Responses

Submitted responses can be inspected for missing values. It is unusual to exclude participants on the grounds that they failed to provide a certain proportion of complete responses, and a more meaningful measure is whether participants have completed certain critical items. In particular, researchers conducting experiments that require a response from participants as a part of the experimental manipulation (e.g., writing about a hypothetical event) may want to specify a certain length or level of detail of responses as a precondition for including a participant's responses.

Credible Responses

One measure of credibility is to simply ask participants whether they are telling the truth, though this is unlikely to be effective (Chandler & Paolacci, 2017). Another option is to use a self-report measure of deception (such as the social desirability or malingering measures discussed earlier) and exclude those individuals with especially discrepant scores (Shapiro et al., 2013).

Researchers can also use a number of strategies to infer whether participants put forth their best effort. The most direct approach is simply to ask them if they were paying attention at the end of the survey, clarifying that the answer will not affect their payment. Some studies indicate that this method might successfully identify inattentive participants (Aust, Diedenhofen, Ullrich, & Musch, 2013; Meade & Craig, 2012), though the rate of observed inattention (3%–5%) might be lower compared to other methods (Curran, 2016).

Attention Check Questions

Of all available methods of ensuring data quality, attention checks are preferable to other measures because they are face valid and reasonably effective. Numerous behavioral measures identify whether participants are making a good-faith effort to complete the survey. One method is to ask questions with verifiable answers that nearly everyone can answer correctly (referred to as "red herrings" or "catch trials"; Beach, 1989). For example, a question might ask if the participant was born on February 30 or if she has ever had a fatal heart attack while watching television (Paolacci et al., 2010). Other researchers simply include items that tell participants which response to select (e.g., "answer strongly disagree to this question"; Meade & Craig, 2012).

Instructional Manipulation Checks (IMCs; Oppenheimer, Meyvis, & Davidenko, 2009) are a widely used method of assessing attentiveness. IMCs test whether participants have read the instructions by suggesting one kind of answer is acceptable through question formatting and providing explicit contradictory instructions within a large block of text. For instance, the question title may ask in which sports activities the participant engages, with several different sports listed as response options. However, embedded within a block of text prior to the question are instructions to ignore the lure question and click the question header instead (Oppenheimer et al., 2009). Participants who follow the text instructions pass the IMC, and those who don't fail it.

Attention checks are popular but somewhat controversial because their reliability is low and pass rates vary greatly depending on item difficulty (Thomas & Clifford, 2017). A broader concern is that there is no principled benchmark of how much attention is "enough" to successfully complete a study. Researchers would normally solve this kind of measurement problem by developing items with known sensitivity and specificity (false-positive and false-negative rates). However, MTurk workers learn commonly used survey methods over time and can likely identify and pass these kinds of checks without needing to pay particularly close attention. For example, in one study, 95% of MTurk workers passed an IMC, compared to only 39% of college students (Hauser & Schwarz, 2016; see also Peer et al., 2017). Researchers who frequently use attention checks could consider using a mixture of old items (to exclude inattentive participants) and new items (to be evaluated for use in future studies).

Researchers should also be careful including attention screeners early in a study. Attention checks can change the way that participants respond to later questions, leading to lower scale reliability and other unintended context effects on later measures (Breitsohl & Steidelmüller, 2018; Hauser & Schwarz, 2015; but also see Kung, Kwok, & Brown, 2018).

Manipulation Checks

In experimental studies with complex instructions, researchers sometimes ask questions about critical instructions prior to exposure to the treatment conditions. For example, if participants can earn different amounts of money depending on the outcome of an economic game, a researcher may quiz them about how much they could earn following each outcome (a factual manipulation check; Kane & Barabas, 2019).

Sometimes, experimenters will directly measure processes that are thought to be caused by the independent variable and are necessary for it to impact the dependent variable of interest (a manipulation check). For example, if a study manipulates anger and then measures risk taking, it may be important to ensure that participants in different conditions self-report the expected differences in anger. Although manipulation checks are common in MTurk research (e.g., Rand et al., 2015), they are not without problems (for a review, see Hauser, Ellsworth, & Gonzalez, 2018). Selecting participants based on whether they pass a manipulation check can invalidate random assignment (for a detailed discussion, see Elwert & Winship, 2014). Manipulation checks can also sometimes impact how people interpret the manipulation itself, leading to spurious findings (Kühnen, 2010).

Anomalous Response Patterns

Low participant credibility can be inferred from unusual response patterns, such as selecting only the most extreme responses, selecting responses in ascending or descending order, or selecting the same response option for every question (straightlining). Data can be visually inspected for these patterns, but anomalous response patterns can also be quantified through multivariate outlier detection tests such as Mahalanobis distance (Huang et al., 2012; Meade & Craig, 2012; Rasmussen, 1988).

Response Speed

Participants who respond too quickly may not be paying attention (Kittur, Chi, & Suh, 2008; Wood, Harms, Lowman, & DeSimone, 2017). For grids of self-report questions that use the same response scale, response times of less than one second per item seem to indicate a sharp decline in data quality (Wood et al., 2017)—though this cutoff will depend on the complexity of the items and potential responses. For studies that do not contain grids, researchers can inspect the total time to complete the study and exclude extreme outliers. Estimates of time to complete should be obtained from the survey platform used to collect data rather than from MTurk because the time between when a task is accepted and submitted may not correspond to how long the worker spent on the study itself.

Researchers can also use any number of the techniques discussed in the "Identifying Individuals Who Provide Poor-Quality Data" section to identify and exclude poor-quality participants. Measures of data quality are weakly (and sometimes negatively) correlated with each other, so different methods will identify different participants as inattentive (Meade & Craig, 2012). For this reason, we recommend following Curran's (2016) advice to use multiple measures to identify low-quality responses.

CAUSES OF AND CURES FOR POOR DATA QUALITY

In this section we present evidence of five different sources of data quality problems—inattentiveness, language comprehension, attrition and selection bias, participant fraud and deception, and nonnaïveté—and potential solutions. We discuss the potential effects of each issue and present remedies to attenuate such effects. Table 5.1 summarizes how these effects relate to the data quality measures described in the previous section. Importantly, the table is necessarily nonexhaustive about the host of possible threats to data quality on Mechanical Turk because some of them may not have been documented yet. The table also does not address the prevalence of these threats in any specific MTurk sample or for any specific research design. Rather, it should be read as a simplified summary of the takeaways of the discussion that follows.

Inattentiveness

Inattentiveness is a subjective evaluation of whether participants have invested enough effort or care into answering a question to make their response "correct." Participant attentiveness exists on a continuum with all (or most) participants inclined to attend to the research study and provide satisfactory answers, but only to a point. Past that point, responses may be based on only the first thoughts that come to mind.

A simple account of inattention would be to treat inattentiveness as "noise" that leads responses to deviate more symmetrically from their true values, increasing measurement error for individual responses and the standard deviation of group responses (though not the mean). Unfortunately, inattentive responses are seldom symmetrically distributed around their true values as would be predicted by this model of error. Instead, "random" inattentive responses to questions tend to be

TABLE 5.1 ⬤ CROSSWALK OF CAUSES AND MEASURES OF DATA QUALITY ISSUES				
	Consistent	Correct	Complete	Credible
Inattentiveness	Low measures of consistency for reverse-coded items	Attenuated correlations between related measures, spurious correlations between unrelated measures	Missing items, brief responses to open-ended questions	Self-reported inattentiveness
Language comprehension	Low measures of consistency for reverse-coded items	Attenuated correlations between related measures, spurious correlations between unrelated measures	Brief responses to open-ended questions	Self-reported low language ability, failure of linguistic aptitude tests
Attrition and selection bias		Participant break-off associated with treatment condition or differentially correlated with participant characteristics within treatment condition	High rates of participant break-off	
Participant fraud and deception	Self-reported characteristics change after learning eligibility criteria	Spurious associations between variables commonly believed to be related		Inflated measures of malingering or social desirability
Nonnaïveté		Participant responses correlated with prior experience		

determined by a unique process from true responses and thus tend to have their own mean and distribution (Chandler, Sisso, & Shapiro, 2019; Huang, Liu, & Bowling, 2015). Further, inattentive responses are not necessarily random responses. Instead, participants may select the same answer to all questions (straightlining) or use a similar strategy.

Including responses drawn from a different distribution can have a large impact on results, especially if the two distributions have very different means. For instance, a single (albeit extreme) outlier in a sample of 29 participants can change a correlation from $r = .99$ to $r = 0$ (Lind & Zumbo, 1993; see also Barnette, 1999). Means are most likely to differ when true responses have a skewed distribution because this increases the maximum possible difference between attentive and inattentive responses. Importantly, when samples with different means are pooled together, correlations between variables that are keyed in the same direction are usually inflated, leading inattentive responses to produce false-positive findings (Barnette, 1999; Chandler et al., 2019; Huang et al., 2015). Correlations between variables keyed in the opposite direction (including reliability measures of reverse-coded items) are often attenuated.

Causes and Remedies

A major challenge of conducting research online is that participants are unsupervised and in an environment that is not controlled by the experimenter. In-person studies are also assumed to create social contact between researchers and participants, which may increase accountability (Johnson, 2005). Compounding this issue, some participants are motivated to complete studies quickly in order to maximize the money they can earn on Mechanical Turk.

Worker Reputation

Restricting studies to high-reputation workers has historically been an effective way of limiting inattention and insufficient effort responding. Compared to low-reputation workers, high-reputation workers (with ≥ 95% HIT approval ratio) pass attention checks at higher rates, have higher scale reliabilities, respond with less socially desirable answers, and show less midpoint bias in scale responses (Peer, Vosgerau, & Acquisti, 2014). However, more recent data show that there are very few low-reputation workers on Mechanical Turk (Robinson, Rosenzweig, Moss, & Litman, 2019). Thus, the use of the 95% HIT approval qualification will only exclude a small proportion of workers (about 2%; Matherly, 2019). The effective use of reputation qualifications, including the 95% approval ratio and the minimum HIT completion qualification, is discussed further in Chapter 7.

Worker Payment

It is widely believed that "you get what you pay for," but this may not be true for data quality. Several studies have examined the effects of payment on MTurk worker responses and have found that for U.S. workers, higher levels of payment increase the speed of recruitment but do not appear to improve data quality (Buhrmester et al., 2011; Litman et al., 2015; Mason & Suri, 2012). Increasing payment (particularly through bonuses) does seem to improve results for tasks in which output is correlated with level of effort and for which quality has some objective standard (Ho, Slivkins, Suri, & Vaughan, 2015), but in practice few psychological or behavioral measures meet these criteria.

Study Length and Engagingness

Long or boring studies are likely to reduce participant attentiveness. The limits of what tasks MTurk workers will tolerate are unknown, but other samples have demonstrated that participants also tend to provide faster, lower-quality responses to later questions. Choices in decision-making tasks become more inconsistent, responses to grids of self-report items become more uniform, and answers to free response questions become shorter (Galesic, 2006; Galesic & Bosnjak, 2009; Savage & Waldman, 2008).

There is little research on what research participants find engaging, but certainly operationalizing research questions so that stimuli are interesting to participants, supplementing text with images and attractive visual design, or creating responsive or interactive study materials (e.g., through the use of games or through providing experimental feedback) should help minimize inattention. There is also little research on the maximum length of study that workers will tolerate, but as a precaution, studies should limit the use of repeated experimental trials, avoid excessively long lists of synonymous self-report items, and generally be no longer than necessary.

Warnings and Trainers

Researchers have experimented with warning MTurk participants to be attentive or training participants to answer carefully (Clifford & Jerit, 2015; Oppenheimer et al., 2009). The evidence for the effectiveness of these techniques is mixed. Oppenheimer et al. (2009) found that IMC trainers that include failure feedback for participants who miss key instructions increased effect sizes on tasks prone to satisficing. On the other hand, Berinsky, Margolis, and Sances (2014) found that IMC trainers only increased IMC pass rates on later IMCs but did not reduce noise in other subsequent tasks. Likewise, evidence suggests that warnings to pay attention can improve data quality on numerous measures (Clifford & Jerit, 2015; Huang et al., 2012), but with the potential cost of increasing socially desirable responding in some populations (Clifford & Jerit, 2015). Quite simply, further research on these techniques is needed and should be focused on their effectiveness and potential adverse effects for MTurk populations.

Language Comprehension

MTurk is used by people from all around the world, only about half of whom speak English as their native language (Pavlick, Post, Irvine, Kachaev, & Callison-Burch, 2014). The resulting issues with language comprehension will often cause the same problems and be detected by the same measures designed to detect inattentive responses (Chandler & Shapiro, 2016; Goodman et al., 2013; Litman et al., 2015; Rashtchian, Young, Hodosh, & Hockenmaier, 2010; Samimi, Ravana, & Koh, 2016), but in some circumstances, researchers may wish to treat language comprehension as a distinct quality issue.

Potential Remedies

Restricting samples by nationality will reduce but not eliminate language comprehension problems. Between 3% and 7% of "U.S." participants complete studies from non-U.S. IP addresses, with a further 10%–30% of "U.S." participants completing studies using virtual private servers located in the United States that effectively conceal their location. Many workers using virtual private servers seem to be from outside the United States (Moss & Litman, 2018). These workers also produce data with serious quality problems (Chandler et al., 2019; Kennedy et al., 2018; Moss & Litman, 2018).

Workers with IP addresses or geolocations associated with virtual private servers can be blocked from studies using tools developed by CloudResearch (Moss & Litman, 2018) and other third parties (Kennedy et al., 2018), while other tools allow researchers to validate the IP addresses of submitted responses (Prims, Sisso, & Bai, 2018). Studies conducted by CloudResearch on an ongoing basis show that these tools are effective at blocking non-U.S. workers, and in eliminating the data quality problems that arise from such participants (Litman, Robinson, Moss, & Gautam, 2018).

Study Design

Survey materials should be written to be accessible to people with a variety of reading levels by minimizing jargon, using the simplest words that convey an intended meaning, and avoiding unnecessarily long or complex sentence structure. Many comprehension issues are best identified through cognitive interviewing. If a certain level of reading comprehension is essential, workers can be required to complete a language comprehension qualification prior to completing the study (Rashtchian et al., 2010, June; Samimi et al., 2016) or embedded within the survey itself. Studies that expect to include people with different native languages (e.g., cross-cultural comparisons) might need to offer the survey in different languages.

Attrition and Selection Bias

Data quality is impacted not only by the responses that participants provide but also by the responses that they do not provide. Participant responses can be missing from a survey either because they decide not to attempt it (selection bias) or they attempt it but then drop out (attrition). If only a certain subpopulation of potential participants completes a survey, important information about those who do not participate may be lost, potentially amplifying the problem of using a nonrepresentative sample (Chapters 7 and 8).

Attrition and selection bias can also impact the validity of research findings. If qualitatively different participants tend to complete different experimental treatments, differences that seem to arise from the experimental treatment may in fact be caused by individual differences between survey participants (Campbell & Stanley, 1963). Zhou and Fishbach (2016) illustrated how differential attrition can impact inferences made from MTurk experiments. In one study, participants who were asked to imagine wearing eyeliner reported weighing less than those who were not. This finding could lead to the conclusion that imagining wearing eyeliner led people to feel thinner. However, this pattern is actually explained by men (who weigh more than women) dropping out of the eyeliner condition more often than the control condition.

Large differences in attrition rates across experimental conditions are a certain warning that attrition threatens the validity of an experiment, but a high overall rate of attrition also increases this risk because it creates the possibility that different kinds of participants are differentially attriting out of different experimental conditions. As a rough approximation, a seven-percentage-point difference in attrition across conditions or an attrition rate above 20% are warning signs, though in practice the tolerable amount of differential and overall attrition could be smaller, depending on the correlation between attrition and responses to the outcome variable (for an overview, see Deke & Chiang, 2017).

Selection bias occurs when participants self-select into a study based on topical interest or other variables like time of day, payment rate, or how long it has been available. Differential selection can occur when participants assigned to different conditions are recruited using different HITs, particularly if one HIT is substantially longer or higher paying than the other, or when different conditions are fielded at different time points (for a detailed discussion, see Casey, Chandler, Levine, Proctor, & Strolovitch,

2017). Differential selection bias might also occur on MTurk because workers share links to some of these HITs, but not others, on worker discussion forums. Selection bias is discussed extensively in Chapter 7.

Potential Remedies

Experimenters should measure and report both overall study attrition and differential attrition across conditions (Crump et al., 2013; Deke & Chiang, 2017). Attrition can be detected by examining survey responses, but it is easy to underestimate for surveys that do not record participants who break off before providing a response (for example, those who only read the consent form or instructions). Researchers should also be careful not to overlook partially completed responses. For example, by default the survey platform Qualtrics leaves partially complete responses open for a week to allow participants time to return and complete them and does not include open responses in data exports (Zhou & Fishbach, 2016). Researchers can also overestimate attrition by assuming that every row of data represents a unique participant without accounting for workers who attempt a survey more than once.

Studies can be designed to limit the potential impact of attrition by encouraging people to break off before random assignment. Placing demographic questions first may help "warm up" participants and commit them to completing the survey. If the experimental and control conditions differ in their expected level of difficulty, a difficult task can be placed prior to random assignment to encourage all participants who are sensitive to difficulty to drop out (Horton, Rand, & Zeckhauser, 2011). Another approach is to focus on the equivalency of participants in different conditions by exposing all of them to all experimental stimuli (either before or after the dependent measures) and analyzing only the data of participants who completed the study (Rand, 2012).

Researchers can also estimate the potential impact of attrition on the inferences made from a study. To do so, they must establish that participants who remained in the study were equivalent at baseline, either on relevant demographic or psychological characteristics or (better yet) on a baseline measure of the dependent variable (Jurs & Glass, 1971; Kazai et al., 2012, October; Schleider & Weisz, 2015). If necessary, robustness to attrition or differential selection can be estimated by imputing the highest and lowest possible values for those who attrite and using the result of these analyses to place upper and lower bounds around a potential effect (Gerber & Green, 2012).

Participant Fraud and Deception

Participants who deceive researchers can threaten data validity. Fraud requires effort and thus fraudulent participants are unlikely to be detected by measures of low-effort responding (Chandler et al., 2019, in press). Though MTurk workers are unlikely to be less honest than other participants, given any propensity to cheat, actual cheating is bound to occur more frequently in online studies than in the laboratory (Clifford & Jerit, 2014).

A common problem is when participants fraudulently misrepresent themselves in order to meet study eligibility criteria (Chandler & Paolacci, 2017; Kan & Drummey, 2018; Sharpe Wessling, Huber, & Netzer, 2017). Participants who misrepresent themselves on screening questions may sometimes try to answer other questions as someone with their assumed identity might (Sharpe Wessling et al., 2017). In some cases, their responses are indistinguishable from honest participants, albeit for deceptive reasons. In other cases, their beliefs about others are incorrect, leading them to respond differently than those who truly possess the identity that they have assumed. For example, workers who falsely claim to be colorblind report difficulty distinguishing blue numbers on a red background, even though red-blue color-blindness is biologically impossible (Kan & Drummey, 2018). Likewise, in the consumer choice studies in Sharpe Wessling et al. (2017), impostors who claimed to be older also claimed to consume more high-fiber foods than those who were actually older, whereas impostors who claimed to be women reported a preference for pink-colored products not shared by actual women.

A second common problem is eliciting honest responses to factual questions from online participants because participants must resist the temptation to look up the answers. People often confuse knowing the correct answer with knowing how to find the correct answer using the Internet (Fisher, Goddu, & Keil, 2015). This problem may be magnified on Mechanical Turk, where there are strong norms to provide correct answers to factual questions using any means necessary. However, the actual prevalence of cheating on factual knowledge questions on MTurk is unknown. Goodman et al. (2013) found that MTurk workers were unusually more likely to correctly estimate the number of countries in Africa than were a community sample that lacked Internet access. Other studies in the domain of political knowledge, however, found low rates of cheating relative to other online samples (Berinsky et al., 2012; Clifford & Jerit, 2016).

Potential Remedies

As a general rule, participants misrepresent themselves for a reason, so deception is best prevented by removing study design features that incentivize it (Chandler & Paolacci, 2017). Researchers should consider carefully whether participants can cheat on survey questions before offering bonuses contingent on a certain response. Screening criteria should always be unobservable, even after the screening has been made, or workers may use this information to reattempt the survey they could not participate in (Chandler & Paolacci, 2017). Rather, the screening variable should be measured as part of a separate study or by advertising the study as a short demographic study and routing eligible workers to a longer study in exchange for a bonus payment (Hydock, 2018). There is also some evidence that deception can be disincentivized by asking participants to complete an honesty pledge (Jacquemet, James, Luchini, Murphy, & Shogren 2019). Unlike inattentiveness, self-report measures are poor at identifying deceptive participants (Chandler & Paolacci, 2017), perhaps because people willing to lie are also willing to lie about lying.

Researchers may also consider monitoring worker discussion forums (Chapter 2) to ensure that eligibility criteria, factual knowledge, or other critical information is not being shared between workers. Sharpe Wessling and colleagues (2017) conducted a study in which participants made a guess that paid $1.00 when correct. A worker shared the correct response on a forum, which was taken down immediately after. In general, when information may circulate that is problematic, researchers should consider asking participants to refrain from doing so and monitor MTurk forums to detect problematic sharing.

Nonnaïveté

Some participants may enter a study with knowledge about its topical contents or the methods that it uses. Though this knowledge can have various consequences (some of which we identify shortly), it is parsimoniously assumed to be bad to rely on participants with substantive research experience. For this reason, traditional convenience samples (like university subject pools or some online panels) include a centralized register of the studies completed by members of the population. This list is used to ensure that the type and frequency of studies that participants complete are regulated.

Participation on MTurk is not regulated and some MTurk workers tend to participate in a huge number of studies—orders of magnitude higher than the number of studies completed by participants in community or undergraduate pools. Mechanical Turk does not report how many tasks workers have completed but surveys that ask participants about the number of studies they complete find that the average MTurk participant might complete dozens of studies every week (Kees et al., 2017; Kennedy et al., 2018). Because workers often stay for years in the population (Stewart et al., 2015), many workers in the typical study sample may have already completed hundreds, if not thousands, of studies in the past (Rand et al., 2014).

"Professional" research participants who complete many studies can cause several threats to data quality. Some researchers speculate that people who complete many surveys are different in important ways from other people. For example, they may only be interested in making money, which would translate into minimizing the time and effort participants put into each task (Ford, 2017), though evidence from other types of MTurk tasks suggests that worker experience is not associated with other indicators of low effort (Hata, Krishna, Fei-Fei, & Bernstein, 2016).

Participants can also learn about research through their experience completing studies (that is, become nonnaïve). Nonnaïveté can be *general* (i.e., about the domains and methods usually employed by the research community) or *specific* to paradigms that may be encountered again (e.g., repeated participation in the same study or common tasks across studies).

The concern that MTurk workers acquire and apply general knowledge about how research is conducted is largely speculative, and it is unclear how knowledge obtained through completing studies on MTurk compares to knowledge obtained by student research participants through their coursework. It is possible that experienced workers learn heuristics about how to answer questions in a way that maximizes their payment. In market research panels, participants have learned to claim that they own the products they are asked about, presumably because it maximizes the chance that they will be allowed to complete studies (Miller, 2006). It is also possible that people who often participate in research may make assumptions about research that have unknown effects on their behavior. For example, economists often worry that frequent exposure to psychology studies that contain deception may lead participants to assume that all social science studies may contain deception (Ortmann & Hertwig, 2002).

There are many demonstrations of MTurk workers applying knowledge gained about specific paradigms or questions to later studies. MTurk workers are often familiar with classic paradigms such as the trolley problem, the prisoner's dilemma, or the Cognitive Reflection Test (Chandler et al., 2014; Thomson & Oppenheimer, 2016). This familiarity is obviously problematic for paradigms that are sensitive to learning effects: by using different popular versions of the Cognitive Reflection Test, Chandler et al. (2014) show that worker productivity predicts performance on a commonly used version, but not an uncommonly used version of the test. Note, however, that Bialek and Pennycook (2018) found that these practice effects did not affect the predictive ability of the test.

Learning can also affect other studies when the impact of a treatment effect is moderated by knowledge. Rand et al. (2014) conducted a series of studies testing whether time pressure makes people more likely to cooperate in interpersonal dilemmas and found that the effect of time pressure declined over time, presumably because participants who had practice completing the task were less affected by the time-pressure manipulation. Similarly, Chandler, Paolacci, Peer, Mueller, and Ratliff (2015) conducted a two-wave study in which participants completed twice a series of two-condition, between-participants experiments in the area of decision making. Effect sizes were smaller in the second wave, particularly when the two waves were close in time (a few days versus a month) and when participants were assigned to the alternative conditions. Although the precise mechanism under which effect size reduction occurs is unclear, these results suggest that participants draw from previous experiences while completing a study (see DeVoe & House, 2016, for a study yielding similar insights).

Potential Remedies

Problems associated with nonnaïveté can be attenuated, and perhaps eliminated entirely, by the careful management of who can access a study (see Robinson et al., 2019). Workers who have previously participated in specific studies can be relatively easy to manage based on the studies they have completed for the experimenter in the past (see Chapters 3 and 4 for details). The way to manage whether workers can access studies on the basis of other research experiences is discussed in depth in Chapter 7. It is also important to note that nonnaïveté is not a problem across the board. Workers do seem to forget information that they saw in studies over time (Chandler, Mueller, & Paolacci, 2014), suggesting that occasional exposure to a particular study is probably benign.

CONCLUSION

Data quality is a goal-dependent, multidimensional concept that generally describes the consistency, correctness, completeness, and credibility of the responses produced by research participants. The popularity of MTurk makes it a primary target of metascientific investigations of data quality. The quality of the data obtained on MTurk is generally comparable to traditional samples, with benchmarking studies showing similar effect sizes and psychometrically sound measurements. However, data collected from MTurk will be of high quality only when active steps are taken to ensure quality.

Fortunately, a growing body of evidence documents the prevalence of and solutions to different data quality issues, both for Internet research in general and for MTurk research in particular. Naturally, these problems apply to different studies to different degrees, and those who conduct or evaluate research should consider whether these issues constitute areas of concern on a case-by-case basis. Importantly, researchers often have tools to prevent these issues, and this chapter reviewed how different facets of data quality can be evaluated and how some causes of data quality problems can be attenuated. As long as researchers measure and are transparent about data quality issues, then crowdsourcing platforms like MTurk can serve as a rich source of data for researchers.

REFERENCES

Arch, J. J., & Carr, A. L. (2017). Using Mechanical Turk for research on cancer survivors. *Psycho-Oncology, 26*(10), 1593–1603. doi:10.1002/pon.4173

Aust, F., Diedenhofen, B., Ullrich, S., & Musch, J. (2013). Seriousness checks are useful to improve data validity in online research. *Behavior Research Methods, 45*(2), 527–535.

Barnette, J. J. (1999). Nonattending respondent effects on internal consistency of self-administered surveys: A Monte Carlo simulation study. *Educational and Psychological Measurement, 59*(1), 38–46. doi:10.1177/0013164499591003

Beach, D. A. (1989). Identifying the random responder. *The Journal of Psychology, 123*(1), 101–103. doi:10.10 80/00223980.1989.10542966

Behrend, T. S., Sharek, D. J., Meade, A. W., & Wiebe, E. N. (2011). The viability of crowdsourcing for survey research. *Behavior Research Methods, 43*(3), 800–813. doi:10.3758/s13428-011-0081-0

Berinsky, A. J., Huber, G. A., & Lenz, G. S. (2012). Evaluating online labor markets for experimental research: Amazon.com's Mechanical Turk. *Political Analysis, 20*(3), 351–368. doi:10.1093/pan/mpr057

Berinsky, A. J., Margolis, M. F., & Sances, M. W. (2014). Separating the shirkers from the workers? Making sure respondents pay attention on self-administered surveys. *American Journal of Political Science, 58*(3), 739–753. doi:10.1111/ajps.12081

Bialek, M., & Pennycook, G. (2018). The cognitive reflection test is robust to multiple exposures. *Behavior Research Methods, 50*(5), 1953–1959. doi:10.3758/s13428-017-0963-x

Breitsohl, H., & Steidelmüller, C. (2018). The impact of insufficient effort responding detection methods on substantive responses: Results from an experiment testing parameter invariance. *Applied Psychology, 67*(2), 284–308. doi:10.1111/apps.12121

Buhrmester, M., Kwang, T., & Gosling, S. D. (2011). Amazon's Mechanical Turk: A new source of inexpensive, yet high-quality, data? *Perspectives on Psychological Science, 6*(1), 3–5.

Campbell, D. T., & Fiske, D. W. (1959). Convergent and discriminant validation by the multitrait-multimethod matrix. *Psychological Bulletin, 56*(2), 81–105. doi:10.1037/h0046016

Campbell, D. T., & Stanley, J. C. (1963). Experimental and quasi-experimental designs for research. In *Handbook of research on teaching.* Chicago, IL: Rand McNally.

Casey, L. S., Chandler, J., Levine, A. S., Proctor, A., & Strolovitch, D. Z. (2017). Intertemporal differences among MTurk workers: Time-based sample variations and implications for online data collection. *SAGE Open, 7*(2). doi:10.1177/2158244017712774

Chandler, J., Mueller, P., & Paolacci, G. (2014). Nonnaïveté among Amazon Mechanical Turk workers: Consequences and solutions for behavioral researchers. *Behavior Research Methods, 46*(1), 112–130. doi:10.3758/s13428-013-0365-7

Chandler, J., & Paolacci, G. (2017). Lie for a dime: When most prescreening responses are honest but most study participants are impostors. *Social Psychological and Personality Science, 8*(5), 500–508. doi:10.1177/1948550617698203

Chandler, J., Paolacci, G., Peer, E., Mueller, P., & Ratliff, K. A. (2015). Using nonnaive participants can reduce effect sizes. *Psychological Science, 26*(7), 1131–1139. doi:10.1177/0956797615585115

Chandler, J., & Shapiro, D. (2016). Conducting clinical research using crowdsourced convenience samples. *Annual Review of Clinical Psychology, 12*(1), 53–81. doi:10.1146/annurev-clinpsy-021815-093623

Chandler, J., Sisso, I., & Shapiro, D. (2019). Participant carelessness and fraud: Consequences for clinical research and potential solutions. *Journal of Abnormal Psychology.*

Clifford, S., & Jerit, J. (2014). Is there a cost to convenience? An experimental comparison of data quality in laboratory and online studies. *Journal of Experimental Political Science, 1*(2), 120–131. doi:10.1017/xps.2014.5

Clifford, S., & Jerit, J. (2015). Do attempts to improve respondent attention increase social desirability bias? *Public Opinion Quarterly, 79*(3), 790–802. doi:10.1093/poq/nfv027

Clifford, S., & Jerit, J. (2016). Cheating on political knowledge questions in online surveys: An assessment of the problem and solutions. *Public Opinion Quarterly, 80*(4), 858–887.

Clifford, S., Jewell, R. M., & Waggoner, P. D. (2015). Are samples drawn from Mechanical Turk valid for research on political ideology? *Research & Politics, 2*(4), 205316801562207. doi:10.1177/2053168015622072

Coppock, A. (2019). Generalizing from survey experiments conducted on Mechanical Turk: A replication approach. *Political Science Research Methods, 7*(3), 613–628.

Cronk, B. C., & West, J. L. (2002). Personality research on the Internet: A comparison of web-based and traditional instruments in take-home and in-class settings. *Behavior Research Methods, 34*(2), 177–180.

Crowne, D. P., & Marlowe, D. (1960). A new scale of social desirability independent of psychopathology. *Journal of Consulting Psychology, 24*(4), 349–354. doi:10.1037/h0047358

Crump, M. J. C., McDonnell, J. V., & Gureckis, T. M. (2013). Evaluating Amazon's Mechanical Turk as a tool for experimental behavioral research. *PLOS ONE, 8*(3), e57410. doi:10.1371/journal.pone.0057410

Curran, P. G. (2016). Methods for the detection of carelessly invalid responses in survey data. *Journal of Experimental Social Psychology, 66*, 4–19. doi:10.1016/j.jesp.2015.07.006

Deke, J., & Chiang, H. (2017). The WWC attrition standard: Sensitivity to assumptions and opportunities for refining and adapting to new contexts. *Evaluation Review, 41*(2), 130–154. doi:10.1177/0193 841X16670047

DeVoe, S. E., & House, J. (2016). Replications with MTurkers who are naïve versus experienced with academic studies: A comment on Connors, Khamitov, Moroz, Campbell, and Henderson (2015). *Journal of Experimental Social Psychology, 67*, 65–67. doi:10.1016/j.jesp.2015.11.004

Elwert, F., & Winship, C. (2014). Endogenous selection bias: The problem of conditioning on a collider variable. *Annual Review of Sociology, 40*(1), 31–53. doi:10.1146/annurev-soc-071913-043455

Fisher, M., Goddu, M. K., & Keil, F. C. (2015). Searching for explanations: How the Internet inflates estimates of internal knowledge. *Journal of Experimental Psychology: General, 144*(3), 674–687. doi:10.1037/xge0000070

Ford, J. B. (2017). Amazon's Mechanical Turk: A comment. *Journal of Advertising, 46*(1), 156–158. doi:10.10 80/00913367.2016.1277380

Galesic, M. (2006). Dropouts on the web: Effects of interest and burden experienced during an online survey. *Journal of Official Statistics, 22*(2), 313.

Galesic, M., & Bosnjak, M. (2009). Effects of questionnaire length on participation and indicators of response quality in a web survey. *Public Opinion Quarterly, 73*(2), 349–360. doi:10.1093/poq/nfp031

Gerber, A. S., & Green, D. P. (2012). *Field experiments: Design, analysis, and interpretation.* New York, NY: Norton.

Goodman, J. K., Cryder, C. E., & Cheema, A. (2013). Data collection in a flat world: The strengths and weaknesses of Mechanical Turk samples. *Journal of Behavioral Decision Making, 26*(3), 213–224. doi:10.1002/bdm.1753

Hamby, T., & Taylor, W. (2016). Survey satisficing inflates reliability and validity measures: An experimental comparison of college and Amazon Mechanical Turk samples. *Educational and Psychological Measurement, 76*(6), 912–932. doi:10.1177/0013164415627349

Harms, P. D., & DeSimone, J. A. (2015). Caution! MTurk workers ahead—Fines doubled. *Industrial and Organizational Psychology, 8*(2), 183–190. doi:10.1017/iop.2015.23

Hata, K., Krishna, R., Fei-Fei, L., & Bernstein, M. S. (2016). A glimpse far into the future: Understanding long-term crowd worker quality. *Proceedings of the 2017 ACM Conference on Computer Supported Cooperative Work and Social Computing*, 889–901.

Hauser, D. J., Ellsworth, P. C., & Gonzalez, R. (2018). Are manipulation checks necessary? *Frontiers in Psychology, 9*, 998.

Hauser, D. J., & Schwarz, N. (2015). It's a trap! Instructional manipulation checks prompt systematic thinking on "tricky" tasks. *SAGE Open, 5*(2), 215824401558461. doi:10.1177/2158244015584617

Hauser, D. J., & Schwarz, N. (2016). Attentive Turkers: MTurk participants perform better on online attention checks than do subject pool participants. *Behavior Research Methods, 48*(1), 400–407. doi:10.3758/s13428-015-0578-z

Ho, C. J., Slivkins, A., Suri, S., & Vaughan, J. W. (2015, May). Incentivizing high quality crowdwork. *Proceedings of the 24th International Conference on World Wide Web*, 419–429.

Holden, C. J., Dennie, T., & Hicks, A. D. (2013). Assessing the reliability of the M5-120 on Amazon's Mechanical Turk. *Computers in Human Behavior, 29*(4), 1749–1754. doi:10.1016/j.chb.2013.02.020

Horton, J. J., Rand, D. G., & Zeckhauser, R. J. (2011). The online laboratory: Conducting experiments in a real labor market. *Experimental Economics, 14*(3), 399–425. doi:10.1007/s10683-011-9273-9

Huang, J. L., Curran, P. G., Keeney, J., Poposki, E. M., & DeShon, R. P. (2012). Detecting and deterring insufficient effort responding to surveys. *Journal of Business and Psychology, 27*(1), 99–114. doi:10.1007/s10869-011-9231-8

Huang, J. L., Liu, M., & Bowling, N. A. (2015). Insufficient effort responding: Examining an insidious confound in survey data. *Journal of Applied Psychology, 100*(3), 828–845. doi:10.1037/a0038510

Hydock, C. (2018). Assessing and overcoming participant dishonesty in online data collection. *Behavior Research Methods, 50*(4), 1563–1567. doi:10.3758/s13428-017-0984-5

International Organization for Standardization/International Electrotechnical Commission. (2008). Software engineering: Software product quality requirements and evaluation (SQuaRe) data quality model. *ISO/IEC, 25012*, 1–13.

Jacquemet, N., James, A., Luchini, S., Murphy, J., & Shogren, J. F. (2019). Lying and shirking under oath. ESI working paper 19-19. Retrieved from https://digitalcommons.chapman.edu/esi_working_papers/278/

Jahnke, S., Imhoff, R., & Hoyer, J. (2015). Stigmatization of people with pedophilia: Two comparative surveys. *Archives of Sexual Behavior, 44*(1), 21–34. doi:10.1007/s10508-014-0312-4

Johnson, J. A. (2005). Ascertaining the validity of individual protocols from web-based personality inventories. *Journal of Research in Personality, 39*(1), 103–129. doi:10.1016/j.jrp.2004.09.009

Jones, D. N., & Paulhus, D. L. (2014). Introducing the short dark triad (SD3): A brief measure of dark personality traits. *Assessment, 21*(1), 28–41.

Jurs, S. G., & Glass, G. V. (1971). The effect of experimental mortality on the internal and external validity of the randomized comparative experiment. *Journal of Experimental Education, 40*(1), 62–66. doi:10.1080/002 20973.1971.11011304

Kan, I. P., & Drummey, A. B. (2018). Do imposters threaten data quality? An examination of worker misrepresentation and downstream consequences in Amazon's Mechanical Turk workforce. *Computers in Human Behavior, 83*, 243–253. doi:10.1016/j.chb.2018.02.005

Kane, J. V., & Barabas, J. (2019). No harm in checking: Using factual manipulation checks to assess attentiveness in experiments. *American Journal of Political Science, 63*(1), 234–249.

Kazai, G., Kamps, J., & Milic-Frayling, N. (2012, October). The face of quality in crowdsourcing relevance labels: Demographics, personality and labeling accuracy. *Proceedings of the 21st ACM International Conference on Information and Knowledge Management*, 2583–2586.

Kees, J., Berry, C., Burton, S., & Sheehan, K. (2017). An analysis of data quality: Professional panels, student subject pools, and Amazon's Mechanical Turk. *Journal of Advertising, 46*(1), 141–155. doi:10.1080/00913367 .2016.1269304

Kennedy, R., Clifford, S., Burleigh, T., Jewell, R., & Waggoner, P. (2018). The shape of and solutions to the MTurk quality crisis. *SSRN Electronic Journal*. doi:10.2139/ssrn.3272468

Kim, H. S., & Hodgins, D. C. (2017). Reliability and validity of data obtained from alcohol, cannabis, and gambling populations on Amazon's Mechanical Turk. *Psychology of Addictive Behaviors, 31*(1), 85–94. doi:10.1037/adb0000219

Kittur, A., Chi, E. H., & Suh, B. (2008). Crowdsourcing user studies with mechanical Turk. *Proceedings of the SIGCHI Conference on Human Factors in Computing Systems*, 453–456.

Kühnen, U. (2010). Manipulation checks as manipulation: Another look at the ease-of-retrieval heuristic. *Personality and Social Psychology Bulletin, 36*(1), 47–58. doi:10.1177/0146167209346746

Kung, F. Y., Kwok, N., & Brown, D. J. (2018). Are attention check questions a threat to scale validity? *Applied Psychology, 67*(2), 264–283. doi:10.1111/apps.12108

Lind, J. C., & Zumbo, B. D. (1993). The continuity principle in psychological research: An introduction to robust statistics. *Canadian Psychology/Psychologie canadienne, 34*(4), 407–414. doi:10.1037/h0078861

Litman, L., Robinson, J., & Rosenzweig, C. (2015). The relationship between motivation, monetary compensation, and data quality among US- and India-based workers on Mechanical Turk. *Behavior Research Methods, 47*(2), 519–528. doi:10.3758/s13428-014-0483-x

Litman, L., Robinson, Y., Moss, A. J., & Gautam, R. (2018, Oct. 29). Moving beyond bots: MTurk as a source of high quality data [blog post]. Retrieved from https://www.cloudresearch.com/resources/blog/moving-beyond-bots-mturk-as-a-source-of-high-quality-data/

Mason, W., & Suri, S. (2012). Conducting behavioral research on Amazon's Mechanical Turk. *Behavior Research Methods*, *44*(1), 1–23.

Matherly, T. (2019). A panel for lemons? Positivity bias, reputation systems and data quality on MTurk. *European Journal of Marketing*, *53*(2), 195–223.

McCredie, M. N., & Morey, L. C. (2019). Who are the Turkers? A characterization of MTurk workers using the personality assessment inventory. *Assessment*, *26*(5), 759–766. doi:10.1177/1073191118760709

Meade, A. W., & Craig, S. B. (2012). Identifying careless responses in survey data. *Psychological Methods*, *17*(3), 437–455. doi:10.1037/a0028085

Miller, J. (2006). Online marketing research. In R. Grover & M. Vriens (Eds.), *The handbook of marketing research* (pp. 110–131). Thousand Oaks, CA: Sage.

Miller, J. D., Few, L. R., Wilson, L., Gentile, B., Widiger, T. A., Mackillop, J., & Keith Campbell, W. (2013). The Five-Factor Narcissism Inventory (FFNI): A test of the convergent, discriminant, and incremental validity of FFNI scores in clinical and community samples. *Psychological Assessment*, *25*(3), 748–758. doi:10.1037/a0032536

Moss, A. J., & Litman, L. (2018). After the bot scare: Understanding what's been happening with data collection on MTurk and how to stop it [blog post]. Retrieved from https://www.cloudresearch.com/resources/blog/after-the-bot-scare-understanding-whats-been-happening-with-data-collection-on-mturk-and-how-to-stop-it/

Mullinix, K. J., Leeper, T. J., Druckman, J. N., & Freese, J. (2015). The generalizability of survey experiments. *Journal of Experimental Political Science*, *2*(2), 109–138. doi:10.1017/XPS.2015.19

Necka, E. A., Cacioppo, S., Norman, G. J., & Cacioppo, J. T. (2016). Measuring the prevalence of problematic respondent behaviors among MTurk, campus, and community participants. *PLoS ONE*, *11*(6), e0157732. doi:10.1371/journal.pone.0157732

Oppenheimer, D. M., Meyvis, T., & Davidenko, N. (2009). Instructional manipulation checks: Detecting satisficing to increase statistical power. *Journal of Experimental Social Psychology*, *45*(4), 867–872. doi:10.1016/j.jesp.2009.03.009

Ortmann, A., & Hertwig, R. (2002). The costs of deception: Evidence from psychology. *Experimental Economics*, *5*(2), 111–131. doi:10.1023/A:1020365204768

Paolacci, G., Chandler, J., & Ipeirotis, P. G. (2010). Running experiments on Amazon Mechanical Turk. *Judgment and Decision Making*, *5*(5), 411–419.

Paulhus, D. L. (2002). Socially desirable responding: The evolution of a construct. In H. I. Braun, D. N. Jackson, & D. E. Wiley (Eds.), *The role of constructs in psychological and educational measurement* (pp. 49–69). Mahwah, NJ: Erlbaum.

Pavlick, E., Post, M., Irvine, A., Kachaev, D., & Callison-Burch, C. (2014). The language demographics of Amazon Mechanical Turk. *Transactions of the Association for Computational Linguistics*, *2*(11), 79–92. doi:10.1162/tacl_a_00167

Peer, E., Brandimarte, L., Samat, S., & Acquisti, A. (2017). Beyond the Turk: Alternative platforms for crowdsourcing behavioral research. *Journal of Experimental Social Psychology, 70,* 153–163. doi:10.1016/j.jesp.2017.01.006

Peer, E., Vosgerau, J., & Acquisti, A. (2014). Reputation as a sufficient condition for data quality on Amazon Mechanical Turk. *Behavior Research Methods, 46*(4), 1023–1031. doi:10.3758/s13428-013-0434-y

Prims, J. P., Sisso, I., & Bai, H. (2018). Suspicious IP online flagging tool, from https://itaysisso.shinyapps.io/Bots (Accessed October 31, 2019).

Rand, D. G. (2012). The promise of Mechanical Turk: How online labor markets can help theorists run behavioral experiments. *Journal of Theoretical Biology, 299,* 172–179. doi:10.1016/j.jtbi.2011.03.004

Rand, D. G., Newman, G. E., & Wurzbacher, O. M. (2015). Social context and the dynamics of cooperative choice. *Journal of Behavioral Decision Making, 28*(2), 159–166. doi:10.1002/bdm.1837

Rand, D. G., Peysakhovich, A., Kraft-Todd, G. T., Newman, G. E., Wurzbacher, O., Nowak, M. A., & Greene, J. D. (2014). Social heuristics shape intuitive cooperation. *Nature Communications, 5*(3677), 1–12. doi:10.1038/ncomms4677

Rashtchian, C., Young, P., Hodosh, M., & Hockenmaier, J. (2010, June). Collecting image annotations using Amazon's Mechanical Turk. *Proceedings of the NAACL HLT 2010 Workshop on Creating Speech and Language Data With Amazon's Mechanical Turk,* 139–147.

Rasmussen, J. L. (1988). Evaluating outlier identification tests: Mahalanobis D squared and Comrey Dk. *Multivariate Behavioral Research, 23*(2), 189–202. doi:10.1207/s15327906mbr2302_4

Robins, R. W., Fraley, R. C., & Krueger, R. F. (Eds.). (2009). *Handbook of research methods in personality psychology.* New York, NY: Guilford Press.

Robinson, J., Rosenzweig, C., Moss, A. J., & Litman, L. (2019). Tapped out or barely tapped? Recommendations for how to harness the vast and largely unused potential of the Mechanical Turk participant pool. *PLOS ONE, 14*(12), e0226394. doi:10.1371/journal.pone.0226394

Samimi, P., Ravana, S. D., & Koh, Y. S. (2016). Effect of verbal comprehension skill and self-reported features on reliability of crowdsourced relevance judgments. *Computers in Human Behavior, 64,* 793–804. doi:10.1016/j.chb.2016.07.058

Savage, S. J., & Waldman, D. M. (2008). Learning and fatigue during choice experiments: A comparison of online and mail survey modes. *Journal of Applied Econometrics, 23*(3), 351–371. doi:10.1002/jae.984

Schleider, J. L., & Weisz, J. R. (2015). Using Mechanical Turk to study family processes and youth mental health: A test of feasibility. *Journal of Child and Family Studies, 24*(11), 3235–3246. doi:10.1007/s10826-015-0126-6

Schönbrodt, F. D., & Perugini, M. (2013). At what sample size do correlations stabilize? *Journal of Research in Personality, 47*(5), 609–612. doi:10.1016/j.jrp.2013.05.009

Shapiro, D. N., Chandler, J., & Mueller, P. A. (2013). Using Mechanical Turk to study clinical populations. *Clinical Psychological Science, 1*(2), 213–220. doi:10.1177/2167702612469015

Sharpe Wessling, K., Huber, J., & Netzer, O. (2017). MTurk character misrepresentation: Assessment and solutions. *Journal of Consumer Research, 44*(1), 211–230. doi:10.1093/jcr/ucx053

Smith, S. M., Roster, C. A., Golden, L. L., & Albaum, G. S. (2016). A multi-group analysis of online survey respondent data quality: Comparing a regular USA consumer panel to MTurk samples. *Journal of Business Research, 69*(8), 3139–3148. doi:10.1016/j.jbusres.2015.12.002

Stewart, N., Ungemach, C., Harris, A. J., Bartels, D. M., Newell, B. R., Paolacci, G., & Chandler, J. (2015). The average laboratory samples a population of 7,300 Amazon Mechanical Turk workers. *Judgment and Decision Making, 10*(5), 479–491.

Thomas, K. A., & Clifford, S. (2017). Validity and Mechanical Turk: An assessment of exclusion methods and interactive experiments. *Computers in Human Behavior, 77*, 184–197. doi:10.1016/j.chb.2017.08.038

Thomson, K. S., & Oppenheimer, D. M. (2016). Investigating an alternate form of the cognitive reflection test. *Judgment and Decision Making, 11*(1), 99–113.

Tourangeau, R., Conrad, F. G., & Couper, M. P. (2013). *The science of web surveys*. New York, NY: Oxford University Press.

Tylka, T. L., & Wood-Barcalow, N. L. (2015). The Body Appreciation Scale-2: Item refinement and psychometric evaluation. *Body Image, 12*, 53–67. doi:10.1016/j.bodyim.2014.09.006

Vehovar, V., Batagelj, Z., Lozar Manfreda, K., & Zalatel, M. (2002). Nonresponse in web surveys. In R. Groves, D. A. Dillman, J. L. Eltinge, & R. J. A. Little (Eds.), *Survey nonresponse* (pp. 229–242). New York, NY: Wiley.

Wood, D., Harms, P. D., Lowman, G. H., & DeSimone, J. A. (2017). Response speed and response consistency as mutually validating indicators of data quality in online samples. *Social Psychological and Personality Science, 8*(4), 454–464. doi:10.1177/1948550617703168

Zhou, H., & Fishbach, A. (2016). The pitfall of experimenting on the web: How unattended selective attrition leads to surprising (yet false) research conclusions. *Journal of Personality and Social Psychology, 111*(4), 493–504. doi:10.1037/pspa0000056

Zwaan, R. A., Pecher, D., Paolacci, G., Bouwmeester, S., Verkoeijen, P., Dijkstra, K., & Zeelenberg, R. (2018). Participant nonnaiveté and the reproducibility of cognitive psychology. *Psychonomic Bulletin & Review, 25*(5), 1968–1972. doi:10.3758/s13423-017-1348-y

WHO ARE THE MECHANICAL TURK WORKERS?

Jonathan Robinson, Leib Litman, and Cheskie Rosenzweig

INTRODUCTION

In the early 2000s, when online research was just beginning to increase in popularity and well before Mechanical Turk existed, some researchers raised major concerns about the prospect of using the web to collect data for scientific research (for a summary, see Gosling et al., 2004). Perhaps the most critical of these concerns was that the Internet lacked diversity. At the time, researchers were concerned that Internet users tended to be male, White, socially maladjusted, and sufficiently different from the general population so as to make data collected from the web ungeneralizable to the population as a whole. Another concern was that online participants' self-reports would be riddled with careless responses that lacked validity and could not be verified independently.

The original concerns researchers had about online data collection were transferred almost directly to the MTurk environment. As with researchers' original attempts to collect data online, fear of the unknown and the idea of an anonymous participant operating in an environment that lacked experimental control—somewhere out there on the Internet—stoked concern and suspicion. And, with Mechanical Turk, these concerns seemed amplified. Researchers wondered, who are these MTurk workers, willing to spend hours participating in studies that pay relatively little? There must be something, the argument went, that makes these people different from most "ordinary" people.

In this chapter we demystify the anonymous MTurk worker. Using a database that consists of more than 16 million completed MTurk assignments and 250,000 workers, we report the basic characteristics of the MTurk population. Although our database represents one of the largest datasets ever compiled to understand MTurk workers, the demographics we report may vary from the actual demographics of Mechanical Turk if there are workers on MTurk who never complete studies posted through CloudResearch. Given the variety of studies conducted on CloudResearch and the number of workers in our database, it is likely that any discrepancies between the demographics we report here and the actual demographics of MTurk workers are small.

Early in the chapter, we focus on the MTurk worker population as a whole and answer the following questions: What is the size of the Mechanical Turk participant pool? How many unique workers participate in studies in any given month? What is the worker turnover rate? Later, we describe the demographics of MTurk workers and some of the attitudes they tend to hold. We present short, self-contained descriptions of common demographics including gender, age, race, family composition, employment, income, education, and religious and political attitudes. For each variable, we describe the distribution on Mechanical Turk and how that distribution compares to the U.S. population as a whole. We additionally address several other key questions: How stable is the demographic over time? How variable are demographics across samples? What is the joint distribution of demographic groups with each other (for example, the distribution of gender within race)? Are there systematic differences in activity levels between different demographic groups?

Although there are some systematic differences between the MTurk population and the U.S. population, in many respects the MTurk population is remarkably similar to the general population of the United States. One key difference is age. The average MTurk worker is in their mid-30s to mid-40s, with male workers being about four years younger than female workers. This is considerably younger than the average age of the U.S. population. Because many demographics, political opinions, and social attitudes correlate with age, it should not be surprising that the MTurk population will differ from the general U.S. population when age is not taken into account. For example, MTurk workers are less likely to be married and to have children. Once we control for age differences, however, MTurk workers are in many respects typical Americans.

This chapter is the first of two chapters whose overall goal is to help researchers understand the demographic distribution their MTurk sample is likely to have and how that distribution is likely to change based on a study's design and sampling methodology. Overall, we show that the demographics of MTurk workers are remarkably stable over time at the platform level. Even so, there is considerable variability in workers' demographics across samples. The composition of a sample depends on more than just the demographics of the MTurk population because any one sample is not randomly drawn from the MTurk worker pool. Samples consist predominantly of active workers, and the demographic distribution of any one sample will strongly depend on several factors that contribute to sampling variability, such as the time of day the study is launched, how much the study pays, and the qualifications used to control data quality. Factors affecting sample composition and sampling best practices are discussed in Chapter 7.

SOURCES OF DATA

Much of the data presented throughout the rest of this book is drawn from the CloudResearch database (formerly TurkPrime), which tracks every assignment completed through CloudResearch. The data we present are drawn from a period of five years, starting in January 2014 and ending in March 2019. During that time, more than 16 million MTurk assignments were completed as part of more than 150,000 unique HITs, taken by more than 250,000 unique MTurk workers. In addition, these HITs were launched by more than 5,000 unique requesters running many types of studies and using various measures and manipulations. The diversity of studies from which the data were drawn increases the generalizability of the results presented in this chapter.

To evaluate the demographic characteristics of Mechanical Turk, we compare MTurk to several nationally representative datasets including the American National Election Studies (ANES), the U.S. Census, and polling by the Gallup Organization and the Pew Research Center. The ANES survey collects nationally representative data before and after every presidential election (ANES, 2012; www.electionstudies.org).

SIZE OF THE MTURK POPULATION

Mechanical Turk is largely an anonymous platform. For that reason, understanding who works on Mechanical Turk is not a trivial task. For many years, Mechanical Turk had advertised that its workforce consists of more than 500,000 registered workers. However, it is not clear whether this number refers to workers who have ever created an account or the number of workers who are available to participate in studies. The number of *available* workers within a specific time period is likely to be significantly smaller than the total number of workers with MTurk accounts, since many workers who have MTurk accounts drop out of the pool and may no longer be active on the platform. Thus, even a seemingly simple question like how many people work on Mechanical Turk is not easy to answer.

The size of the MTurk worker population has significant research implications. Researchers wishing to conduct large studies need to be aware of the upper limit on the number of participants they are likely to recruit. The size of the subject pool affects the likelihood of workers cross-participating in studies from multiple labs, which influences their familiarity with typical study protocols (Chandler, Paolacci, Peer, Mueller, & Ratliff, 2015). Additionally, the size of the total pool influences the likelihood of researchers being able to sample minority groups and to selectively target hard-to-reach participants. For example, if a researcher wants to recruit participants with a medical condition that occurs with 1% frequency in the general population, the likelihood of being able to do that will depend on the size of the available participant pool.

Data from the CloudResearch database show that the number of unique workers who participated in at least one study posted through CloudResearch was 250,810 (see Robinson, Rosenzweig, Moss, & Litman, 2019). Of these workers, 226,000 were from the United States. Because U.S.-based workers are by far the largest active group on MTurk, and because most researchers sample from U.S.-based participants, the demographics presented in this chapter are based exclusively on participants from the United States.

From 2016 to 2018, between 81,000 and 86,000 unique U.S.-based workers participated in studies each year (Figure 6.1). Furthermore, approximately 50,000 to 60,000 new workers joined the platform each year (see Figure 6.1). In any given month, there were between 25,000 and 30,000 unique MTurk workers who completed assignments

FIGURE 6.1 ● U.S. WORKERS TAKING A HIT THROUGH CLOUDRESEARCH FROM 2016 TO 2018

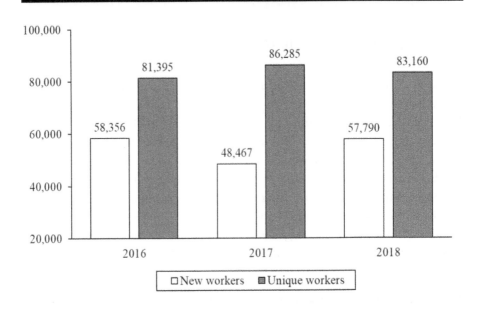

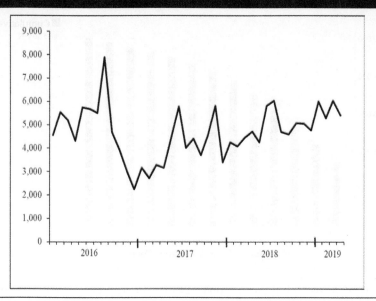

FIGURE 6.2 ● NEW U.S. WORKERS WHO ARE ACTIVE FOR THE FIRST TIME EACH MONTH ON THE CLOUDRESEARCH PLATFORM

and approximately 4,500 new workers who joined the pool (see Figure 6.2). Thus, these data show that the MTurk worker pool is significantly larger than previously estimated (see Difallah, Filatova, & Ipeirotis, 2018; Stewart et al., 2015) and, more importantly, that the worker pool is constantly replenishing. Several thousand new participants join the pool each month, making it possible to recruit participants who have had little prior exposure to social science stimuli and procedures.

Given that there are approximately 30,000 active participants per month, how many of them can a researcher expect to recruit? To examine this question, we opened a study to 10,000 participants to see how long it took for the study to complete. Figure 6.3 shows that it took two weeks to recruit 10,000 workers. The vast majority of workers participated in the first several days, with more than 3,000 participating on the first day. Toward the last several days of data collection, only a few hundred participants could be reached each day. This suggests that about a third of the active 30,000 participants can be recruited within a two- to four-week time span. However, recruitment speed depends on many factors, including the length of the study, how much it pays, and the reputation of the requester account (see Chapter 2). The ability to recruit 10,000 people within two weeks will depend on optimal sampling conditions.

Although the size of the MTurk participant pool is large enough to accommodate many types of research studies, Mechanical Turk is significantly smaller than other sources of research participants. Market research platforms (see Chandler,

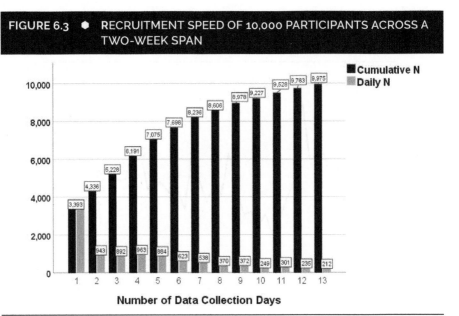

FIGURE 6.3 ● RECRUITMENT SPEED OF 10,000 PARTICIPANTS ACROSS A TWO-WEEK SPAN

Rosenzweig, Moss, Robinson, & Litman, 2019), which are described in more detail in Chapter 10, have tens of millions of participants. Such large participant pools make it possible to recruit tens of thousands of people within short time periods (typically days), and to selectively recruit participants from specific cities or zip codes. They also make it possible to selectively recruit hard-to-reach groups, including participants with specific medical conditions, from specific professions and industries, and with specific consumer preferences. The trade-offs between sampling from Mechanical Turk versus market research platforms are discussed in Chapter 10.

LOCATION OF WORKERS IN THE UNITED STATES

Where in the United States are MTurk workers located? To examine the distribution of workers in the United States, we plotted the 16 million assignments completed on CloudResearch (see Figure 6.4). Each worker's location was verified by IP address location matching. The distribution of workers in each state is virtually identical to the distribution of the U.S. population, based on the U.S. Census. The correlation between the proportion of the U.S. population in each state and the proportion of assignments completed in each state is $r = .97$. The largest difference between the proportion of a state's population and the proportion of assignments completed in that state was in Florida, where the difference was 1.63%. Other than Florida, virtually all other states had less than a 1% difference from the U.S. population.

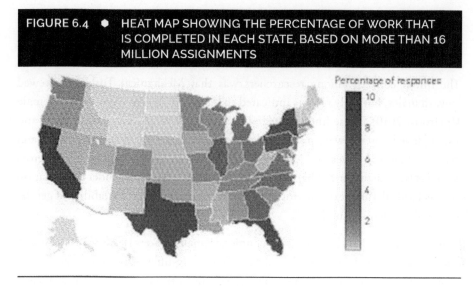

FIGURE 6.4 ● HEAT MAP SHOWING THE PERCENTAGE OF WORK THAT IS COMPLETED IN EACH STATE, BASED ON MORE THAN 16 MILLION ASSIGNMENTS

Note: All data were verified by IP address location matching.

These results show that the actual distribution of MTurk workers is fairly representative of all U.S. geographic regions. This is consistent with research showing that the rural-urban distribution of MTurk workers is also virtually identical to that of the general U.S. population (see Huff & Tingley, 2015). Thus, the distribution of MTurk workers is remarkably consistent with the overall distribution of the U.S. population across all 50 states.

DEMOGRAPHICS OF MTURK WORKERS

Gender

Basic Demographics

Virtually every study in the social and behavioral sciences reports the gender distribution of its samples (see Clayton & Tannenbaum, 2016). Gender is commonly examined as a moderator of many psychological and social processes such as social support (Wohlgemuth & Betz, 1991), consumer behavior (Kolyesnikova, Dodd, & Wilcox, 2009), and mental health (Greer, Laseter, & Asiamah, 2009), among many others (e.g., Card, Stucky, Sawalani, & Little, 2008; Gaub & Carlson, 1997; Leaper & Smith, 2004). For these reasons, understanding whether a population is heavily skewed toward one gender is important.

Many traditional sources of research participants have been disproportionately female. For example, between 70% and 80% of participants recruited through university subjects pools are female (Gosling et al., 2004). Market research platforms likewise disproportionately consist of women, and for that reason the standard practice on market research platforms is to use a 50-50 gender quota.

The initial concern among researchers was that Mechanical Turk was skewed toward males, but early reports indicated that around 70% of workers were female (Ipeirotis, 2010). These findings were interpreted to mean that stay-at-home and unemployed parents were more available to participate in MTurk studies. Later reports, however, revealed significant variability in gender composition across samples (see Chandler & Shapiro, 2016). Here, we report the gender composition of Mechanical Turk at the platform level and also examine the variability of gender composition across samples.

Figure 6.5 shows that the percentage of unique female workers is close to 58%. It also shows that the gender distribution of MTurk workers differs substantially across age groups. The proportion of women among MTurk workers increases almost linearly with age, and for workers over age 50, almost 70% are women.

These data show the importance of examining the joint distribution of demographic variables on Mechanical Turk, such as the proportion of men and women within different age groups. The joint distribution of gender and age does not follow the same pattern as in the general population. The proportion of female MTurk workers increases with age at a much higher rate on Mechanical Turk compared to the general population, where the female to male ratio is within 4%

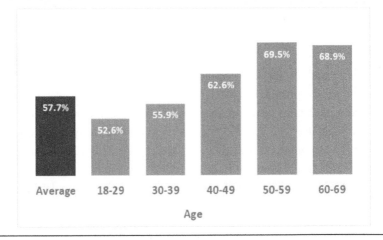

FIGURE 6.5 ● UNIQUE FEMALE WORKERS ACROSS AGE GROUPS

Note: N (unique workers) > 100,000.

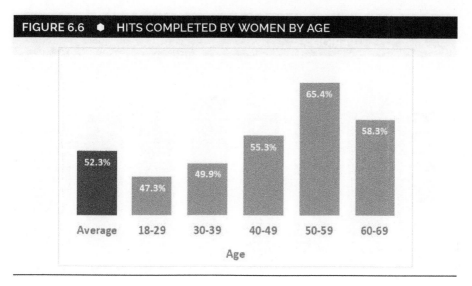

FIGURE 6.6 ● HITS COMPLETED BY WOMEN BY AGE

Note: N (assignments) > 16 million.

until after age 70, when it begins to increase dramatically (U.S. Census Bureau, 2016a).

Another important characteristic of MTurk workers is that demographic groups can differ with regard to participation rates. This is because some groups of workers are more active than others. Figure 6.6 shows the percentage of assignments that are completed by women on the platform, and across different age groups. Women complete 52.3% of assignments, which is 5% less than would be expected based on their percentage of the worker pool. This discrepancy shows that men are more active and tend to participate in more studies on average than women. As a comparison of Figures 6.5 and 6.6 shows, the observation that men are more active than women is consistent across all age groups. Women complete between 5% and 10% fewer HITs within every age group than would be expected based on their proportion of the MTurk population.

Consistency Over Time

Figure 6.7 shows that the gender distribution of completed HITs is highly consistent over time. Across a four-year time span, there is a slight yet persistent female advantage in the number of completed HITs. Although there is a high level of consistency in gender distribution across time, the gender composition of individual studies is highly variable. Figure 6.8 shows the gender composition of more than 100,000 studies. Across studies, the standard deviation of the percentage of women in studies is 9%. As can be seen from the histogram, studies typically range between 25% and 75% of the sample consisting of women.

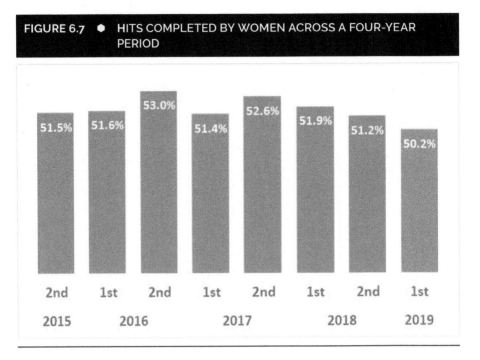

FIGURE 6.7 ● HITS COMPLETED BY WOMEN ACROSS A FOUR-YEAR PERIOD

Note: Data are presented for the first and second half of each year. *N* (assignments) > 16 million.

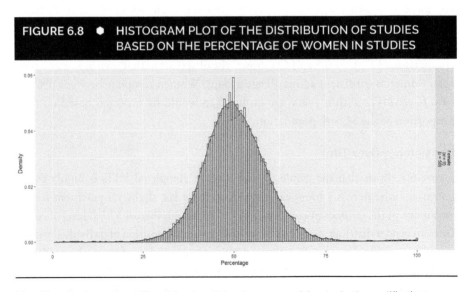

FIGURE 6.8 ● HISTOGRAM PLOT OF THE DISTRIBUTION OF STUDIES BASED ON THE PERCENTAGE OF WOMEN IN STUDIES

Note: All studies have at least 30 participants and do not use any participant selection qualifications, except reputation qualifications (approval rating and HIT completion). *N* (studies) > 100,000.

Implications for Sampling

Men tend to complete more HITs than women relative to their demographic distribution, demonstrating that any one study on Mechanical Turk is not a random sample of the MTurk population. Workers have preferences and choose which HITs to participate in. These individual choices can significantly alter the demographic distribution of any one sample.

The joint distribution of age and gender provides insight into one of the potential sources of between-sample variability in gender. Because the proportion of women differs substantially across different age groups, studies that recruit older workers are significantly more likely to have a high proportion of women. Other factors such as time of day (Fordsham et al., 2019), pay rate (Litman et al., 2020), and the use of the approval rating qualifications also play a role. The way in which these factors contribute to sampling variability, and the way in which they contribute to variability in the distribution of gender across samples, is discussed more fully in Chapter 7.

Age

Basic Demographics

Figure 6.9 shows the distribution of MTurk workers by age and the percentage of assignments completed by workers of different age groups. The age distribution on Mechanical Turk differs substantially from the U.S. population. MTurk workers are predominantly in their 20s and 30s and few workers are older than 50. In the general U.S. population, approximately 32% of people are in their 20s and 30s, whereas on MTurk close to 67% of workers are in this younger cohort. When

FIGURE 6.9 ● AGE DISTRIBUTION OF WORKERS

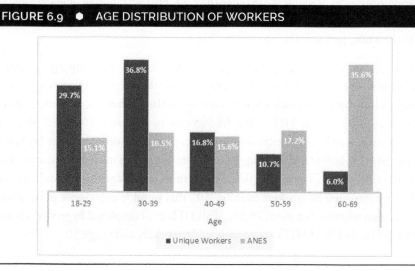

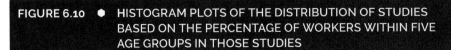

FIGURE 6.10 ● HISTOGRAM PLOTS OF THE DISTRIBUTION OF STUDIES BASED ON THE PERCENTAGE OF WORKERS WITHIN FIVE AGE GROUPS IN THOSE STUDIES

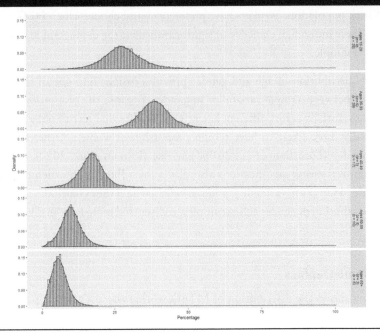

Note: All studies have at least 30 participants and do not use any participant selection qualifications, except reputation qualifications (approval rating and HIT completion). *N* (studies) > 100,000.

examining workers aged 50 or older, the opposite pattern is observed. In the U.S. population, more than 50% of people are aged 50 or older. On Mechanical Turk, however, only 17% of workers are older than 50. Furthermore, people over age 60 are particularly underrepresented on Mechanical Turk, where only 6% of workers are in their 60s, and just 1% are in their 70s.

As with gender, the average percentage of HITs taken by different age groups is highly stable over time. Across a four-year period, the averages of each age group do not change by more than a few percentage points. There is, however, considerable variability across HITs. The histograms in Figure 6.10 reveal the variance across more than 100,000 studies for each age group. The distribution of completed HITs across different age groups reveals an even more dramatic age bias. More than 74% of HITs are completed by workers under age 40, and only 11% of HITs are completed by workers over age 50. This trend is even more pronounced for men than women. For men, 78.5% of all HITs are completed by workers below age 40, and only 8% of HITs are completed by workers above age 50.

Implications for Sampling

Age is one of the key ways in which the MTurk population systematically differs from the general population. Knowing that Mechanical Turk consists primarily of adults under age 40, it is not reasonable to expect Mechanical Turk to mirror the general population on variables that are systematically associated with age. For example, family composition, including marital status and number of children, is strongly correlated with age. Because most MTurk workers are young, it should not be surprising to find that MTurk workers have fewer children compared to the general population. Differences like this do not mean that MTurk workers are a qualitatively *different kind* of people than the general population. Because age is associated with multiple demographic and behavioral variables, including family composition, political attitudes, education levels, income levels, and numerous clusters of psychologically relevant factors, these differences demonstrate the importance of comparing the representativeness of Mechanical Turk to the general population within specific age groups. In addition, solutions such as quota sampling are available to researchers who want to recruit a representative number of people across age groups in a study on Mechanical Turk.

Like gender, the distribution of age is highly stable at the platform level across time. The percentage of workers within specific age groups does not vary by more than a few points across a four-year period. There is considerable variability, however, across samples. This means that specific studies can expect to see significant variability in age and gender, even though across all studies the average remains stable. The pattern of stable platform-level demographic distributions and variable between-sample distributions is consistent across all of the demographics presented in the sections that follow. Specifically, for all demographics, no changes were observed beyond a few percentage points over time. Due to the high level of consistency of this pattern of results, figures for the variability across time and samples are not presented for the rest of the variables discussed in this chapter.

Race

Basic Demographics

Figure 6.11 shows the racial and ethnic distribution of MTurk workers, compared to that of the U.S. population (U.S. Census Bureau, 2016b) presented for comparison. Close to 80% of MTurk workers are White, which is a few percentage points higher than the U.S. population based on the census. African Americans constitute 9.1% of MTurk workers, which is slightly lower than the U.S. population. Asian workers are overrepresented on MTurk compared to their share of the U.S. population, and Latino workers constitute just over 20% of the MTurk worker pool. Overall, racial and ethnic groups appear to be well represented, with the exception of African Americans, which are slightly underrepresented.

FIGURE 6.11   ●   RACE AND ETHNICITY

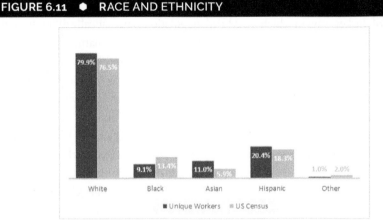

Note: N > 100,000. Following the approach of the U.S. Census, ethnicity (Hispanic) was asked as a separate question, since Latino/a individuals may identify as White, African American, or other race. Thus, the racial and ethnic percentages are greater than 100%.

Although the racial and ethnic differences between MTurk workers and the U.S. population are relatively small, there are significant disparities in racial composition across age groups. The proportion of White workers increases with age (see Figure 6.12) while the proportion of all other groups decreases with age. For example, the proportion of White participants over age 60 is close to 90%.

Implications for Sampling

Overall, these data show that racial diversity on Mechanical Turk is similar to that found in the general U.S. population. There is no evidence that White workers are significantly overrepresented on Mechanical Turk. Whereas some minority groups such as African Americans are slightly underrepresented, other minority groups are slightly overrepresented, and the overall proportion of Whites is similar to that found in the general U.S. population.

A more complex picture of racial and ethnic diversity does emerge across age, however. White workers are overrepresented in the 40–59 age category by 10% and in the 60 or older category by 18% compared to the U.S. population. Thus, while researchers who are sampling from the general MTurk population should expect the racial distribution of their sample to match the U.S. population within a few percentage points, researchers whose focus is on studying older adults are likely to attain disproportionately White samples. This further complicates research with older adults on Mechanical Turk. Not only are there very few workers over age 50, but they also lack racial diversity as the vast majority of older workers are predominantly White.

FIGURE 6.12 ● PERCENTAGE OF HITS COMPLETED BY WHITES WITHIN DIFFERENT AGE GROUPS

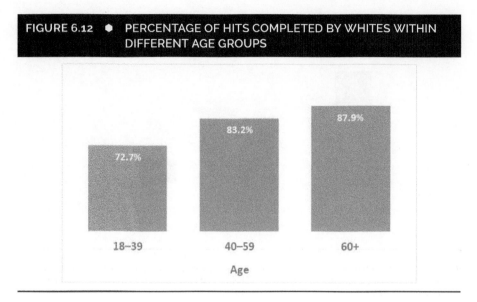

Note: N (assignments) > 16 million.

Family Composition

Figure 6.13 shows the distribution of marital status on MTurk and a nationally representative sample. Figure 6.14 shows the number of children that MTurk workers have. MTurk workers are less likely to be married or to have children compared to the general population. According to the U.S. Census Bureau (2016c), 45% of the U.S.

FIGURE 6.13 ● FAMILY COMPOSITION: MARITAL STATUS

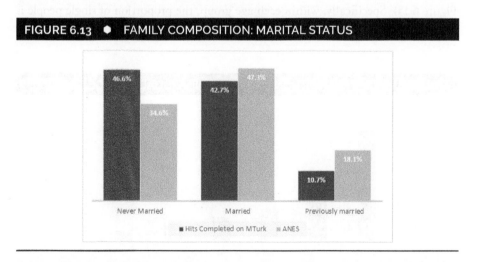

Note: Dark bars show the percentage of completed MTurk assignments (> 16 million) based on the marital status of workers who completed those assignments. Light bars show marital status family composition for a representative sample of U.S. adults, based on the ANES.

FIGURE 6.14 ● FAMILY COMPOSITION: NUMBER OF CHILDREN

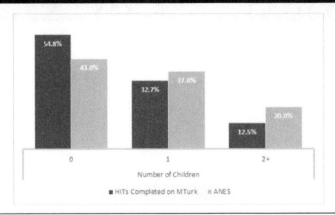

Note: Dark bars show the percentage of completed MTurk assignments (> 16 million) based on the number of children of workers who completed those assignments. Light bars show the number of children for a representative sample of U.S. adults, based on the ANES.

population over age 18 is unmarried, while this proportion is about 57% on MTurk. On MTurk, approximately 55% of workers do not have any children, which is much higher than in the U.S. population.

Although MTurk workers are predominantly single, the joint distribution of family composition and age reveals that, once age is taken into account, MTurk is not biased toward single people. The distribution of single people on Mechanical Turk within each age group is virtually identical to that found in the U.S. population (see Figure 6.15). Specifically, within each age group, the proportion of single people is never different by more than five percentage points between the MTurk population

FIGURE 6.15 ● PROPORTION OF SINGLE INDIVIDUALS BY AGE GROUPS

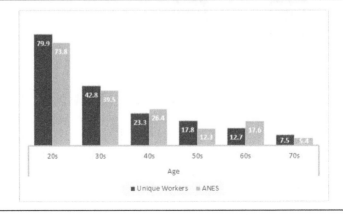

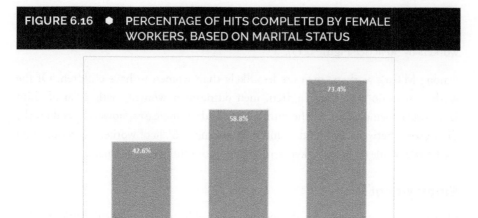

FIGURE 6.16 ● PERCENTAGE OF HITS COMPLETED BY FEMALE WORKERS, BASED ON MARITAL STATUS

Note: N (assignments) > 16 million.

and the ANES sample. Thus, although the proportion of single participants on Mechanical Turk is higher than in the general population, there is no evidence of family composition bias on Mechanical Turk when age is taken into consideration.

The distribution of gender varies significantly depending on marital status (see Figure 6.16) and number of children (see Figure 6.17). Among MTurk workers who have never married, 42.6% are women (see Figure 6.16). However, among workers who are currently married, 58.8% are women; and among workers who have been

FIGURE 6.17 ● PERCENTAGE OF HITS COMPLETED BY FEMALE WORKERS, BASED ON NUMBER OF CHILDREN

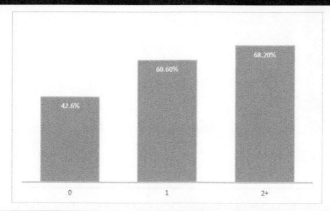

Note: N (assignments) > 16 million.

married in the past, 73.4% are women. Thus, although there is an even gender distribution for unmarried workers, previously married female workers outnumber male workers by 30% (see Figure 6.15).

Among MTurk workers, men are less likely than women to have children. Of the workers who do not have children, men outnumber women, with 42% of childless workers being male. As the number of children increases, however, so does the discrepancy between men and women. For example, 60% of workers with one child are female, while 68% of workers with two or more children are female.

Employment

One particularly interesting demographic variable on Mechanical Turk is what workers do for employment. Because MTurk itself is a way to earn money, some may assume that people with time to spend on MTurk are likely unemployed. The data in Figure 6.18 show this is not the case. Compared to the general U.S. population, MTurk workers are equally likely to be employed. Almost 68% of workers are employed, compared to 60% in the general population. There are, however, significantly fewer retired workers on Mechanical Turk than there are in the general population. And, importantly, the proportion of students is only five percentage points higher on Mechanical Turk than in the general population, a finding that is surprising, given that most MTurk workers are younger than the U.S. population.

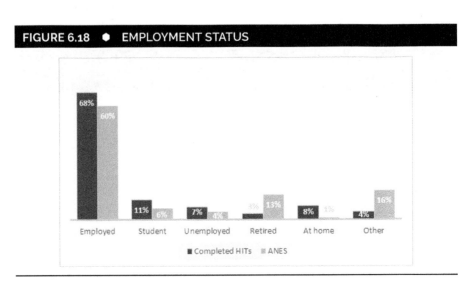

FIGURE 6.18 ● EMPLOYMENT STATUS

Note: Dark bars show the percentage of completed MTurk assignments (> 16 million) based on the employment of workers who completed those assignments. Light bars show the percentage of the U.S. population across employment categories based on the ANES national sample.

The data in Figure 6.18 seem to contradict the common perception that MTurk workers are largely unemployed. There is also no evidence that MTurk workers who are unemployed are spending more time on Mechanical Turk than are workers who are employed. Indeed, examining the proportion of HITs completed by each group suggests the opposite is true. Employed workers complete more HITs relative to their numbers, whereas people who stay at home and students complete fewer HITs relative to their numbers.

Income

The overall income distribution among MTurk workers differs from that of the general population (see Figure 6.19). There are significantly more MTurk workers in the very low income bracket and fewer MTurk workers in the highest income bracket. In particular, there are more workers making less than $20,000 per year on Mechanical Turk compared to the general population. There are also more people in the general population making more than $100,000 compared to MTurk workers. That doesn't mean MTurk workers are predominantly from the lowest income brackets. Although 25% of MTurk workers report having an income lower than $20,000, compared to 22% in the general population, the distribution of medium income brackets among MTurk workers is relatively similar to that of the general population. Importantly, workers from the lower income brackets do not disproportionately complete more HITs than other workers.

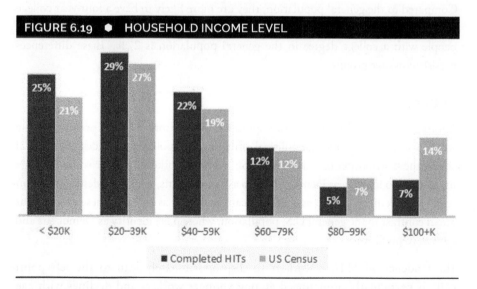

FIGURE 6.19 ● HOUSEHOLD INCOME LEVEL

■ Completed HITs ■ US Census

Note: Dark bars show the percentage of completed MTurk assignments (> 16 million) based on the income of workers who completed those assignments. Light bars show the percentage of the U.S. population across household income levels, based on the ANES national sample.

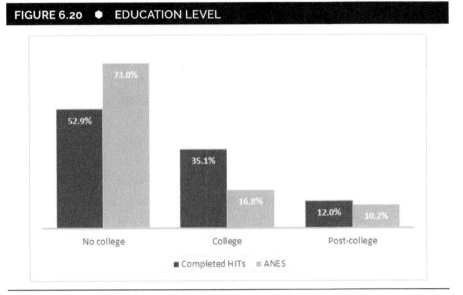

FIGURE 6.20 ● EDUCATION LEVEL

Note: Dark bars show the percentage of completed MTurk assignments (> 16 million) based on the education level of workers who completed those assignments. Light bars show the percentage of the U.S. population across education levels based on the ANES national sample.

Education

MTurk workers are more educated than the general population (see Figure 6.20). Compared to the general population, they are more likely to have a four-year college degree. Whereas 35% of MTurk workers have a college degree, the proportion of people with a college degree in the general population is 27%. These differences persist across age groups.

Politics

Another way in which the MTurk population differs from the U.S. population as a whole is in the distribution of political affiliation and political attitudes. Figure 6.21 shows the distribution of party affiliation. MTurk workers are approximately 20% more likely to identify as Democrats than as Republicans, with 46% describing themselves as a Democrat, 28% as a Republican, and 26% as "other." These proportions are in contrast to the general U.S. population, where 33% identify as Democrats and 29% as Republicans.

The tendency of MTurk workers to disproportionately lean to the left politically is particularly pronounced among younger workers and declines with age. Workers in their 20s favor Democrats over Republicans by 25 percentage points.

FIGURE 6.21 ● POLITICAL PARTY AFFILIATION

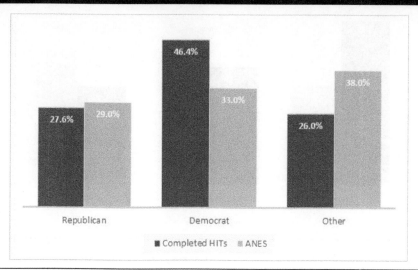

Note: Dark bars show the percentage of completed MTurk assignments (> 16 million) based on the political party affiliation of workers who completed those assignments. Light bars show the percentage of the U.S. population across political party affiliations based on the ANES national sample.

In contrast, workers in their 40s and 50s favor Democrats by just eight percentage points. Although the overall tendency to favor Democrats over Republicans decreases with age, the Democratic advantage remains high at any age compared to the general population. The Gallup Poll consistently shows that people aged 40 or older are more likely to identify as Republican than as Democratic in the general U.S. population. On Mechanical Turk, however, a Republican advantage is not observed at any age.

A similar left-leaning advantage is observed for political orientation (see Figure 6.22). The majority of MTurk workers identify as liberal (43%) as opposed to conservative (26%). This is in stark contrast to national trends. Although the tendency of the U.S. population to identify as liberal has increased steadily in the past two decades, the vast majority of the U.S. population still identifies as moderate and conservative. As of 2014, 35% of the U.S. population identified as conservative and 26% identified as liberal, according to the Gallup Poll.

The tendency of MTurk workers to be more likely to identify as liberal is most pronounced for workers in their 20s, 46% of whom identify as either liberal or very liberal and only 20% of whom identify as conservative or very conservative. This pattern decreases dramatically with age. For workers over age 40, there is only a five-percentage-point liberal advantage.

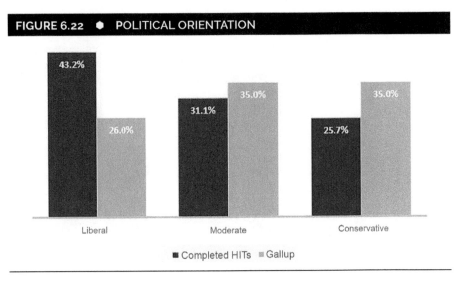

FIGURE 6.22 ● POLITICAL ORIENTATION

■ Completed HITs   ▪ Gallup

Note: Dark bars show the percentage of completed MTurk assignments (> 16 million) based on the political orientation of workers who completed those assignments. Light bars show the percentage of the U.S. population across political orientations based on the Gallup Poll. For the Gallup, the values do not add to 100% because the "other" category is omitted.

Religion

Figure 6.23 shows the distribution of religious affiliation. Compared to the general population, MTurk workers are far less likely to describe themselves as religious. On MTurk, 41% of workers describe themselves as religious, 20% as spiritual, 21% as agnostic, and 16% as atheist. The atheist and agnostic self-identifications are much higher on Mechanical Turk than in the general U.S. population.

As is the case in the general population, the rate of atheism and agnosticism on Mechanical Turk decreases steadily with age whereas religiosity increases steadily. Only 36% of workers in their 20s and 30s describe themselves as religious; by contrast, the proportion describing themselves as religious is close to 50% for workers over age 40.

The religious affiliation of MTurk workers is predominantly Christian: 52% of workers describe themselves as a Christian. Although other religions such as Buddhism, Hinduism, Islam, and Judaism are represented on Mechanical Turk, they make up less than 3% of workers combined. The percentage of workers who identify as Christian grows linearly with age: 40% of workers in their 20s identify as Christian, whereas close to 70% of workers in their 50s and older identify as Christian. The opposite pattern is observed among those who do not identify with any religion. Close to 50% of workers in their 20s do not identify with any religion, whereas only 20% of workers in their 70s do not identify with any religion. This is in line with

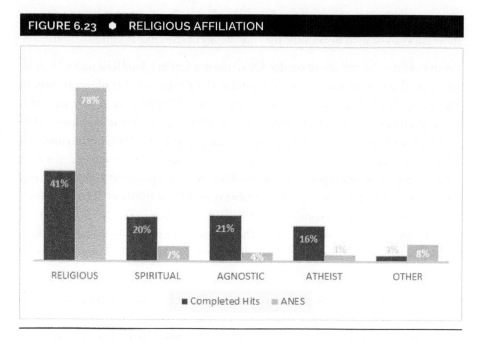

FIGURE 6.23 ● RELIGIOUS AFFILIATION

Note: Dark bars show the percentage of completed MTurk assignments (> 16 million) based on the religious affiliation of workers who completed those assignments. Light bars show the percentage of the U.S. population across religious affiliations based on the ANES national sample.

worldwide trends that indicate that young people are increasingly less likely to identify with a religion (Pew Research Center, 2018).

RELIABILITY AND VALIDITY

In the previous several sections we described the demographic and behavioral characteristics of the MTurk population. All data presented here relied on self-report, which leads to an important question: Is self-reported information on Mechanical Turk reliable? In other words, can we trust what MTurk workers tell us about themselves? Here we address this question as it relates to the data we just reported.

Reliability refers to whether the participants are consistent in the way they describe themselves over time. To assess whether workers are consistent in their self-reports, CloudResearch dynamically allocates demographic questions to workers based on the response information already in the database for those workers. This means, for example, that if a worker answered a question about his or her gender prior to taking one HIT, the question about gender would be less likely to be displayed again in the future, but the probability would remain greater than zero. Over time, workers answer the same questions multiple times, which means CloudResearch's database contains workers' answers to demographic questions asked on multiple occasions and those data can be used to examine the consistency of self-reported information.

Let us consider the variable of gender. Of all the workers in CloudResearch's database who provided information about their gender, the average number of reports was 15. The average internal consistency for these workers' self-reports of gender was 99%. More specifically, 92.2% of all workers provided 100% consistent information, while 96.5% of workers provided consistent information more than 90% of the time, and 97.8% of workers provided consistent information more than 80% of the time. In an examination of self-reports of race, 88.8% of workers provided 100% consistent information and 93.7% were consistent more than 90% of the time. There are several factors that can lower the consistency of self-reports somewhat on Mechanical Turk. Most important, some workers share their account with family members, which explains why responses can sometimes differ across time periods. Overall, however, the consistency of self-reports is very high.

One way to examine the validity of workers' responses is by the correlations between multiple self-reported variables. Among the variables discussed in this chapter, correlations between related constructs are consistent with expectations. For example, older MTurk workers tend to be more religious and more conservative, a pattern that is consistent with the general U.S. population. Marital status and the reported number of children correlates strongly with age and family status. Religiosity correlates with political party affiliation, and age correlates with religiosity, political party affiliation, and employment status. Importantly, the CloudResearch database consists of responses that individuals provide over many different studies that are separated by long time periods. It is thus unlikely that there is large-scale misrepresentation of basic demographics, as the majority of participants would have to be familiar with national population statistics and create fictitious profiles to match those trends. At the same time, specific individuals may misrepresent who they are, particularly when they are financially motivated to do so. Chapter 5 discusses ways to minimize such misrepresentation.

CONCLUSION

We started this chapter by describing common concerns about MTurk workers that the research community has shared. Common preconceptions are that MTurk workers lack diversity, are predominantly White, male, unemployed, and not representative of the United States geographically, and may provide nonsense responses due to lack of oversight. Additional concerns are based on published reports suggesting that the MTurk worker pool is very small.

The data presented in this chapter paint a different picture. The size of the MTurk worker pool is larger than previously thought. As many as 86,000 unique, U.S.-based MTurk workers participate in research studies every year. In any given month, approximately 30,000 unique workers participate in research studies, and 4,500 new workers enter the pool.

MTurk workers are also surprisingly diverse. They come from a variety of racial groups, occupations, and geographic locations. Contrary to common beliefs, MTurk workers are not any more likely to be White than is the general U.S. population. The gender distribution is approximately even. Workers are more likely to be employed, and not substantially more likely to be students, compared to the general U.S. population. Additionally, the distribution of MTurk workers across all 50 states almost perfectly matches the distribution of the U.S. population.

One key difference between the MTurk population and the general population of the United States is age. Close to 70% of MTurk workers are below age 40. For this reason, any comparison of the MTurk pool to the general U.S. population should be made within specific age groups. For example, while MTurk workers are less likely to be married and have children relative to the U.S. population, this bias is alleviated when age is controlled for. Within each age group, family composition is remarkably similar on Mechanical Turk compared to the U.S. population.

Age also plays an important role in the distribution of gender and race. The proportion of White workers increases dramatically with age. The distribution of White workers among workers below age 40 is similar to the proportion of Whites in the United States. Among older workers, however, there is a disproportionately high number of White workers and a disproportionately low number of minorities, particularly Asian and Hispanic participants. Gender distribution likewise varies dramatically across age groups, with the proportion of women increasing among older workers.

Overall, the data presented in this chapter show that MTurk workers are significantly more diverse in terms of race, age, family background, and gender compared to other sources of convenience samples, including traditional sources of participants such as the university subject pool.

At the same time, MTurk workers are different from the U.S. population in certain ways. Even when controlling for age, MTurk workers are more liberal politically, less religious, and more educated. These differences raise questions about when the data collected on Mechanical Turk are generalizable. The topic of generalizability is addressed in Chapter 8.

Although this chapter shows that MTurk workers as a whole are not that different from the U.S. population, the composition of any one sample is not necessarily representative of the MTurk population. Rather, samples are likely to disproportionately consist of the most active workers and those workers who saw the study first. In the next chapter we discuss how sampling methodology may affect sample composition as well as sampling best practices.

REFERENCES

American National Election Studies (ANES). (2012). Time Series Study [dataset]. Stanford University and the University of Michigan [producers]. *PLOS ONE*.

Card, N. A., Stucky, B. D., Sawalani, G. M., & Little, T. D. (2008). Direct and indirect aggression during childhood and adolescence: A meta-analytic review of gender differences, intercorrelations, and relations to maladjustment. *Child Development, 79*(5), 1185–1229. doi:10.1111/j.1467-8624.2008.01184.x

Chandler, J., Paolacci, G., Peer, E., Mueller, P., & Ratliff, K. A. (2015). Using nonnaive participants can reduce effect sizes. *Psychological Science, 26*(7), 1131–1139. doi:10.1177/0956797615585115

Chandler, J., Rosenzweig, C., Moss, A. J., Robinson, J., & Litman, L. (2019). Online panels in social science research: Expanding sampling methods beyond Mechanical Turk. *Behavior Research Methods, 51*(5), 2022–2038.

Chandler, J., & Shapiro, D. (2016). Conducting clinical research using crowdsourced convenience samples. *Annual Review of Clinical Psychology, 12*(1), 53–81. doi:10.1146/annurev-clinpsy-021815-093623

Clayton, J. A., & Tannenbaum, C. (2016). Reporting sex, gender, or both in clinical research? *JAMA, 316*(18), 1863–1864.

Difallah, D., Filatova, E., & Ipeirotis, P. (2018). Demographics and dynamics of Mechanical Turk workers. *Proceedings of the Eleventh ACM International Conference on Web Search and Data Mining*, 135–143.

Fordsham, N., Moss, A. J., Krumholtz, S., Roggina, T., Jr., Robinson, J., & Litman, L. (2019). Variation among Mechanical Turk workers across time of day presents an opportunity and a challenge for research. Retrieved from https://doi.org/10.31234/osf.io/p8bns

Gaub, M., & Carlson, C. L. (1997). Gender differences in ADHD: A meta-analysis and critical review. *Journal of the American Academy of Child & Adolescent Psychiatry, 36*(8), 1036–1045. doi:10.1097/00004583-199708000-00011

Gosling, S. D., Vazire, S., Srivastava, S., & John, O. P. (2004). Should we trust web-based studies? A comparative analysis of six preconceptions about Internet questionnaires. *American Psychologist, 59*(2), 93–104. doi:10.1037/0003-066X.59.2.93

Greer, T. M., Laseter, A., & Asiamah, D. (2009). Gender as a moderator of the relation between race-related stress and mental health symptoms for African Americans. *Psychology of Women Quarterly, 33*(3), 295–307. doi:10.1177/0361684309033300305

Huff, C., & Tingley, D. (2015). "Who are these people?" Evaluating the demographic characteristics and political preferences of MTurk survey respondents. *Research & Politics, 2*(3), 2053168015604648. doi:10.1177/2053168015604648

Ipeirotis, P. (2010). *Demographics of mechanical Turk. CeDER-10–01 working paper.* New York, NY: New York University.

Kolyesnikova, N., Dodd, T. H., & Wilcox, J. B. (2009). Gender as a moderator of reciprocal consumer behavior. *Journal of Consumer Marketing, 26*(3), 200–213. doi:10.1108/07363760910954136

Leaper, C., & Smith, T. E. (2004). A meta-analytic review of gender variations in children's language use: Talkativeness, affiliative speech, and assertive speech. *Developmental Psychology, 40*(6), 993–1027. doi:10.1037/0012-1649.40.6.993

Litman, L., Robinson, J., Rosen, Z., Rosenzweig, C., Waxman, J., & Bates, L. M. (2020). The persistence of pay inequality: The gender pay gap in an anonymous online labor market. *PLOS ONE, 15*(2), e0229383. doi:10.1371/journal.pone.0229383

Pew Research Center. (2018). The age gap in religion around the world. Retrieved from https://www.pewforum.org/2018/06/13/young-adults-around-the-world-are-less-religious-by-several-measures/

Robinson, J., Rosenzweig, C., Moss, A. J., & Litman, L. (2019). Tapped out or barely tapped? recommendations for how to harness the vast and largely unused potential of the mechanical Turk participant pool. *PLOS ONE, 14*(12), e0226394. doi:10.1371/journal.pone.0226394

Stewart, N., Ungemach, C., Harris, A. J., Bartels, D. M., Newell, B. R., Paolacci, G., & Chandler, J. (2015). The average laboratory samples a population of 7,300 Amazon Mechanical Turk workers. *Judgment and Decision Making, 10*(5), 479.

U.S. Census Bureau. (2016a). Quick facts, United States. Retrieved from https://factfinder.census.gov/faces/tableservices/jsf/pages/productview.xhtml?src=bkmk

U.S. Census Bureau. (2016b). Quick facts, United States. Retrieved from https://www.census.gov/quickfacts/fact/table/US/PST045216

U.S. Census Bureau. (2016c). FFF: Unmarried and single Americans, Week: Sept. 18-24, 2016. Retrieved from https://www.census.gov/newsroom/facts-for-features/2016/cb16-ff18.html

Wohlgemuth, E., & Betz, N. E. (1991). Gender as a moderator of the relationships of stress and social support to physical health in college students. *Journal of Counseling Psychology, 38*(3), 367–374. doi:10.1037/0022-0167.38.3.367

SAMPLING MECHANICAL TURK WORKERS

Problems and Solutions

Leib Litman, Jonathan Robinson, and Cheskie Rosenzweig

INTRODUCTION

Sampling refers to the process of recruiting individuals from a larger pool of potential participants. As part of the sampling process, researchers may choose to allow all participants to enter a study on a first-come, first-served basis, with minimal effort to control sample composition. Such samples are referred to as *convenience samples* (see Baker et al., 2013). Alternatively, researchers may wish to set specific recruitment criteria in order to attain greater control over the composition of the sample. This later type of sampling, in which significant effort is made to control sample composition, is referred to as *purposive sampling*. Purposive sampling is used to mitigate against potential sources of sampling bias.

We begin this chapter by describing the sampling methods used by the vast majority of researchers on Mechanical Turk. We refer to this as *standard sampling*. We then discuss several limitations of standard sampling and suggest approaches to purposive sampling that can mitigate against the biases that sometimes arise from standard samples.

As part of our discussion, it is important to keep in mind that not all studies are threatened by sampling bias to the same extent. Whether a particular source of sampling bias poses a threat to the validity of a study depends on the study's aims and objectives. What constitutes a source of bias in one study—say, the time of day when a study is launched—may not constitute a problem for another study. As a result, our discussion highlights the most common sources of sampling bias on Mechanical Turk and outlines steps researchers can take to ameliorate such bias.

SAMPLING ON MECHANICAL TURK

When a study is launched on Mechanical Turk, it becomes visible on workers' dashboards within a few minutes. However, not all workers are eligible to participate. Requesters can control which workers are able to participate in a study by using qualifications. The qualifications that are available for requesters to choose from are described in Chapters 3 and 4.

The vast majority of research studies on Mechanical Turk use three qualifications. The first qualification is the country from which participants are recruited; most researchers sample participants from the United States and Canada. The other two qualifications commonly used in standard samples are collectively known as reputation qualifications. The *number of HITs approved* qualification is the number of HITs a worker has successfully completed in the past. The *approval rating* qualification is the percentage of prior HITs that have been approved by requesters (see Chapter 2).

Requesters can use worker reputation qualifications to selectively recruit workers with a minimum or maximum number of completed HITs and a minimum or maximum approval rating. The standard practice for behavioral research on Mechanical Turk is to select workers who have completed at least 100 prior HITs and who have an approval rating of 95% or higher. These reputation metrics are used to control data quality (e.g., Peer, Vosgerau, & Acquisti, 2014).

To summarize, the standard sample on Mechanical Turk selectively recruits participants using the following three qualifications: (1) workers should be based in the United States or Canada, (2) workers should have completed at least 100 HITs, and (3) workers should have an approval rating of at least 95%.

As we discuss in more detail in Chapters 5 and 8, standard MTurk samples have been shown to produce highly reliable results in a very large number of studies. Thus, using standard samples is an effective sampling strategy. That doesn't mean, however, that the sampling process cannot be improved. In this chapter we discuss several biases that arise in standard samples and ways to mitigate these biases.

SOURCES OF SAMPLING BIAS

Sampling bias occurs when the group of participants who may take a study are not all equally likely to be sampled. Sampling bias is particularly problematic when the dependent variables are correlated with demographic and other characteristics of excluded participants. For example, online participants from the West Coast are more likely to be excluded when a study is launched early in the morning on the East Coast, due to regional time differences (Casey, Chandler, Levine, Proctor, & Strolovitch, 2017). People on the West Coast differ from those in the East in terms of a number of cultural attitudes, including attitudes toward social norms (e.g., Plaut, Markus, Treadway, & Fu, 2012), climate, and terrain. Thus, a region-specific sampling bias is likely to be correlated with region-specific cultural attitudes such as attitudes toward climate change (Casey et al., 2017) and well-being (Plaut et al., 2012).

As a result, studies that seek to explore attitudes that differ by region may want to minimize region-specific sampling bias and strive to obtain a geographically diverse sample (see case study 1 in Chapter 9). Controlling for sampling bias requires an awareness of the factors that give rise to various forms of bias on Mechanical Turk and the tools and methods that are available for attaining greater control over the sampling process. Factors that cause sampling bias can be grouped into three categories: coverage bias, nonresponse bias, and self-selection bias.

Coverage Bias

Coverage bias occurs when some part of the target population does not have the ability to participate in a study. This can occur on Mechanical Turk because of the time a HIT is launched (Casey et al., 2017) and can also result from the qualifications requesters set for HITs, such as restricting a HIT to workers who have completed at least 100 HITs.

Nonresponse Bias

Nonresponse bias occurs when workers who choose not to participate in a study are systematically different from those who choose to participate. Various aspects of a HIT, such as its length and wage, can make it less attractive to specific workers, leading them to avoid the study.

Self-Selection Bias

Self-selection bias is the opposite of nonresponse bias. Self-selection bias occurs when some workers are more likely than others to self-select into a HIT. The main source of self-selection bias on Mechanical Turk comes from superworkers. Superworkers are highly active workers who are more likely to self-select into many HITs. Superworkers pose a special kind of sampling challenge on Mechanical Turk and other online platforms more generally.

THE PROBLEM OF SUPERWORKERS

We begin our discussion of sampling bias with the problem of superworkers. Of all the biases that arise from sampling on Mechanical Turk, the problem of superworkers stands out as particularly important. Indeed, at least some observers have suggested that other platforms may be better suited for social science research because of this issue (Peer, Brandimarte, Samat, & Acquisti, 2017). For this reason, we explore the problem of superworkers in considerable detail. The overall message of this section is simply that superworker bias on Mechanical Turk is largely due to current sampling practices in the field and can easily be mitigated. The problem arises not due to any flaw in Mechanical Turk. Instead, it arises because of the way in which researchers typically sample participants. A simple change in sampling methodology can eliminate the problem.

The superworker bias on Mechanical Turk begins the moment a HIT is launched. This is because the workers' dashboard serves as the main communication channel between workers and requesters (see Chapter 2, Figure 2.1). A HIT posted on Mechanical Turk is visible only to workers who are looking at the dashboard at the time it is posted. Workers who are not on Mechanical Turk when a HIT is posted will not know the HIT is available and thus will not be able to participate in the study.

To get around this limitation, workers use several apps that notify them about attractive HIT opportunities (see Chapter 2), or use such apps to automatically accept HITs. Workers also use various forums to share information about desirable HITs including the HIT's pay rate, user experience, and the reputation of the requester who posted it.

While HIT notification apps and worker forums are routine parts of the MTurk worker's experience, they also contribute to sample bias by skewing sample composition toward more experienced participants. Because experienced workers are more likely than less experienced workers to spend time monitoring the dashboard, use HIT notification apps, and monitor worker forums for good HIT opportunities, experienced workers are more likely to learn about HITs immediately when they are posted. This problem is exacerbated for high-paying HITs because workers seek to participate in the most attractive and well-paying studies.

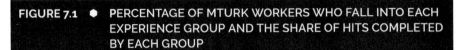

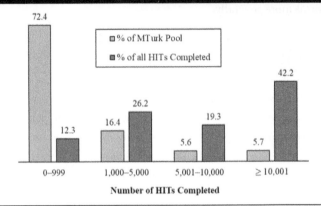

The Scale of the Superworker Problem

Every study run on Mechanical Turk consists of a disproportionately high number of experienced workers that we refer to as superworkers. As shown in Figure 7.1, the most active 5.2% of workers complete 42% of all assignments (Robinson, Rosenzweig, Moss, & Litman, 2019). The proportion of superworkers is even higher for high-paying HITs, as we discuss below. Superworkers are highly experienced, often having completed more than 10,000 prior HITs.

Not all of these HITs are social science studies. MTurk workers complete a variety of different tasks (see Chapter 2), many of which are not research related. At the same time, a correlation exists between a worker's overall MTurk activity and the likelihood of participation in research studies.

The least active workers who have completed fewer than 1,000 HITs constitute 72% of the MTurk worker pool. This group of workers completes only 12% of all assignments. Robinson et al. (2019) found that in studies open to all workers (without any restrictions on the number of previously completed HITs), only 14% of the sample will have completed fewer than 1,000 HITs (see Figure 7.2). Effectively, the average study pulls close to half of its participants from about 5% of the available MTurk participant pool. Additionally, 72% of MTurk workers barely have a chance to participate because they are crowded out of HITs by more experienced superworkers.

The superworker bias raises important questions about how the disproportionately high percentage of active workers in MTurk samples affects study outcomes and about best practices for sampling on Mechanical Turk (see Appendix A). If close to half of participants in standard samples are likely to be highly active superworkers,

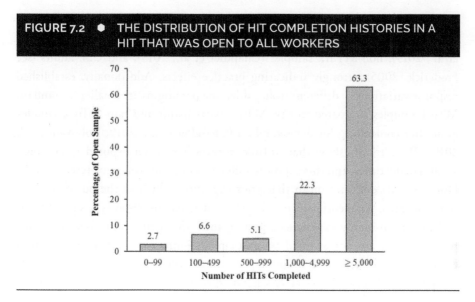

FIGURE 7.2 ● THE DISTRIBUTION OF HIT COMPLETION HISTORIES IN A HIT THAT WAS OPEN TO ALL WORKERS

do their data systematically differ from those of other workers? Further, are there sampling practices that would allow researchers to limit or exclude superworkers and still collect quality data on Mechanical Turk?

The Practical Impact of the Superworker Bias

Experienced workers are much more likely to have participated in many social and behavioral research studies. As a result, they are not naïve to study protocols, which can lead to changes in their response patterns (Bialek & Pennycook, 2017; Chandler, Paolacci, Peer, Mueller, & Ratliff, 2015; DeVoe & House, 2016; Rand et al., 2014; Zwaan et al., 2017).

Several studies have examined how participants in typical MTurk samples respond to common stimuli compared to new MTurk participants (Robinson et al., 2019) and participants on other online panels (Chandler, Rosenzweig, Moss, Robinson, & Litman, 2019). Participants in typical MTurk samples self-report having previously seen many stimuli that are commonly used in social and behavioral research studies. For example, 75% of MTurk participants in standard samples report having seen the Cognitive Reflection Test (a commonly used measure in decision-making research), 60% report having previously seen the trolley dilemma, and 30% report being familiar with the "Asian disease" problem (Chandler et al., 2019; Robinson et al., 2019).

Previous exposure to study stimuli directly affects the outcomes of some studies, particularly those that use common measures. Several common measures have been directly examined with regard to nonnaïveté. Performance on the Cognitive

Reflection Test is multiple standard deviations higher among participants in standard MTurk samples compared to samples of new MTurk participants (Robinson et al., 2019), non-MTurk samples (Chandler et al., 2019), and U.S. adults (see Frederick, 2005), strongly indicating practice effects. Additionally, established response variations to different trolley dilemma paradigms are smaller in standard MTurk samples compared to new MTurk participants and non-MTurk samples, even after controlling for demographics (Chandler et al., 2019; Robinson et al., 2019). These results show that MTurk workers have been exposed to common stimuli many times, and this exposure influences outcomes on some research tasks. However, this does not mean that prior exposure influences the outcome of all research tasks. As mentioned in Chapter 5, it is parsimoniously assumed to be bad to rely on highly experienced participants. That being said, there are many measures that are not affected by participant nonnaïveté and many measures for which researchers have simply not examined whether prior exposure affects responses (see Hauser, Paolacci, & Chandler, 2019).

Finally, the speed with which participants from standard MTurk samples complete tasks is significantly faster compared to new MTurk workers. Robinson et al. (2019) showed that a HIT consisting of typical psychological stimuli was completed by new workers in an average of 18 minutes, while the same HIT was completed by a standard sample of MTurk participants in under 13 minutes. This is consistent with previous findings, showing that highly experienced participants complete tasks faster, likely as a result of satisficing, or taking shortcuts in order to maximize hourly wages (Toepoel, Das, & Van Soest, 2008).

Causes of the Superworker Problem

Researchers have long been suspicious of data quality on Mechanical Turk. One common way this concern is addressed is by the use of reputation qualifications. These qualifications allow researchers to select experienced participants with a high percentage of previously approved HITs. In this section we explain how reputation qualifications, as commonly used in standard samples, have the unintended consequence of exacerbating the problem of superworkers. We then describe an alternative way of using the reputation system to eliminate the superworker problem without compromising data quality.

Most researchers restrict their studies to only those workers who have an approval rating above 95% and a minimum of 100 HITs completed (e.g., Peer et al., 2014). Although the use of these reputation metrics to select participants is intended to improve data quality, recent studies suggest that they confer little benefit to data quality for two reasons. First, the number of MTurk workers with low approval ratings is negligible, thus bringing into question the need to restrict participation based on approval ratings. The second, and related, reason is that the data quality of samples that use standard approval ratings is similar to those that do not use them.

The CloudResearch database (previously TurkPrime) shows that only 1.8% of the more than 200,000 U.S.-based workers (see Chapter 6) who have ever taken a HIT posted through CloudResearch had an approval rating below 90%. Robinson et al. (2019) further showed that when no approval rating qualifications were used to sample participants (open sample), 100% of the sample still had approval ratings above 90% and 98.4% of the sample had approval ratings above 95%. The data quality of these participants was also indistinguishable from the standard sample that used the 95% qualification rating and 100 HIT completion minimum. Since close to 98% of MTurk workers have high approval ratings, the reputation qualifications are effectively being used to screen out a very small percentage of workers, with little to no impact on the overall data quality.

The use of approval ratings is intended to select high-quality, experienced workers. However, this qualification does little to improve data quality. Instead, using approval ratings to exclude hypothetical unscrupulous workers increases the likelihood that workers who complete the study will be highly active superworkers. These super-workers will have a disproportionately high level of familiarity with standard scientific protocols, increasing the likelihood of obtaining attenuated effect sizes across multiple types of research studies. Most importantly, this practice does not exclude enough bad-quality workers to justify its use.

Alternative Sampling Strategies: Sampling From Inexperienced Workers

The vast majority of the MTurk participants are relatively inexperienced (see Figure 7.1) and take a while to find HITs. When the 95% approval rating and 100 HIT completion minimum (standard qualifications) are used, most of the sample will consist of superworkers because they find HITs very quickly. Indeed, the sample will consist predominantly of superworkers even when no reputation qualifications are used and the sample is open to everyone (see Figure 7.2).

There are several strategies by which the problem of superworker bias can be overcome. They involve simply limiting highly experienced workers from HITs. To do so, the reputation qualifications should be used to select low-active workers, including workers who do not have an established approval rating due to having completed fewer than 100 HITs. Using these qualifications will open the pool to the many workers who are typically crowded out of HITs by more experienced superworkers.

A recent study (Robinson et al., 2019) examined data quality from less experienced participants and found that these workers provide high-quality data as indicated by pass rate on attention checks, replication of multiple classic experiments, and scale reliabilities. This study also examined levels of nonnaïveté by assessing familiarity with common measures. Across all indicators of data quality, the inexperienced workers performed as well as the more experienced standard sample workers with established approval ratings. At the same time, the inexperienced workers were much less familiar with commonly used measures.

These results demonstrate that there is little reason to be suspicious of the data quality of novice workers. Thus, there is little reason to use the 100 HIT completion minimum. Indeed, there are many reasons to prefer novice workers over more experienced workers as research participants. Novice workers are motivated primarily to increase their reputation ratings so that they can be selected for future high-paying HITs. Thus, even though their approval ratings have not been established, they are motivated primarily to perform well and to have their work approved so that they can be paid more for their work and be more likely to qualify for future HITs.

How to Use Reputation Qualifications Effectively

Using HIT Completion History Effectively

The standard use of the worker reputation qualifications on Mechanical Turk has multiple negative consequences: there are not enough low-reputation workers to justify the use of approval ratings, there is no discernible impact on data quality for typical studies, and standard samples consist predominantly of superworkers. This leads to the question of whether worker reputation qualifications should be used at all, and, if so, how? We suggest that rather than using qualifications to exclude workers with a low approval rating and low number of HITs, qualifications should be used to either exclude superworkers or to limit their participation by stratifying the sample. The downside of excluding superworkers is that it may slow down the speed of data collection. Stratifying the sample can avoid this problem by limiting the number of superworkers to 30% of the sample, or some other smaller segment of the sample (see Robinson, Rosenzweig, Moss, & Litman, 2019). This approach has the advantage of maintaining the speed of data collection while balancing the participation of both experienced and inexperienced participants.

What is the right threshold for the maximum number of previously completed HITs? We recommend using 5,000 completed HITs as the exclusion threshold. This threshold is likely to provide enough naïve workers while excluding the most active superworkers who effectively make it all but impossible for less experienced workers to participate. As Figure 7.1 shows, excluding workers who have completed more than 5,000 HITs will prevent approximately 11% of workers who complete close to 60% of all HITs from participating. The other 90% of workers will still be eligible to participate.

Using the Approval Rating Effectively

As mentioned earlier, the approval rating qualification does not improve data quality appreciably on typical studies in the social and behavioral sciences because only a negligible percentage of workers have approval ratings below 90%. However, there is no harm in using the approval ratings in tandem with setting a maximum HIT completion threshold. It must be noted, however, that workers who have completed fewer than 100 HITs, and who have an unknown approval rating, should still be eligible to participate. Thus, the approval rating, when used this way, will be applied only to a subsample of the workers who have completed more than 100 HITs.

This approach has the advantage of simultaneously allowing novice workers (i.e., those with fewer than 100 completed HITs) into the sample, while also selectively vetting the approval ratings of more experienced workers (i.e., those who have completed more than 100 HITs) and excluding highly experienced superworkers (i.e., either excluding those who have completed more than 5,000 HITs, or stratifying the sample).

What about bad-quality workers? Undoubtedly, workers who participate in any research study will range in their levels of attentiveness. Chapter 5 described several techniques that researchers can use to vet the attentiveness of participants. We suggest that every study should employ attention screeners and other data validation measures described in Chapter 5 to make sure participants are adequately attending to task demands.

Overall, using worker reputation qualifications to exclude highly active workers while also using several attention checks to exclude inattentive participants is a sampling strategy that balances the need for quality participants on the one hand and addresses the superworker sampling bias on the other.

Studies That Should Selectively Recruit Superworkers

Although most social and behavioral research studies should restrict the proportion of superworkers in their samples, some studies should selectively seek out superworkers. The experience of superworkers makes them skilled at performing many different types of tasks, particularly those requiring a high degree of prolonged attentiveness and focus. Superworkers are particularly good at providing open-ended essay responses, solving complex tasks, working interactively together, and overcoming challenges. In addition, superworkers are significantly less likely to attrite from longitudinal studies, as we discuss further in Chapter 10. Thus, researchers should weigh the costs of nonnaïveté against the benefits of experience and willingness to engage in challenging tasks in deciding whether to tilt their sample toward or away from superworkers.

TIME-OF-DAY EFFECTS

In addition to the problem of superworkers, researchers may wish to control for several other forms of sampling bias. One advantage of conducting research on Mechanical Turk is the speed with which data can be collected. A HIT open to, say, 200 workers can be completed within a few hours or less (see Figure 6.3). However, the speed with which data are collected can also introduce sampling bias. Because most studies are completed within a few hours, MTurk samples tend to consist of workers who are active during the time of day in which the HIT began. This raises the potential problem of time-related coverage bias. Do workers who participate in HITs at specific times differ from each other in systematic ways? For example, are workers who take HITs in the evening different from workers who take HITs in the morning? Because research shows reliable individual differences in time-of-day preferences, this question applies to both the demographics and the psychosocial characteristics of workers.

To appreciate why time-related sampling bias is a more vexing problem in online platforms than in more traditional research settings, it helps to situate Mechanical Turk within the emerging "gig economy." The gig economy is characterized by a distributed and dynamic workforce in which workers are free to choose their tasks and the time at which to work on those tasks. In traditional labor markets, most jobs typically require employees to work at specific times, such as from 9 a.m. to 5 p.m. In the gig economy, however, people are free to choose when they want to work. This produces a potentially critical difference in work patterns between the traditional and gig economies, in that gig economy work patterns are much more likely to be aligned with employees' time-of-day preferences. Studies launched in the evening, for example, will tend to be completed by workers who prefer to work in the evening. Similarly, studies launched in the morning are more likely to be completed by people who have a morning preference.

To examine the temporal profile of work patterns on Mechanical Turk, we used the CloudResearch database to plot the activity levels of workers over the 24-hour period. Figure 7.3 shows worker activity across the day separated by gender. As is clearly visible, worker activity varies significantly across a 24-hour period. The least active time on Mechanical Turk is between midnight and 5 a.m. Thereafter, activity increases steadily and peaks at 10 a.m. Starting at 2 p.m., activity begins to decline.

FIGURE 7.3 ● DISTRIBUTION OF HITS ACROSS TIME OF DAY

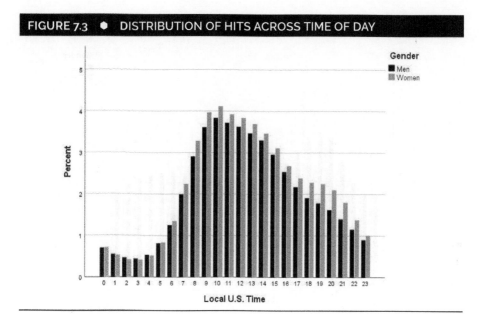

Worker activity on Mechanical Turk is in some ways consistent with traditional work environments. People on Mechanical Turk are most active during the early morning and in the afternoon. At the same time, however, a considerable amount of work on Mechanical Turk is done in the late evening and at night, a time when work is typically not performed in traditional work environments. Close to 25% of HITs on Mechanical Turk are completed between 10 p.m. and 5 a.m.

Figures 7.3 and 7.4 plot gender and age differences in activity patterns across a 24-hour period. From midnight until roughly 5 a.m., the proportion of assignments completed by men and women is almost identical. After around 5 a.m., however, women are consistently more active than men, with around 55% of assignments completed by women.

The temporal distribution of age across studies is also affected by time of day (see Figure 7.4). Older participants tend to prefer early morning, and younger participants prefer late evening. The diurnal age distribution of activity on Mechanical Turk is largely consistent with activity levels of adults in the general population. Research shows that evening and morning preferences are strongly correlated with age (Carrier, Monk, Buysse, & Kupfer, 1997). Older adults tend to be more active in the morning, starting around 4 a.m. Younger adults tend to be more active in the evening, with the most active time being between midnight and 3 a.m. Thus, the activity level of workers on Mechanical Turk closely mirrors findings about evening and morning preferences across age groups.

FIGURE 7.4 ● DISTRIBUTION OF AGE AND GENDER ACROSS TIME OF DAY

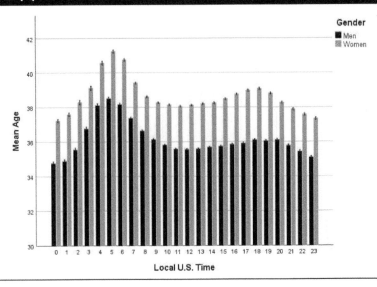

Because time-of-day preference is likely to play a major influence on when workers participate in HITs, Fordsham et al. (2019) used time-of-day preference as the organizing principle around which to explore time-related self-selection bias in behavioral, personality, and clinical outcomes. In this study, the researchers hypothesized that participants who choose to take studies in the evening would be more likely to have evening-type personalities than those who choose to take studies in the morning. Importantly, the study also examined whether morning and evening activity on Mechanical Turk was associated with a large cluster of demographic, personality, and clinical variables that research has shown are related to time-of-day preference, including anxiety (Antypa, Vogelzangs, Meesters, Schoevers, & Penninx, 2016), depression (Merikanto et al., 2013), Internet compulsion (Randler, Horzum, & Vollmer, 2014), procrastination (Díaz-Morales, Ferrari, & Cohen, 2008), and erratic nighttime behavior and sleep patterns (Collado Mateo, Díaz-Morales, Escribano Barreno, Delgado Prieto, & Randler, 2012).

To examine whether evening-active and morning-active MTurk participants differ on these variables, Fordsham et al. (2019) sampled workers across different times of the 24-hour period. As predicted, the results showed that workers who participated in the evening were more likely to have evening-type personalities and were also significantly more likely to have higher levels of internet compulsion, procrastination, erratic nighttime sleep behavior, anxiety, and depression. Evening participants were also more likely to report lower levels of conscientiousness and higher levels of neuroticism. The correlations between time-of-day work preferences and morning-versus-evening personality were very high.

This research shows that morning and evening preference is associated not only with age and gender but also with a cluster of other variables that include clinical, personality, and behavioral factors. These findings suggest that sampling online participants at any one point in time may introduce sampling bias, particularly in the early morning and evening, which is when demographic and psychosocial profiles of active workers tend to differ most dramatically.

Researchers should consider several sampling options to avoid time-of-day sampling bias. One option is to collect data during the most active hours, which are between 10 a.m. and 4 p.m. However, this approach has the disadvantage of excluding participants who are active in the morning and evening, workers whose psychosocial profiles should be of interest to those conducting research in personality, social, clinical, and related fields. Thus, collecting data at one specific point in time is not the optimal strategy for research in these areas. Rather, researchers should use a staggered sampling approach, where studies are broken up into smaller samples and data are collected across different times of the day and days of the week. Tools that are available for automatically spreading out HITs across different times of the day are described in Chapter 4.

PAY RATE

The selection of tasks based on wages is another aspect that differentiates gig economy markets from more traditional marketplaces. On Mechanical Turk, workers are free to choose their work and tend to select tasks based primarily on wages. The ability of workers to select high-paying tasks depends on the resources they have to quickly find high-paying HITs, their amount of free time, and their motivation to pursue such work. As a result, the compensation associated with any one HIT affects sample composition in important ways.

Pay Rate and the Superworker Bias

As described earlier, superworkers are disproportionately likely to participate in standard-sample HITs on Mechanical Turk. Even so, the pay rate of a HIT has an outsized influence on the number of superworkers who participate in a study. In this section, we describe how wages affect the number of superworkers in a sample. To do so, we examined the proportion of superworkers who participate in HITs with different payment levels, using the CloudResearch database. Table 7.1 shows a grid that divides HITs based on both their dollar value and their hourly wage. The leftmost column consists of all

HITs that paid less than $1. Because those HITs differ in length, their hourly wages vary significantly. For example, if a HIT paying $1 takes 10 minutes or less to complete, the hourly wage is $6 per hour or more.

The proportion of superworkers in a sample can vary by as much as 30% depending on both the HIT's dollar value and the hourly wage. For HITs paying $1 that took 1 hour or more to complete, and thus had an hourly wage of less than $1 per hour, only 36% of the sample consisted of superworkers. On the other side of the spectrum, for HITs that pay more than $6 and whose hourly wage is more than $6 per hour, the proportion of superworkers increases to 65%.

Both the dollar value and the hourly wage affect the participation rates of superworkers. Focusing on just the HITs whose dollar value is less than $1, participation rates can vary between 36% and 50% depending on the hourly wage. This shows that by keeping the dollar value of a HIT constant, HITs that have higher hourly wages will attract higher numbers of superworkers. Focusing on HITs whose hourly wages are $6 per hour or more, the dollar value of those HITs also influences superworkers' participation rates. Specifically, HITs whose dollar value is less than $1 will have 50% superworker composition. When the dollar value of those HITs is $6 or higher the participation rate of superworkers increases to 65%.

These data show that the superworker bias is even bigger in studies that pay higher wages, making it even more important to minimize this bias by using maximum HIT completion qualifications.

TABLE 7.1 ● PROPORTION OF SUPERWORKERS IN A STUDY AS A FUNCTION OF HOW MUCH A STUDY PAYS AND THE STUDY'S HOURLY WAGE

Hourly Wage	Dollar Value of HIT				
	$0–1	$1–3	$3–5	$5–6	$6+
$0–1/hr.	35.8%	N/A	N/A	N/A	N/A
$1–3/hr.	41.9%	47.0%	N/A	N/A	N/A
$3–5/hr.	47.9%	51.0%	48.7%	N/A	N/A
$5–6/hr.	49.3%	52.6%	63.9%	57.2%	N/A
$6+/hr.	50.1%	55.3%	61.0%	61.3%	65.1%

Note: N (studies) = 100,000+

Pay Rate and the Gender Bias

The self-selection of high-active workers into most MTurk research studies also affects the demographic composition of the sample. Most superworkers are male, and they tend to be younger in age compared to less active workers. Table 7.2 shows that the proportion of males in any given HIT can range between 38% and 52% depending on the HIT's dollar value. Interestingly, the proportion of males is driven primarily by the hourly wage of a HIT and less so by its dollar value. It appears that males are more likely to self-select into HITs that offer a higher hourly wage independent of how much those HITs actually pay.

These results are consistent with findings by Litman et al., 2020, who showed that women earn less than men on Mechanical Turk. Critically, this gender wage bias exists across all age levels, family composition types, education levels, and racial groups.

Pay Rate and the Age Bias

In addition to gender, pay rate also affects the age distribution of samples. The age of workers who take high-paying HITs is systematically lower. This pattern of high-paying HITs being completed disproportionately by younger males is consistent with the demographic distribution of superworkers. Workers who complete more HITs are more likely to be male and younger.

Sampling Practices to Avoid Pay-Related Bias

The exact causal factors responsible for the emergence of a gender wage gap in an economic market that is anonymous, and mostly devoid of structural factors that lead to gender-based wage discrepancies in traditional labor markets, remains to be

TABLE 7.2 ● PROPORTION OF MALES IN A STUDY AS A FUNCTION OF A STUDY'S HOURLY WAGE					
	Dollar Value of HIT				
Hourly Wage	$0–1	$1–3	$3–5	$5–6	$6+
$0–1/hr.	38.9%	N/A	N/A	N/A	N/A
$1–3/hr.	42.7%	42.7%	N/A	N/A	N/A
$3–5/hr.	47.7%	47.2%	45.2%	N/A	N/A
$5–6/hr.	49.7%	48.9%	48.8%	49.8%	N/A
$6+/hr.	50.1%	50.2%	50.4%	50.2%	51.9%

Note: N (studies) = 100,000+

explored. Litman et al. (2020) hypothesize that women may take tasks that pay less on Mechanical Turk due, in part, to discrimination in more traditional labor markets, which leads women to undervalue their labor and have lower reservation wages (Caliendo, Lee, & Mahlstedt, 2017).

Whatever the causal mechanisms of the gender wage gap on Mechanical Turk, it raises important questions about sampling methodology and ethics. The problem of men being more likely to self-select into high-paying HITs can be easily resolved with a simple quota-based sampling approach. One possibility is to cap participation by each gender at 50%. Both MTurk and CloudResearch provide the ability to selectively target workers based on gender. This simple solution will minimize the gender-based sampling bias that results from males being more likely to self-select into high-paying HITs. This approach will also create a more equitable work environment for women on Mechanical Turk, and if adopted in the gig economy more broadly, in other nontraditional marketplaces as well. The ethical implications of this issue are discussed in more detail in Chapter 11.

Overall, higher pay rates bias samples toward young male superworkers. These problems can be alleviated if studies exclude superworkers by applying a maximum HIT completion qualification, as discussed earlier, in combination with a gender-based quota sample. Quota samples can also be used to distribute the age of workers more equally.

DROPOUT

So far in this chapter, sampling bias has been discussed from the perspective of coverage bias, nonresponse, and self-selection into a study. However, just as workers can self-select into a study, they can also self-select out of a study—a phenomenon referred to as dropout or attrition. Dropout rates on Mechanical Turk can vary significantly from study to study, and they depend on multiple factors. In some cases, dropout can reach 80% or more, making dropout a significant threat to external validity.

The most serious threat posed by high dropout is to the internal validity of randomized experimental studies. Internal validity refers to the ability to make sound causal inferences. An experiment enables causal inference because potential confounds are randomly distributed across experimental conditions by random assignment. High dropout can invalidate the internal validity of experiments in several ways. The first threat to internal validity occurs if dropout rates are different across conditions. Condition-specific dropout is likely to occur when one of the conditions is either more difficult or less interesting to some participants. Zhou and Fishbach (2016) demonstrated that condition-specific dropout on Mechanical Turk can be dramatic. For example, one of their experiments had two conditions to which subjects were randomly assigned. In the *ego-depletion* condition, subjects had to write a 100-word paragraph without using letters *A* or *N*. In the second, *non-ego-depletion* condition, subjects had to write a 100-word paragraph without using letters *X* or *Y*. The more difficult, ego-depletion condition had a dropout rate of almost 80% compared to the easier non-ego-depletion condition, in which dropout was 23%.

Zhou and Fishbach (2016) also showed that participants who do not drop out are systematically different from those who do. In the ego-depletion condition, participants who did not drop out reported less overall fatigue prior to the study compared to those who did drop out. The very purpose of the ego-depleting condition is to make subjects more tired. Thus, this manipulation can be completely invalidated if the tired subjects self-select out of the ego-depletion condition and the ones who started out being less tired are the ones who stick with it to the end.

In a series of well-designed experiments conducted on Mechanical Turk, Zhou and Fishbach (2016) demonstrated that the threat of differential condition-specific dropout is not just a theoretical concern. Across more than 20 experimental manipulations, they found that dropout can pose severe challenges to causal inference, both when the dropout rate is condition specific and when the dropout rate is the same across experimental conditions. They also found that instructing participants about the importance of not dropping out of a study had only a modest effect in reducing dropout rates.

Researchers have long recognized that dropout is a particularly critical threat to the validity of online research. More traditional research settings such as face-to-face studies (see Birnbaum, 2004), phone interviews (see Galesic, 2006), and university subject pools (Zhou & Fishbach, 2016) tend to see significantly less dropout compared to online settings. In some online studies outside of Mechanical Turk, dropout has been documented to be as high as 80% (O'Neil, Penrod, & Bornstein, 2003) and has been reported to be 30% on average (see Bosnjak & Tuten, 2001; Galesic, 2006; Manfreda & Vehovar, 2002; Vehovar, Batagelj, Manfreda, & Zaletel, 2002). In contrast, dropout is typically as low as 5% in face-to-face interviews (see Galesic, 2006) and is mostly nonexistent in university subject pools (Zhou & Fishbach, 2016). This is likely because in online studies participants have few barriers to terminating a study, whereas in face-to-face laboratory settings they have to interact with a researcher and are thus less likely to walk out in the middle of a study.

Calculated based on over 100,000 HITs in the CloudResearch database, the dropout rate on Mechanical Turk is 18.5% on average with a standard deviation of 19%. For some studies the dropout rate is dramatic, reaching above 95%. At the same time, more than 20% of studies have a dropout rate of less than 5%, and 45% of studies have a dropout rate of less than 10%. Thus, a low dropout rate on Mechanical Turk is not uncommon. Additionally, the dropout rate is not random across studies but can be predicted based on study characteristics. Factors that increase dropout include inaccurate task descriptions and setting a lower expected study duration in the study description than the actual duration of a study. Factors that decrease dropout include higher wages and providing a bonus.

As shown in Table 7.3, both the wage and duration can have dramatic effects on the dropout rate. For studies that are shorter than 5 minutes, dropout ranges between 19% and 12%, depending on the wage. Studies that are longer than 30 minutes can have dropout rates as high as 60% when the hourly wage is less than $3. However, even when HITs are longer than 1 hour, dropout can be as low as 16% when the wage is greater than $6 per hour.

In addition to wage and pay rate, dropout is associated with the discrepancy between the advertised and actual length of a HIT. This means that once workers see that a HIT is taking longer than it was supposed to, they are much more likely to drop out. Additionally, a significant percentage of variance in dropout is due to systematic differences between requesters. This means that some requesters tend to consistently have more dropout than others. This may be due to many factors, including that some requesters pay more, tend to have longer studies, or have more technical issues with their HITs. It is also likely that having a good requester reputation makes workers more likely to want to complete their HITs.

TABLE 7.3 ● DROPOUT AS A FUNCTION OF A HIT'S LENGTH AND WAGE

	Duration				
Wage	< 5 min	5–10 min	10–30 min	30–60 min	> 1 hour
$0–1/hr	16.9%	24.4%	34.4%	57.6%	44.4%
$1–3/hr	19.3%	21.3%	35.0%	41.2%	59.3%
$3–5/hr	13.7%	20.1%	30.7%	45.2%	33.8%
$5–6/hr	14.6%	23.2%	27.1%	33.3%	25.1%
$6+/hr	12.0%	20.4%	24.5%	21.1%	15.8%

Note: Each cell shows the average percentage of workers who drop out of studies with the given duration and wage. *N* (studies) = 100,000+

TABLE 7.4 ● MTURK SAMPLING SETUP: USES, ADVANTAGES, AND DISADVANTAGES				
	Standard Sampling	**Purposive Sampling**	**Advantages**	**Disadvantages**
U.S./Canada only	☑	☑	Avoids data quality and language barrier problems.	
100 HITs minimum	☑		Excludes workers with an unverified approval rating.	Excludes naïve workers. Reduces the size of the available pool. Majority of the sample will consist of superworkers.
95% approval rating	☑	☑	Excludes workers with a low approval rating.	Very few workers have low approval ratings. No evidence that data quality improves appreciably.
5,000 HITs maximum		☑	Expands the available pool. Increases naïveté of participants.	Expands the available pool. Increases naïveté of participants. Excludes all superworkers. Data collection may be slower.
Stratified samples based on three levels of experience		☑	Expands the available pool. Increases naïveté of participants.	Data collection may be slower, particularly for large samples.
50/50 gender split		☑	Avoids gender pay gap. Creates more equitable ecosystem.	More expensive.
High pay rate		☑	Reduces dropout. Reduces nonresponse bias.	Increases superworkers bias. Can be avoided when 5,000 HIT maximum is used concurrently.

(Continued)

TABLE 7.4 ● *(Continued)*				
	Standard Sampling	Purposive Sampling	Advantages	Disadvantages
Slow release across time of day		☑	Reduces coverage bias.	Slower data collection.

Overall, these results paint a positive picture of dropout rates on Mechanical Turk. Average dropout on Mechanical Turk is lower than what has previously been reported for other online platforms. More than 20% of studies on Mechanical Turk have virtually no dropout, and this proportion increases dramatically with higher wages. Importantly, dropout rates are not random. Requesters have significant control over dropout levels of HITs. Paying an appropriate wage, accurately describing a HIT's length and task requirements, and providing an overall positive user experience for the workers can reduce dropout rates to negligible levels.

At the same time, there is a need to be extremely cautious, as there is potential for high dropout rates to invalidate an experiment without researchers ever knowing about it. When requesters are not careful to monitor and take precautions against dropout, dropout can be dramatic, reaching 80% or higher. What poses an even greater level of concern is that Mechanical Turk does not report dropout. Thus, researchers whose studies have high dropout levels may not be aware that this problem is presenting a threat to the internal validity of their studies. For this reason, it is important to use tools that make it possible to monitor dropout. As described in Chapter 4, several API-based tools are available to monitor dropout (see bounce rate in Figure 4.14). Although API-based tools can help to monitor overall levels of dropout at the study level, stimulus development platform tools have to be used in order to monitor condition-specific dropout levels. Researchers should also report dropout levels in their manuscripts in order to alleviate reviewers' concerns about the potential threat of dropout to both the internal and the external validity of the research.

CONCLUSION

The central theme of this chapter is that there is high potential for sampling bias in any single study on Mechanical Turk if specific precautions are not employed. At the population level, Mechanical Turk has more than 30,000 workers who participate in studies each month. New workers are constantly joining the platform, with close to 4,500 fresh workers entering the pool each month (see Chapter 6). However, when sampling from the MTurk population, researchers are likely to access only a small fraction of these workers (e.g., Stewart et al., 2015), if they rely on current standard sampling techniques, which rely on minimum HIT completion criteria. Most samples will consist primarily of highly active superworkers. This problem becomes exacerbated as a HIT's wages increase because highly active workers are experts at finding high-paying HITs quickly. Superworkers differ in their demographic composition from other workers and are more likely to be young and male. Additionally, superworkers are more likely to have been influenced by their prior exposure to numerous research studies, thus leading to higher levels of satisficing and lower effect sizes.

Additional sampling challenges occur when workers are sampled at one time point. The time of day during which workers choose to participate in studies is correlated with multiple psychosocial and clinical outcomes, thus potentially biasing the external validity of studies. Finally, high dropout on MTurk is not uncommon and poses additional threats to both internal and external validity, particularly for longer HITs with lower wages in which dropout rates exceed 80%.

Although the potential for sampling bias on Mechanical Turk is high, bias can be ameliorated with the judicious use of tools available on MTurk and third-party API platforms. Requesters should use worker reputation qualifications and maximum HIT completion criteria to reduce participation rates among superworkers. Wages should be kept relatively high so as to reduce coverage bias and dropout. Researchers should also consider the use of gender-based quotas in order to create a more equitable sampling environment, particularly for high-paying HITs. The sampling best practices described in this chapter are summarized in Table 7.4 and can be used to set up studies in tandem with Appendix A at the end of Chapter 3 (see also Appendix A at the end of this chapter). Following these best practices can significantly reduce sampling bias and dropout rates and is likely to lead to higher levels of both internal and external validity when conducting research on Mechanical Turk.

APPENDIX A: BEST PRACTICES FOR SAMPLING

1. Use HIT completion history to exclude highly active workers rather than inactive workers.

   a. Exclude workers who have completed more than 5,000 HITs.

2. Allow workers who have completed fewer than 100 HITs into your study; the data quality of these workers is as good as that of others. These workers should be sought after because of high levels of naïveté.

   a. Do not rely on selectively recruiting workers with approval ratings as an effective way of screening out inattentive participants.

3. Set gender-based quotas to avoid male opt-in bias toward high-paying HITs.

4. Sample across multiple times of day and days of the week.

5. Be particularly careful about not collecting data at unusual times such as late at night or early in the morning.

6. Increase pay rates to avoid nonresponse bias among low-active workers (in tandem with 1a).

7. Experimental studies that randomly assign subjects to conditions should do the following:

   a. Monitor studies for high dropout rates.

   b. Increase hourly wages to significantly reduce dropout.

   c. Monitor differential dropout rates across conditions.

   d. Report overall dropout and differential dropout rates.

REFERENCES

Antypa, N., Vogelzangs, N., Meesters, Y., Schoevers, R., & Penninx, B. W. J. H. (2016). Chronotype associations with depression and anxiety disorders in a large cohort study. *Depression and Anxiety, 33*(1), 75–83.

Baker, R., Brick, J. M., Bates, N. A., Battaglia, M., Couper, M. P., Dever, J. A., . . .Tourangeau, R. (2013). Summary report of the AAPOR task force on non-probability sampling. *Journal of Survey Statistics and Methodology, 1*(2), 90–143.

Bialek, M., & Pennycook, G. (2017). The Cognitive Reflection Test is robust to multiple exposures. *Behavior Research Methods*, 1–7.

Birnbaum, M. H. (2004). Human research and data collection via the Internet. *Annual Review of Psychology, 55*(1), 803–832. doi:10.1146/annurev.psych.55.090902.141601

Bosnjak, M., & Tuten, T. L. (2001). Classifying response behaviors in web-based surveys. *Journal of Computer-Mediated Communication, 6*(3), JCMC636. doi:10.1111/j.1083-6101.2001.tb00124.x

Caliendo, M., Lee, W.-S., & Mahlstedt, R. (2017). The gender wage gap and the role of reservation wages: New evidence for unemployed workers. *Journal of Economic Behavior & Organization, 136*, 161–173.

Carrier, J., Monk, T. H., Buysse, D. J., & Kupfer, D. J. (1997). Sleep and morningness-eveningness in the "middle" years of life (20-59y). *Journal of Sleep Research, 6*(4), 230–237. doi:10.1111/j.1365-2869.1997.00230.x

Casey, L. S., Chandler, J., Levine, A. S., Proctor, A., & Strolovitch, D. Z. (2017). Intertemporal differences among MTurk workers: Time-based sample variations and implications for online data collection. *SAGE Open, 7*(2). doi:10.1177/2158244017712774

Chandler, J., Paolacci, G., Peer, E., Mueller, P., & Ratliff, K. A. (2015). Using nonnaive participants can reduce effect sizes. *Psychological Science, 26*(7), 1131–1139. doi:10.1177/0956797615585115

Chandler, J., Rosenzweig, C., Moss, A. J., Robinson, J., & Litman, L. (2019). Online panels in social science research: Expanding sampling methods beyond mechanical Turk. *Behavior Research Methods, 51*(5), 2022–2038.

Chelminski, I., Ferraro, F. R., Petros, T. V., & Plaud, J. J. (1999). An analysis of the "eveningness-morningness" dimension in "depressive" college students. *Journal of Affective Disorders, 52*(1-3), 19–29.

Collado Mateo, M. J., Díaz-Morales, J. F., Escribano Barreno, C., Delgado Prieto, P., & Randler, C. (2012). Morningness-eveningness and sleep habits among adolescents: Age and gender differences. *Psicothema, 24*(3), 410–415.

DeVoe, S. E., & House, J. (2016). Replications with MTurkers who are naïve versus experienced with academic studies: A comment on Connors, Khamitov, Moroz, Campbell, and Henderson (2015). *Journal of Experimental Social Psychology, 67*, 65–67. doi:10.1016/j.jesp.2015.11.004

Díaz-Morales, J. F., Ferrari, J. R., & Cohen, J. R. (2008). Indecision and avoidant procrastination: The role of morningness-eveningness and time perspective in chronic delay lifestyles. *The Journal of General Psychology, 135*(3), 228–240.

Fordsham, N., Moss, A. J., Krumholz, S. J., Roggina, T., Robinson, J., & Litman, L. (2019). Variation among mechanical Turk workers across time of day presents an opportunity and a challenge for research. *PsychArxiv.* doi:10.31234/osf.io/p8bns

Frederick, S. (2005). Cognitive reflection and decision making. *Journal of Economic Perspectives, 19*(4), 25–42. doi:10.1257/089533005775196732

Galesic, M. (2006). Dropouts on the web: Effects of interest and burden experienced during an online survey. *Journal of Official Statistics, 22*(2), 313.

Hauser, D., Paolacci, G., & Chandler, J. J. (2019). Common concerns with MTurk as a participant pool: Evidence and solutions. In *Handbook of research methods in consumer psychology.* New York: Routledge.

Litman, L., Robinson, J., Rosen Z., Rosenzweig, C., Waxman, J., & Bates, L.. (2020). The persistence of pay inequality: The gender wage gap in an anonymous online labor market. *PLOS ONE.*

Manfreda, K. L., & Vehovar, V. (2002). Survey design features influencing response rates in web surveys. In *The International Conference on Improving Surveys Proceedings* (pp. 25–28).

Merikanto, I., Lahti, T., Kronholm, E., Peltonen, M., Laatikainen, T., Vartiainen, E., . . .Partonen, T. (2013). Evening types are prone to depression. *Chronobiology International, 30*(5), 719–725.

O'Neil, K. M., Penrod, S. D., & Bornstein, B. H. (2003). Web-based research: Methodological variables' effects on dropout and sample characteristics. *Behavior Research Methods, Instruments, & Computers, 35*(2), 217–226. doi:10.3758/BF03202544

Peer, E., Brandimarte, L., Samat, S., & Acquisti, A. (2017). Beyond the Turk: Alternative platforms for crowdsourcing behavioral research. *Journal of Experimental Social Psychology*, *70*, 153–163. doi:10.1016/j.jesp.2017.01.006

Peer, E., Vosgerau, J., & Acquisti, A. (2014). Reputation as a sufficient condition for data quality on Amazon Mechanical Turk. *Behavior Research Methods*, *46*(4), 1023–1031. doi:10.3758/s13428-013-0434-y

Plaut, V. C., Markus, H. R., Treadway, J. R., & Fu, A. S. (2012). The cultural construction of self and well-being: A tale of two cities. *Personality and Social Psychology Bulletin*, *38*(12), 1644–1658.

Rand, D. G., Peysakhovich, A., Kraft-Todd, G. T., Newman, G. E., Wurzbacher, O., Nowak, M. A., & Greene, J. D. (2014). Social heuristics shape intuitive cooperation. *Nature Communications*, *5*(1). doi:10.1038/ncomms4677

Randler, C., Horzum, M. B., & Vollmer, C. (2014). Internet addiction and its relationship to chronotype and personality in a Turkish university student sample. *Social Science Computer Review*, *32*(4), 484–495.

Robinson, J., Rosenzweig, C., Moss, A. J., & Litman, L. (2019). Tapped out or barely tapped? Recommendations for how to harness the vast and largely unused potential of the Mechanical Turk participant pool. *PsyArXiv*.

Stewart, N., Ungemach, C., Harris, A. J., Bartels, D. M., Newell, B. R., Paolacci, G., & Chandler, J. (2015). The average laboratory samples a population of 7,300 Amazon Mechanical Turk workers. *Judgment and Decision Making*, *10*(5), 479.

Toepoel, V., Das, M., & Van Soest, A. (2008). Effects of design in web surveys: Comparing trained and fresh respondents. *Public Opinion Quarterly*, *72*(5), 985–1007.

Vehovar, V., Batagelj, Z., Manfreda, K. L., & Zaletel, M. (2002). Nonresponse in web surveys. *Survey Nonresponse*, 229–242.

Zhou, H., & Fishbach, A. (2016). The pitfall of experimenting on the web: How unattended selective attrition leads to surprising (yet false) research conclusions. *Journal of Personality and Social Psychology*, *111*(4), 493–504. doi:10.1037/pspa0000056

Zwaan, R. A., Pecher, D., Paolacci, G., Bouwmeester, S., Verkoeijen, P., Dijkstra, K., & Zeelenberg, R. (2017). Participant nonnaiveté and the reproducibility of cognitive psychology. *Psychonomic Bulletin & Review*, 1–5.

DATA REPRESENTATIVENESS OF ONLINE SAMPLES

Leib Litman, Jonathan Robinson, and Cheskie Rosenzweig

INTRODUCTION

Within the social sciences, concern about the representativeness and external validity of research samples has been described as a "near obsession" (Clifford, Jewell, & Waggoner, 2015). It thus comes as no surprise that the topic of Mechanical Turk's representativeness has received considerable attention in both peer-reviewed literature (e.g., Landers & Behrend, 2015) and the popular press (Searles & Ryan, 2015).

In this chapter we discuss issues pertaining to the representativeness of data collected on Mechanical Turk. The chapter begins with a broad overview of how representative samples are obtained, how surveys are conducted, and common sources of bias associated with creating sample frames. We then introduce the focal point of this chapter: the empirical fit-for-purpose framework. This framework avoids dichotomizing sample sources as either valid or invalid and instead takes an empirically driven approach to understanding when and under what conditions a sample source provides accurate estimates, given the project's specific measurement goals.

Researchers from different fields across the social sciences have different measurement goals and approach the topic of representativeness very differently as a result. For example, most psychologists and consumer researchers conduct studies that rely on students from university subject pools, a form of convenience sampling. The unrepresentativeness of these samples is typically not viewed as a problem by researchers within these fields because their goal is often to test theoretical ideas, by demonstrating that a predicted effect is observed, but not to estimate the size of an effect in the general population. In other fields, however, such as political science, sample representativeness is often extremely important because researchers sometimes seek to accurately estimate population parameters (e.g., Mutz, 2016).

This leads us to describe a simple taxonomy that categorizes research studies into two types of measurement goals—population oriented versus theory oriented—and three types of designs—those aimed at measuring frequency, experimental treatment effects, and association. This taxonomy can be used to identify the conditions under which MTurk samples provide a good "fit" to answer specific research questions.

Within this context, we evaluate the representativeness of data collected on Mechanical Turk. We review empirical evidence that compares the similarity of effect size estimates obtained in studies conducted on Mechanical Turk with those obtained in probability-based, nationally representative samples. Based on this research, MTurk samples have been shown to provide surprisingly similar, accurate estimates of population-level effect sizes, particularly for experimental studies. In the vast majority of experiments, the effects obtained in both samples are virtually identical. At the same time, at least in some cases, MTurk samples need to be adjusted through quota sampling to control for sample bias. The key points of this chapter are summarized in Table 8.2 and in Appendix A at the end of the chapter.

REPRESENTATIVENESS, SURVEYS, AND SURVEY SAMPLING

With the rise of modern societies in the Age of Enlightenment, countries increasingly sought to understand the demographics, behavior, and attitudes of their populations. As early as the 1600s, attempts were made in Germany and England to use birth and death rate data to estimate the size and growth rates of populations (Jahoda, 2007). Initially, it was thought that to accurately characterize a population it was necessary to conduct a census, a process whereby data are collected from each individual in the population. It was subsequently realized that measurements on each individual were not necessary and that small samples could be used to make valid population-level inferences. Survey methodology and survey sampling theory were developed to support the process of obtaining valid population estimates from smaller samples drawn from survey data.

In the beginning of the 20th century, several methods of sampling were considered to yield "representative" data (Neyman, 1934). One method was referred to as purposive selection. As described in an early report of the International Statistical Institute, *purposive selection* consists of "groups of units which it is presumed will give the sample the same characteristics as the whole" (Bowley, 1926). Purposive selection aims to match the sample to the population based on known attributes of the population such as age, education, and family composition. Today, purposive selection is referred to as *quota sampling* (see Baker et al., 2013).

The second method is known as *random* or *probability-based sampling*. In probability-based sampling, every member of the population has an equal chance of being in the sample. Rather than using a top-down approach in which the researcher assembles a sample to fit the demographic characteristics of the population, as is done in quota sampling, in probability-based sampling the randomly selected units naturally take on the distributional characteristics of the population. In the early part of the 20th century, Fisher (1922) developed the mathematical foundations of probability sampling. Purposive sampling, by contrast, did not rest on a solid theoretical foundation. Further, purposive sampling was repeatedly demonstrated to produce biased and inaccurate results compared to the results of probability-based sampling approaches. Due to the wealth of empirical evidence showing the superiority of random sampling compared to purposive sampling (Biemer & Lyberg, 2003; Groves & Lyberg, 2010), by the 1950s the random sampling approach had been firmly established as the gold standard method for obtaining representative samples (Seng, 1951).

While survey methodology has evolved in the past 80 years (see Converse, 2017; Frankel & Frankel, 1987; Groves et al., 2009, for a review), probability sampling continues to be the most widely used methodology for acquiring representative samples today (Couper, Dever, & Gile, 2013). Indeed, as described by Baker et al. (2013), there is currently a general consensus that the terms *probability sampling* and *scientific study* are synonymous, and that a sample should not be referred to as being representative unless the sample was acquired using a probability-based sampling approach.

THE METHODOLOGY OF SURVEY SAMPLING

Survey studies are a particular kind of study whose goal is to accurately estimate population-level parameters, such as opinions about political candidates and consumer products, or the prevalence of behaviors and states such as unemployment. These studies are conducted in four distinct steps (see Couper & Nicholls, 1998):

1. **Identifying a population of interest.** For example, a population may be all residents of the United States, breast cancer patients, or likely voters.

2. **Selecting a sampling frame.** A sampling frame is a specific group of people from which the sample will be drawn. A sampling frame might consist of

undergraduates at a specific university taking introductory psychology courses, Mechanical Turk, an opt-in online panel, or a national registry of telephone numbers. A sampling frame differs from a population in that, under almost all circumstances, not every individual in the population will be reachable by the survey. Individuals who cannot be reached are not part of the sampling frame. For example, if a survey uses random digit dialing, then only people with a telephone will be part of the sampling frame. While it is not ideal, it is unavoidable that the sampling frame from which the sample is obtained will not be the same as the population. To the extent the frame differs from the population on variables that will be measured in the survey, there is coverage error for those variables. Selecting a sampling frame that closely corresponds to the population is a critical component of probability sampling. Indeed, random sampling from a non representative sampling frame will yield results that are as biased as the frame.

3. **Drawing a sample from the sampling frame.** Samples can be drawn in a variety of ways, including random sampling, quota sampling, or convenience sampling. The way in which a sample is drawn from the frame can further introduce multiple forms of bias (see Chapter 7).

4. **Collecting and analyzing data.** Post–data collection adjustment can have a significant impact on the representativeness of results. In both probability based and nonprobability samples, data can be weighted to obtain more accurate population estimates. A variety of adjustment techniques such as propensity matching and raking are commonly used for this purpose (for an overview, see Callegaro, Villar, Krosnick, & Yeager, 2014sizes of experimental manipulations Association).

MECHANICAL TURK AS A SAMPLING FRAME

When researchers sample participants from Mechanical Turk they are using Mechanical Turk as a sampling frame. A key feature of Mechanical Turk as a sampling frame is that workers choose to join the platform. Thus, Mechanical Turk can be thought of as an opt-in panel because participants "opt in" rather than being selected by a random process. Sampling frames that consist of participants who opted in to a panel suffer from specific sources of bias, including coverage bias, self-selection bias, and attrition bias (see Tourangeau, Conrad, & Couper, 2013). Due to these biases, Mechanical Turk cannot be considered a sampling frame of the U.S. population. In other words, samples drawn from Mechanical Turk cannot be considered to represent the people in the United States who are not on Mechanical Turk.

Bias Associated With the Opt-In Process

Factors that systematically covary with the opt-in process bias the sampling frame. If younger people are more likely to opt in to a panel, as is the case on Mechanical Turk, then the panel will not be representative of the U.S. population in terms of age and variables that covary with age such as political opinions, marital status, number of children, income, multiple attitudinal factors (e.g., Alwin, Cohen, & Newcomb, 1991; Oxley et al., 2008), as well as many psychological outcomes (e.g., Ng & Feldman, 2010; Rhodes, 1983). In addition to observed sources of bias, such as age, there may be myriad unobserved variables that bias the sample in ways that are unexpected and difficult to measure.

For these reasons, all sampling frames in which individuals choose to become members are biased by the opt-in process. Chapter 6 described the demographic composition of the MTurk population. We saw that the MTurk population differs from the general population of the United States along multiple dimensions. Most strikingly, MTurk workers are younger, more educated, less politically diverse, less religious, and less likely to be married and have children relative to the U.S. population (Berinsky, Huber, & Lenz, 2012; Clifford et al., 2015; Krupnikov & Levine, 2014; Paolacci et al., 2010). The extent to which these demographic biases pose a challenge to the validity of data collected on Mechanical Turk will depend on several factors, including the nature of the study and its measurement goals.

THE FIT-FOR-PURPOSE FRAMEWORK

Mechanical Turk samples can be subject to various forms of bias. This presence of bias is sometimes used as an a priori justification for treating results obtained on Mechanical Turk as being nonrepresentative or, in extreme cases, invalid (see Kahan, 2013). This approach sees representativeness as a dichotomy according to which a sample is either bias free and thus valid or contains bias and thus is invalid. An alternative approach was articulated at the 1989 presidential address of the American Association of Public Opinion Research (Mitofsky, 1989). This approach laid the foundation for what would later become known as the fit-for-purpose framework (Baker et al., 2013). The address articulated three key principles: (a) sampling methodology evolves, (b) evaluating a sampling methodology involves a consideration of trade-offs, and (c) sampling methodology should fit a study's purpose.

Sampling Methodology Evolves With Technological Innovation

Probability-based sampling methodology has shifted dramatically over the years. Probability-based sampling originally was based on at-home and face-to-face interviews.

By the 1970s, however, the predominant method became telephone interviews in which lists of telephone numbers were obtained from national registries and respondents were selected using random digit dialing (RDD) (see Lyberg et al., 1997). In subsequent decades the cost of interviewers and the labor-intensive nature of running a data collection center, which are requirements of RDD sampling, caused the field to shift toward using computer-assisted survey information collection (CASIC). Initially, CASIC involved the use of digitized voice presentation to replace the human interviewer. As the number of survey organizations grew dramatically from the 1970s to the 1990s, the use of electronic questionnaires became dominant. Eventually, some companies started using electronic online panels in place of phone interviews altogether. In 1986, using a random sampling frame, researchers recruited participants in Dutch households into the first online probability-based sample. These households were provided with computers and a telephone-based dial-up connection, so that they could submit their survey responses electronically. These kinds of efforts in turn led to the growth of online probability-based sampling panels that use online respondents exclusively (Berrens, Bohara, Jenkins-Smith, Silva, & Weimer, 2003; Best, Krueger, Hubbard, & Smith, 2001; Hays, Liu, & Kapteyn, 2015; Saris & de Pijper, 1986) (see Chapter 10 for further details about online probability-based samples).

Considering Trade-Offs

Every technological development within sampling methodology was initially met with deep suspicion. Even the switch from in-home to telephone interviews—something that is standard in the most rigorous probability-based samples today—was considered unreliable by the "elder statesmen" (Mitofsky, 1989) in the field. Indeed, some observers even considered the use of statistical weights to be "cooking the data" (Mitofsky, 1989). However, technological advances also provided multiple methodological advantages. For example, telephone interviews provided the ability to have supervision of interviewers, something not feasible with the more methodologically pure at-home interviews. Similarly, while deviating in some ways from previously established and accepted standards, every technological innovation described above carried with it significant advantages of scale, speed of data collection, reductions in cost, and often the ability to reach populations that otherwise would not be feasible. Thus, while some techniques introduced what at first appeared to be less rigorous practices, consideration of their advantages eventually led to their widespread adoption, ultimately benefiting the field.

Fitting a Sampling Methodology to a Study's Purpose

These considerations led to the key principle of the fit-for-purpose framework: different studies have different purposes, and sampling methodology should correspond to the purpose of the survey, rather than to a theoretical gold standard. As articulated by Mitofsky (1989), "It is reasonable for a researcher to conduct his or her research using any design that fits the problem, provided there is proper disclosure of their methods and its limitations." A sample that has bias may still be appropriate to use despite its limitations, if that sampling methodology offers considerable other advantages and allows researchers to answer the specific questions they are asking. Within this framework, "frequently, legitimate conclusions are possible and sometimes those conclusions are important" even when probability-based methods are not used at all (Mitofsky, 1989).

Recent technological advances have put online convenience samples like Mechanical Turk at researchers' fingertips. What are the advantages of these new methodological resources? Although MTurk samples are not probability based, which conclusions derived from these convenience samples can be considered legitimate?

Empirically Driven Fit-for-Purpose Framework

Within the fit-for-purpose framework, sampling methodology should be considered within the context of the research questions that are addressed. Here, we describe a simple taxonomy that will help to identify the categories of research that are "fit" to be conducted on Mechanical Turk and other online platforms. This taxonomy is driven by both theoretical considerations and empirical evidence. As such, this *empirically driven fit-for-purpose framework* is subject to modification over time, as new evidence about data quality and validity emerges in this fast-paced field.

Representativeness: Is It Important, and If So, When?

Despite the near universal acceptance of probability-based sampling as the most accurate survey method for obtaining population estimates, the vast majority of studies in the social and behavioral sciences do not use probability-based sampling for sample acquisition. Consistent with the fit-for-purpose framework, for the vast majority of studies, researchers do not see probability-based sampling as necessary, given the goals of most social and behavioral research.

In the early years of social psychology research, participants were recruited from a diverse range of sources (see Sears, 1986, for a review). Beginning in the 1960s, the field shifted toward the use of the undergraduate subject pool as an almost exclusive source of participant recruitment. Sears (1986) reported that 85% of published articles in major social psychology journals used undergraduate research participants in the 1980s. This trend continued in subsequent decades and across other fields. Peterson (2001) reported a similar rate of 87% in the field of consumer research.

As the use of undergraduate subject pools, and convenience samples more broadly, became more widespread across the social and behavioral sciences, a considerable literature emerged on the debate about the use of convenience samples in scientific research. As early as the 1960s, strong opinions were expressed both for (Schultz, 1969) and against (McGuire, 1967; Oakes, 1972) the use of undergraduate samples in psychology and other fields (Dill, 1964). A full review of this vast literature is beyond the scope of this book. This debate spans many decades and disciplines and continues to this day (e.g., Abelman, 1996; Ashton & Kramer, 1980; Baker et al., 2013; Barr & Hitt, 1986; Basil, 1996; Covin & Brush, 1993; Dobbins, Lane, & Steiner, 1988a, 1998b; Gordon, Slade, & Schmitt, 1986; Greenberg, 1987; Hayes, 2017; Henrich, Heine, & Norenzayan, 2010; Oakes, 1972; Remus, 1986; Schultz, 1969; Slade & Gordon, 1988; Sparks, 1995a, 1995b; Tourangeau, Conrad, & Couper, 2013).

The debate about the representativeness of undergraduate subject pools is relevant for evaluating Mechanical Turk as a valid source of data for a number of reasons. First, the choice of using Mechanical Turk is almost never made at the expense of using probability-based representative samples. Instead, the choice is typically between using one type of convenience sample (undergraduate subject pool) and another (Mechanical Turk). Additionally, the literature that has emerged from the discussions of validity of the undergraduate participant pool provides important theoretical considerations to inform and contextualize the current discussion about the use of Mechanical Turk and, more broadly, other online and offline nonprobability samples. The main themes that emerged from this literature are that the importance of representativeness critically depends on (a) the study's measurement goals and (b) the study's design.

Measurement Goals and Design Types

Measurement Goals

Measurement goals have typically been divided into two types: (a) studies whose goal is to arrive at precise population estimates with generalizable data and (b) studies that have the goal of testing a theory in a context that has the potential to provide evidence for or against the theory. Calder, Phillips, and Tybout (1981) refer to this distinction as effects-oriented research and theory-oriented research, respectively. Here, rather than using the term *effects-oriented research,* we will refer to *population-oriented research.* Specifically, population-oriented research focuses on accurately describing a population. *Theory-oriented research* focuses on testing the predictions of theories.

Design Types

Study designs are typically divided into three types: (a) studies that aim to describe the frequencies or proportions with which something occurs, (b) experimental studies that use random assignment for causal inference, and (c) studies of association between variables of interest. Evaluating the fit of Mechanical Turk depends on both the study type (population oriented versus theory oriented) and the study's measurement goals (frequency versus experimental effect versus association). In the discussion that follows we provide a framework for evaluating Mechanical Turk's representativeness, given the specific goal and design of a research study.

Study Type 1: Measuring Frequency
Population-Oriented Frequency Studies

Some research is designed to measure the frequency or the proportion with which something occurs in a population. Political polls are the most common examples of such studies. Political polls aim to provide measurements that are as precise as possible, and they usually have an applied component. Their goal is to measure the percentage of the population that is likely to support a specific political party, candidate, or policy, with as much precision as possible.

Frequency studies are the least common type of study in social and behavioral science fields such as psychology and consumer research. However, there are times when measuring the frequency with which a phenomenon occurs in a population becomes an important research topic in any field.

For example, Simons and Chabris (2011) examined the percentage of the U.S. population that has misconceptions about how memory works. This question has critical implications for forensic psychology, eyewitness testimony, and memory research more broadly. Specifically, it is important, for both theoretical and practical reasons, to understand the extent to which facts that are known about memory from psychological science are understood by the general public, especially when such information is relevant for the way in which juries evaluate evidence.

Notably, Simons and Chabris (2011) found that 52% of the U.S. population believes that hypnosis is useful in helping witnesses accurately recall details of crimes; 38% of the U.S. population believes that the testimony of one confident eyewitness should be enough to convict a defendant of a crime; and 47% of the general public believes that once a person forms a memory, that memory does not change. In contrast, not a single memory expert believed these statements to be true.

Two aspects of this study are noteworthy with regard to methodological considerations of representativeness. First, the study was designed to measure the frequency with which people hold certain beliefs about memory. Second, the measurement goal was to provide a precise assessment of these beliefs in the general population. Thus, this study is categorized as a *population-oriented frequency study*.

When the goal is to measure precisely the frequency with which something occurs in the population, Mechanical Turk should not be considered a good fit for the purpose of the study. Indeed, Simons and Chabris (2011) did not use Mechanical Turk to collect their data, nor did they use any other convenience or opt-in sample. Instead, a random-digit-dialing methodology was used to acquire a probability sample, from which the results could be extrapolated accurately to the general U.S. population.

Theory-Oriented Frequency Studies

For some frequency studies, precise measurement is not the goal. Instead, the goal of such studies might be to provide initial data that can be useful for evaluating a theory, or to get an initial very general estimate of the frequency with which something might occur in the population. For example, Zigerell (in press) examined the frequency with which people in the U.S. population hold beliefs about eugenics. The goal of the study was not to measure precisely this belief in the U.S. population. Instead, the goal was to present initial evidence for the hypothesis that there may be nontrivially high levels of support for eugenics among the U.S. general public. Because providing precise measurement was not this study's goal, it should be categorized as *a theory-oriented frequency study*.

Zigerell (in press) conducted the study using a sample of 500 MTurk workers. The findings indicated that close to 40% of participants believe that people who commit crimes, have low intelligence scores, or are poor should not have children. Because this study was collected on a nonprobability MTurk sample, the frequency estimate of 40% cannot be relied on to be a precise measure of how common such beliefs are in the U.S. population. At the same time, the findings provide initial evidence that such beliefs in the U.S. population are likely to be nontrivially high. Even this interpretation should be made cautiously. There are at least some cases in which the frequency of a phenomenon measured on Mechanical Turk can be vastly inflated relative to the U.S. population. For example, rates of technology use or participation in the gig economy are likely to be significantly higher on Mechanical Turk compared to the general population. Thus, this interpretation should be made with caution.

Consistent with the advice of Mitofsky (1989) described previously, Zigerell (in press) reports that a key limitation of this study was that it used "a convenience sample, so strong inferences should not be drawn about patterns in the population." The contribution of the study was to show that future studies of belief in eugenics using probability samples are likely warranted to provide a more precise measurement. The advantages of using Mechanical Turk to provide such initial estimates of population frequencies is that the data can be collected very quickly and inexpensively. Data collected from such studies can offer an initial glimpse that can guide decisions about the allocation of resources for more resource-intensive probability-based samples.

Accuracy of Frequency Studies on Mechanical Turk

At least some researchers have attempted to use Mechanical Turk for population-oriented frequency studies (Emerson Polling, 2019). The accuracy of such studies is of interest because it provides a way to gauge how closely attitudes and behaviors of MTurk participants match those of the general population. To examine the accuracy of population-oriented frequency studies conducted on MTurk samples, CloudResearch conducts ongoing MTurk polls with question wording that is identical to contemporaneous probability-based samples. The goal of these polls is to compare the results of MTurk samples directly to national probability-based studies. The results of these polls are available on the CloudResearch website (https://metrics.cloudresearch.com/).

In one series of studies, CloudResearch conducted a presidential approval poll every week for 12 weeks from March to June 2019. The basis for comparison was FiveThirtyEight.com, a polling aggregate that averages across dozens of probability polls including Ipsos, YouGov, Harris, Rasmussen and others. The results revealed a reasonable level of agreement between the results of Mechanical Turk and probability-based samples. In every case, the MTurk sample accurately indicated that more people disapproved of President Trump than approved. Across all 12 weeks, the MTurk samples differed by three percentage points on average for the approval and disapproval ratings compared to the polling aggregate (see Table 8.1). On most weeks, the results did not differ from the national probability samples by more than three percentage points, with the highest difference in any of the weeks being six percentage points. While this level of discrepancy might seem high given some recent razor-thin electoral outcomes, this can be considered a reasonably good outcome, given that there is a wide range of variability among the different probability polls themselves. Indeed, many of the probability polls deviate from the aggregated average by more than five percentage points on any given day.

All polling data collected by CloudResearch were weighted by multiple demographic variables. When the results are not weighted, the difference between MTurk polls and probability samples can be substantial. For example, Richey and Taylor (2012) polled more than 500 MTurk participants on the day of the 2012 presidential election. They found that 73% of MTurk participants voted for President Barack Obama and only 15% voted for former Massachusetts governor

TABLE 8.1 ● A LONGITUDINAL PRESIDENTIAL APPROVAL POLL CONDUCTED ON MTURK AND PROBABILITY-BASED SAMPLES						
	MTurk		Poll Aggregate (FiveThirtyEight.com)		Difference	
Survey Date	Approve	Disapprove	Approve	Disapprove	Approve	Disapprove
3.10.2019	47	49	41	53	−6	4
3.17.2019	44	51	41	54	−3	3
3.24.2019	41	55	42	53	1	−2
3.31.2019	46	49	42	53	−4	4
4.07.2019	38	57	42	53	4	−4
4.14.2019	43	53	42	53	−1	0
4.21.2019	47	49	42	53	−5	4
4.28.2019	38	57	41	53	3	−4
5.05.2019	42	54	43	52	1	−2
5.12.2019	41	54	42	53	1	−1
5.19.2019	40	55	42	53	2	−2

Note: Values show the percentage of approval and disapproval of President Trump.

Mitt Romney. In the actual election, 47.2% of people voted for Romney. Thus, the unweighted MTurk data underestimated support for Romney by more than 32 percentage points.

These results demonstrate an important principle about the MTurk population. Although the proportion of liberal, younger, and less religious individuals is higher on Mechanical Turk compared to the U.S. population, they behave similarly. In other words, the political opinions of liberal and conservative individuals on Mechanical Turk are similar to the opinions of liberals and conservatives outside of Mechanical Turk. For this reason, adjusting for the proportions with which subgroups appear in a sample by weighting the data or by quota sampling can substantially improve the accuracy of results.

At the same time, a key limitation of quota sampling is that it is impossible to know which subgroups should be used for weighting in any specific case. For some polls, political affiliation is the only variable that matters, whereas for others the relevant subgroups can be regional or even occupation specific.

Because of the uncertainty about how cases should be weighted, studies that have evaluated the accuracy of nonprobability online samples are consistent in showing that statistical adjustment generally removes only part of the bias. Tourangeau et al. (2013) reviewed seven studies that compared the results of online nonprobability samples to probability-based national surveys. In each study, the nonprobability sample was drawn from a large online opt-in panel typically used for market research. In each case, the data were statistically corrected based on weighting and other techniques (see Tourangeau et al., 2013). Following statistical adjustment, most studies significantly reduced some but not all of the overall error (see Levay, Freese, & Druckman, 2016, for similar results). These results reinforce the general principle outlined at the beginning of the chapter, which is that quota sampling is not a substitute for probability sampling in population-oriented frequency research.

To summarize, the political attitudes of major demographic subgroups on Mechanical Turk are similar to those outside of Mechanical Turk. But the proportions with which these demographic groups appear in MTurk samples differ substantially from the U.S. population. Weighting the data can substantially increase accuracy, often producing results that are indistinguishable from probability-based samples. However, because it is not possible to know how the data should be weighted for any specific case, the results of polls from nonprobability samples cannot be relied on to produce accurate estimates of the U.S. population. For these reasons, research that aims to measure population frequencies precisely (population-oriented frequency research) should not be considered a good fit for Mechanical Turk. However, when the goal is to provide initial estimates that can guide future research (theory-oriented frequency research), Mechanical Turk's fit-for-purpose is high.

Study Type 2: Measuring Experimental Treatment Effects

In the previous section we discussed population frequency research, where the goal is to measure the frequency or proportion with which something occurs in the population. A much more common research goal in the social and behavioral sciences is to examine causal relationships between variables. Causal relationships are established by experiments, in which participants are randomly assigned to different levels of an independent variable. Multiple factors make experimental research different from frequency research with regard to considerations of representativeness.

First, it is rarely important to measure the size of an experimental effect precisely as it appears in the population. In most cases, the goal of an experiment is to evaluate a specific theory by showing that a manipulation produces an effect in some sample. Theories make predictions about whether or not a manipulation will produce a statistically significant difference between groups, and they often do not address the specific size of the effect. Thus, so long as the likelihood of committing a Type I error (finding a difference between groups where one does not exist) or Type II error (not finding a difference between groups where one does exist) is sufficiently small, a sample's fit-for-purpose should be considered to be high. Because the goal of most experimental studies does not include precise measurement of effects sizes but, rather, involves an evaluation of the predictions of theories regarding group differences, the vast majority of experimental studies are classified as theory-oriented experimental research.

Second, confounding variables that might normally bias a sample are equally distributed across experimental conditions. The role that random selection plays in eliminating bias in surveys is accomplished by random assignment in experimental manipulations (Callegaro et al., 2014; Kish, 2004). Thus, even though the precise measure of an effect in experimental studies is less important, convenience samples are typically expected to match probability-based samples more closely in results of effect sizes than they might in results of frequency studies.

Finally, experimental effects are much less susceptible to group differences than are measurements of frequency. This is referred to as the *general homogeneity of treatment effects* assumption (see Hayes, 2017, p. 5). For example, if an experimental effect is the same across liberal and conservative participants, then the proportion of liberal participants in a sample will not affect the outcome. However, if an effect is much stronger for conservatives than for liberals and a sample has few conservatives, then the effect will be weakened by the composition of the sample. The homogeneity of treatment effects assumption states that experimental treatment effects are the same across demographic groups.

Because experiments are typically considered theory oriented, and because experimental effects are assumed to be homogeneous across demographic groups, experiments are commonly conducted on convenience samples. This is true in both the social and behavioral sciences, as well as in medical clinical trials.

There are, however, times when the goal of experiments is to measure precisely an effect as it appears in a population. For example, in political polling the goal may be to randomly assign subjects to different versions of a political message and to measure the percentage of the population that is affected by such changes in wording. In such studies, a difference of a few percentage points can mean the difference in allocating millions of dollars toward a specific campaign within a particular region of the country.

Such experimental studies would be categorized as population-oriented experimental research. Such experiments are becoming increasingly common and are reviewed in depth by Mutz (2016). In the sections that follow, we examine Mechanical Turk's fit-for-purpose for both theory-oriented and population-oriented experimental research.

Theory-Oriented Experimental Research

One way to examine the validity of experimental results obtained on Mechanical Turk is to compare those results to similar studies conducted on probability-based samples. Because of the increasing frequency with which probability-based experimental studies are currently being conducted, it is now possible to see how Mechanical Turk and other convenience samples compare to probability-based samples in terms of effect sizes of experimental manipulations.

In one series of studies, 23 experiments including 36 treatment effects were conducted on Mechanical Turk and the TESS nationally representative probability-based sample (Mullinix, Leeper, Druckman, & Freese, 2015). The studies on Mechanical Turk and TESS samples used the exact same language and design, allowing for direct comparisons of treatment effects to be made. These experiments are particularly instructive because they range across a wide spectrum of the social and behavioral sciences, including eight in political science, six in sociology, three in psychology, and several others from communications, education, law, and public health.

The results showed that in more than 80% of experimental effects, MTurk samples perfectly replicated the results of nationally representative studies. Further, in none of the cases were the MTurk results opposite to the probability-based results. These findings show that in the overwhelming number of cases, experimental effects observed on Mechanical Turk replicate the effects of probability-based samples (very low Type I error) and do not produce results that are not observed in probability-based samples (very low Type 2 error). Thus, because the likelihood of Type I and Type II errors on MTurk samples is low, extant empirical evidence supports the claim that Mechanical Turk has a high level of fit-for-purpose for *theory-oriented experimental research*.

The Homogeneity of Treatment Effects Assumption

As mentioned multiple times throughout this book, the proportion of many major demographic subgroups on Mechanical Turk differs substantially from that of the U.S. population. How does this difference in the proportion with which certain groups appear in the MTurk population affect the outcomes of experimental manipulations? This question is not specific to Mechanical Turk but, rather, applies to any source of convenience samples, including the undergraduate subject pool. As such, this question has been the source of debate in the social and behavioral sciences for decades. One aspect of this debate relies on the homogeneity of treatment effects assumption. If treatment effects are the same across demographic groups, then the proportions with which those groups appear in the sample will not affect the outcome of an experiment.

To examine the homogeneity of treatment effects assumption, Coppock, Leeper, and Mullinix (2018) compared 27 experimental treatment effects on Mechanical Turk and a probability sample. Each of these effects was compared across different demographic groups, including different age, education, gender, political ideology, political party affiliation, and race groups, for a total of 394 subgroup comparisons. Out of all these analyses, every result within every subgroup was in the same direction on Mechanical Turk that it was in the probability-based sample, and in only 15% of the studies were the results significantly different in magnitude.

These results show that experimental treatment effects tend to be the same no matter what the composition of the sample. For most experiments, whether they are conducted on young, old, liberal, conservative, white, or minority participants, the results will remain largely the same. Thus, whether a convenience sample will have more or fewer participants from any of these groups compared to the U.S. population will not change the outcome of the study. These findings provide strong support for the homogeneity of treatment effects assumption (e.g., Hayes, 2017), showing that in the vast majority of cases, experimental treatments are mostly homogeneous across subgroups.

Exceptions to the Homogeneity of Treatment Effects Assumption

The studies described in the preceding section demonstrated that experimental treatment effects are largely the same across demographic groups (Coppock et al., 2018). However, there are exceptions to this general rule. In a study reported by Mullinix et al. (2015), a probability sample's support for abortion decreased significantly after participants were asked to think about God's attitude toward abortion. The same effect could not be replicated on Mechanical Turk across multiple attempts (Chandler, Rosenzweig, Moss, Robinson, & Litman, 2019; Mullinix et al., 2015).

In a series of follow-up studies, Litman et al. (2019) found that less religious people's opinions about abortion are not affected by a God-oriented prime and in fact can produce results in the opposite direction. Because Mechanical Turk consists of participants who are overwhelmingly less religious than the general population, it is not surprising that such experimental effects would be reduced with samples drawn from the MTurk population. Importantly, however, when quota sampling was used to match the proportion of religious participants on MTurk to the U.S. population, the results on Mechanical Turk replicated the probability sample's findings.

These results show that there are exceptions to the homogeneity of treatment effects assumption. There are specific studies in which the demographic composition of the sample directly influences experimental outcomes. The violation of the homogeneity of treatment effects assumption matters most for those studies in which the demographics that bias the study (e.g., religiosity) are systematically skewed on Mechanical Turk. Specifically, in the current example, religious groups are both less common on Mechanical Turk compared to the general population and less affected by the experimental manipulation.

MTurk studies that are most likely to be affected by treatment effects heterogeneity are those in which the experimental treatment effect may be correlated with variables such as political orientation, age, education, religiosity, family composition, and general knowledge. As Coppock et al. (2018) showed, the vast majority of studies are immune to such influences. However, when researchers suspect that outcomes may be correlated with these demographics, the use of quota sampling to control for their distribution is warranted.

Population-Oriented Experimental Studies

Although most experimental studies are categorized as theory oriented, there are increasingly more studies that are being conducted to measure the precise effect that an experiment has in the general population. Such studies are common when the goal is to examine how different messages may influence attitudes toward a political candidate or how different messages may influence attitudes based on different versions of a health-oriented public service announcement (Mutz, 2016). In such studies, the goal is often not merely to establish that a change in the message will produce a statistically significant effect but, instead, to measure how large that effect will be and how many people in the general population such changes are likely to influence. Such studies would be classified as *population-oriented experimental studies.*

Because the outcomes of experiments are affected by demographics in at least some cases, the outcomes of the experiments conducted on convenience samples, including Mechanical Turk, cannot be relied on to produce exact population estimates. This is especially true because, as with frequency studies, the specific demographic groups that will influence the outcome of an experiment cannot be known for certain a priori.

As extant data demonstrate, Mechanical Turk is a reliable staging ground for experimental pilot studies in which the goal is to demonstrate whether a particular experimental treatment produces a statistically significant effect. When care is taken to control for key demographics, the likelihood of an experimental finding observed on Mechanical Turk replicating on a probability sample is high. Thus, researchers conducting population-oriented experimental studies may consider using Mechanical Turk to pilot their experiments. Such pilot studies can be conducted quickly and inexpensively, and they are likely to produce results that closely match those of probability-based samples. For population-oriented research, such pilot studies should be followed up with a probability-based sample for a more precise measurement of the treatment effects.

Study Type 3: Association Studies

Like experimental studies, studies of association are less likely to be influenced by sample bias than are studies of frequency. Unlike experimental and frequency studies, fewer systematic attempts have been made to compare associative effects on Mechanical Turk to those obtained on probability-based benchmarks. The studies that have been done are limited to political science research, but they are generally consistent with the findings on experimental treatment effects.

Clifford et al. (2015) compared the association between various political attitudes of MTurk workers to those found in data collected through the nationally representative ANES. The political attitudes included egalitarianism, moral traditionalism, authoritarianism, racial resentment, as well as other social and economic attitudes. An examination of 72 effect sizes found that 68 were similar on both platforms, with just 4 effect sizes being statistically different. For example, authoritarianism predicted social ideology more strongly on Mechanical Turk than in the ANES sample. However, even these effect sizes were in the same direction on Mechanical Turk as in the ANES sample.

More research needs to be conducted to compare effect sizes of association studies on Mechanical Turk to probability samples of the U.S. population in areas other than political science. However, the results obtained thus far are highly encouraging and consistent with the conclusion that studies that sample from Mechanical Turk are likely to come to the same conclusion as studies that sample from probability samples in both association and experimental studies (Clifford et al., 2015). This is true, so long as the goal of the research is theory oriented rather than population oriented.

Putting It All Together

The previous section distinguished among three types of studies: studies designed to measure frequency, studies designed to measure effect sizes of experimental manipulations, and studies designed to measure associations. In addition to these three design types, studies can also be categorized based on their measurement goals (population-oriented research versus theory-oriented research). Design types and measurement goals can be crossed, thus making a 2 × 3 framework shown in Table 8.2. This

TABLE 8.2 ● APPLYING THE FIT-FOR-PURPOSE FRAMEWORK TO DATA COLLECTION ON MTURK AND OTHER PLATFORMS			
Study Type			
Purpose of Research	**Frequency**	**Experimental**	**Association**
Population-Oriented Research (accurately describing a population)	Not fit-for-purpose. Fit for piloting initial data, with caution. Quota sampling and/or weighting must be used.	Fit for piloting initial data.	Fit for piloting initial data.
Theory-Oriented Research (testing the predictions of theories)	Rare. Fit to explore general hypotheses about prevalence, with caution. Quota sampling and/or weighting must be used.	Highest fit-for-purpose.	Fit-for purpose.

framework can be useful for evaluating the fit of Mechanical Turk and other sample sources to specific studies, given their design and measurement goals.

There is almost universal agreement that a distinction should be made between studies that aim to precisely measure a population value and those that do not. When the goal is to accurately describe population parameters—whether they be frequencies, experimental treatment effects, or associations—Mechanical Turk should not be relied on to achieve a high level of precision.

This is particularly true for studies of population frequencies. Even when the sample is adjusted by quota sampling or by statistical adjustments after data collection, there is often considerable discrepancy between Mechanical Turk and probability-based sample estimates. The magnitude of such discrepancies is likely to be highest in studies of population frequencies, but in both experimental and correlational research, parameter estimates obtained from Mechanical Turk should not be relied on to accurately describe the population.

At the same time, MTurk data can be used meaningfully to inform effects-oriented research programs. As Levay et al. (2016) suggest, "If used with care, observational researchers can use MTurk for developing a research program in that the data will generate useful inferences on which to build (i.e. they should not generate an unusual number of false negatives or false positives)." Probability-based data collection is very expensive and labor intensive. MTurk data can thus be usefully employed as a first-pass approximation that can point toward useful avenues to pursue in more expensive research efforts.

Many scientific studies do not see the precise estimates of the population as their primary goal. Rather, research in the social and behavioral sciences often falls into what Calder et al. (1981) referred to as theory-oriented research. The measurement goals of theory-oriented research are to collect data that provide evidence for or against a theory being tested. The research reviewed in this chapter shows that MTurk results are, in most cases, comparable to probability-based studies in terms of both directionality and effect sizes across a wide range of social and behavioral science fields. This research thus compellingly demonstrates that Mechanical Turk is "fit" to study such theory-oriented effects.

Many of the experimental treatment effects in the social sciences are homogeneous across demographic groups. However, some treatment effects are moderated by specific demographic or attitudinal variables that are highly skewed in the MTurk population. Extant research suggests that such moderation effects are rare and in many cases correctable. Over the many hundreds of effect sizes that have now been compared between Mechanical Turk and probability-based samples, there are, to our knowledge, no known cases in which discrepancies exist that cannot be corrected for by quota sampling or other statistical techniques.

At the same time, the possibility that bias may affect study outcomes always exists, and attempts should be made to replicate effects across other sample sources. As has been stressed with regard to undergraduate subject pools and other convenience samples, "it is critical to emphasize the importance of replications in the generation of knowledge" (Peterson, 2001).

CONCLUSION

This chapter described an empirically driven fit-for-purpose framework. This framework emphasizes that the extent to which a specific sampling methodology is fit for the purposes of a specific research project should be determined by empirical evidence. This evidence takes the form of comparing the sample source to previously validated probability-based benchmarks. The extent to which Mechanical Turk has been validated by such tests is perhaps surprising. Hundreds of effect sizes measured using samples drawn from Mechanical Turk have now been compared to probability-based, nationally representative benchmarks. The results of these studies compellingly demonstrate that the theory-oriented conclusions derived from studies conducted on Mechanical Turk will in most cases be the same as the conclusions drawn from studies conducted on probability-based samples. As such, Mechanical Turk should be viewed in the historical context of other technological developments, many of which were at first viewed with suspicion but subsequently became commonly used and, among many circles of researchers, indispensable. As long as MTurk samples are used to inform theory-oriented research, and reasonable attempts are made to control for known sources of bias, currently available evidence suggests that results obtained on Mechanical Turk will yield highly accurate and replicable effects in the large majority of cases.

APPENDIX A: BEST PRACTICES FOR ENSURING DATA REPRESENTATIVENESS

1. The empirically driven fit-for-purpose framework advocates considering the trade-offs between advantages of nonprobability samples against probability-based representative samples, and the use of replication, quota sampling, and statistical adjustment for improved external validity of convenience samples.

2. Convenience samples—including subject pools, Mechanical Turk, and non-probability-based online panels—should not be used to precisely estimate population frequencies.

3. Studies of experimental treatment effects and association replicate on Mechanical Turk in the vast majority of cases.

4. Effect sizes on Mechanical Turk closely match those of probability-based representative samples in the vast majority of cases.

5. Effect sizes on Mechanical Turk may not replicate, or may be significantly attenuated, when the dependent variable is strongly correlated with highly unrepresentative demographic variables such as religiosity and political attitudes.

6. Quota sampling and/or statistical adjustment after data collection may significantly improve replicability and should be strongly considered when the dependent variable is correlated with highly unrepresentative demographic variables such as religiosity and political attitudes.

REFERENCES

Abelman, R. (1996). Standpoint: Can we generalize from generation X? Not! *Journal of Broadcasting & Electronic Media, 40*(3), 441–446. doi:10.1080/08838159609364365

Alwin, D. F., Cohen, R. L., & Newcomb, T. M. (1991). *Political attitudes over the life span: The Bennington women after fifty years.* Madison: University of Wisconsin Press.

Ashton, R. H., & Kramer, S. S. (1980). Students as surrogates in behavioral accounting research: Some evidence. *Journal of Accounting Research, 18*(1), 1–15. doi:10.2307/2490389

Baker, R., Brick, J. M., Bates, N. A., Battaglia, M., Couper, M. P., Dever, J. A., . . .Tourangeau, R. (2013). Summary report of the AAPOR task force on non-probability sampling. *Journal of Survey Statistics and Methodology, 1*(2), 90–143. doi:10.1093/jssam/smt008

Barr, S. H., & Hitt, M. A. (1986). A comparison of selection decision models in manager versus student samples. *Personnel Psychology, 39*(3), 599–617. doi:10.1111/j.1744-6570.1986.tb00955.x

Basil, M. D. (1996). The use of student samples in communication research. *Journal of Broadcasting and Electronic Media, 40*(Summer), 431–440.

Berinsky, A. J., Huber, G. A., & Lenz, G. S. (2012). Evaluating online labor markets for experimental research: Amazon.com's Mechanical Turk. *Political Analysis, 20*(3), 351–368. doi:10.1093/pan/mpr057

Berrens, R. P., Bohara, A. K., Jenkins-Smith, H., Silva, C., & Weimer, D. L. (2003). The advent of Internet surveys for political research: A comparison of telephone and Internet samples. *Political Analysis, 11*(1), 1–22. doi:10.1093/pan/11.1.1

Best, S. J., Krueger, B., Hubbard, C., & Smith, A. (2001). An assessment of the generalizability of Internet surveys. *Social Science Computer Review, 19*(2), 131–145. doi:10.1177/089443930101900201

Biemer, P. P., & Lyberg, L. E. (2003). *Introduction to survey quality.* Hoboken, NJ: Wiley.

Bowley, A. L. (1926). Measurement of the precision attained in sampling. *Bulletin of the International Statistical Institute, 54*(1), 1–62.

Calder, B. J., Phillips, L. W., & Tybout, A. M. (1981). Designing research for application. *Journal of Consumer Research, 8*(2), 197–207. doi:10.1086/208856

Callegaro, M., Villar, A., Krosnick, J., & Yeager, D. (2014). A critical review of studies investigating the quality of data obtained with online panels. In M. Callegaro, R. Baker, J. Bethlehem, A. Goritz, J. Krosnick, & P. Lavrakas (Eds.), *Online panel research: A data quality perspective* (pp. 23–53). Hoboken, NJ: Wiley.

Chandler, J., Rosenzweig, C., Moss, A. J., Robinson, J., & Litman, L. (2019). Online panels in social science research: Expanding sampling methods beyond Mechanical Turk. *Behavior Research Methods, 51*(5), 2022–2038.

Clifford, S., Jewell, R. M., & Waggoner, P. D. (2015). Are samples drawn from Mechanical Turk valid for research on political ideology? *Research & Politics, 2*(4), 2053168015622072. doi:10.1177/2053168015622072

Converse, J. M. (2017). *Survey research in the United States: Roots and emergence 1890-1960.* London, U.K.: Routledge.

Coppock, A., Leeper, T. J., & Mullinix, K. J. (2018). Generalizability of heterogeneous treatment effect estimates across samples. *Proceedings of the National Academy of Sciences, 115*(49), 12441–12446.

Couper, M. P., Dever, J. A., & Gile, K. J. (2013). *Report of the AAPOR task force on non-probability sampling.* Oakbrook Terrace, IL: AAPOR.

Couper, M. P., & Nicholls, W. L. (1998). The history and development of computer assisted survey information collection methods. *Computer Assisted Survey Information Collection*, 1–21.

Covin, T. J., & Brush, C. C. (1993). A comparison of student and human resource professional attitudes toward work and family issues. *Group & Organization Management, 18*(1), 29–49. doi:10.1177/1059601193181003

Dill, W. R. (1964). Desegregation or integration? Comments about contemporary research on organizations. *New Perspectives in Organization Research*, 39–52.

Dobbins, G. H., Lane, I. M., & Steiner, D. D. (1988a). A further examination of student babies and laboratory bath water: A response to Slade and Gordon. *Journal of Organizational Behavior, 9*(4), 377–378. doi:10.1002/job.4030090410

Dobbins, G. H., Lane, I. M., & Steiner, D. D. (1988b). A note on the role of laboratory methodologies in applied behavioural research: Don't throw out the baby with the bath water. *Journal of Organizational Behavior, 9*(3), 281–286. doi:10.1002/job.4030090308

Emerson Polling. (2019). June national poll: All eyes on the Democratic debates. Retrieved from http://emersonpolling.com/2019/06/24/june-national-poll-all-eyes-on-the-democratic-debates-biden-sanders-and-warren-separate-from-the-field/

Fisher, R. A. (1922). On the mathematical foundations of theoretical statistics. *Philosophical Transactions of the Royal Society of London. Series A, Containing Papers of a Mathematical or Physical Character, 222*(594-604), 309–368.

Frankel, M. R., & Frankel, L. R. (1987). Fifty years of survey sampling in the United States. *Public Opinion Quarterly, 51*(4 Pt. 2), S127–S138. doi:10.1093/poq/51.4_PART_2.S127

Gordon, M. E., Slade, L. A., & Schmitt, N. (1986). The "science of the sophomore" revisited: From conjecture to empiricism. *Academy of Management Review, 11*(1), 191–207.

Greenberg, J. (1987). The college sophomore as guinea pig: Setting the record straight. *Academy of Management Review, 12*(1), 157–159. doi:10.5465/amr.1987.4306516

Groves, R. M., Fowler, F. J., Couper, M. L., Lepkowski, J. M., Singer, E., & Tourangeau, R. (2009). *Survey methodology* (2nd ed.). Hoboken, NJ: Wiley.

Groves, R. M., & Lyberg, L. (2010). Total survey error: Past, present, and future. *Public Opinion Quarterly, 74*(5), 849–879. doi:10.1093/poq/nfq065

Hayes, A. F. (2017). *Introduction to mediation, moderation, and conditional process analysis: A regression-based approach.* New York, NY: Guilford.

Hays, R. D., Liu, H., & Kapteyn, A. (2015). Use of Internet panels to conduct surveys. *Behavior Research Methods, 47*(3), 685–690. doi:10.3758/s13428-015-0617-9

Henrich, J., Heine, S. J., & Norenzayan, A. (2010). The weirdest people in the world? *Behavioral and Brain Sciences, 33*(2-3), 62–135. doi:10.1017/S0140525X0999152X

Jahoda, G. (2007). *A history of social psychology: From the eighteenth-century Enlightenment to the Second World War*. Cambridge, U.K.: Cambridge University Press.

Kahan, D. M. (2013). What's a "valid" sample? Problems with Mechanical Turk study samples, Part 1. Cultural Cognition Project Blog. Retrieved from http://www.culturalcognition.net/blog/2013/7/8/whats-a-valid-sample-problems-with-mechanical-turk-study-sam.html

Kish, L. (2004). Representation, randomization, and realism. In *Statistical design for research*. Hoboken, NJ: Wiley-Interscience.

Krupnikov, Y., & Levine, A. S. (2014). Cross-sample comparisons and external validity. *Journal of Experimental Political Science*, *1*(1), 59–80. doi:10.1017/xps.2014.7

Landers, R. N., & Behrend, T. S. (2015). An inconvenient truth: Arbitrary distinctions between organizational, Mechanical Turk, and other convenience samples. *Industrial and Organizational Psychology*, *8*(2), 142–164. doi:10.1017/iop.2015.13

Levay, K. E., Freese, J., & Druckman, J. N. (2016). The demographic and political composition of Mechanical Turk samples. *SAGE Open*, *6*(1), 215824401663643.

Litman, L., Rosenzweig, C., Robinson, J., & Moss, AJ. (2019). Composition of online participant pools moderates effect sizes of experimental manipulations *Association for Psychological Science, 31st Annual Convention*, Washington, DC.

Lyberg, L., Biemer, P., Collins, M., de Leeuw, E., Dippo, C., Schwarz, N., & Trewin, D. (1997). Data collection methods and survey quality: An overview. In *Survey measurement and process quality* (pp. 197–220). New York, NY: Wiley Interscience.

McGuire, W. J. (1967). Some impending reorientations in social psychology: Some thoughts provoked by Kenneth Ring. *Journal of Experimental Social Psychology*, *3*(2), 124–139. doi:10.1016/0022-1031(67)90017-0

Mitofsky, W. J. (1989). Presidential address: Methods and standards: A challenge for change. *Public Opinion Quarterly*, *53*(3), 446–453. doi:10.1093/poq/53.3.446

Mullinix, K. J., Leeper, T. J., Druckman, J. N., & Freese, J. (2015). The generalizability of survey experiments. *Journal of Experimental Political Science*, *2*(2), 109–138.

Mutz, D. C. (2016). *In-your-face politics: The consequences of uncivil media*: Princeton University Press.

Neyman, J. (1934). On the two different aspects of the representative method: The method of stratified sampling and the method of purposive selection. *Journal of the Royal Statistical Society*, *97*(4), 558–625. doi:10.2307/2342192

Ng, T. W., & Feldman, D. C. (2010). The relationships of age with job attitudes: A meta-analysis. *Personnel Psychology*, *63*(3), 677–718. doi:10.1111/j.1744-6570.2010.01184.x

Oakes, W. (1972). External validity and the use of real people as subjects. *American Psychologist*, *27*(10), 959–962. doi:10.1037/h0033454

Oxley, D. R., Smith, K. B., Alford, J. R., Hibbing, M. V., Miller, J. L., Scalora, M., . . .Hibbing, J. R. (2008). Political attitudes vary with physiological traits. *Science*, *321*(5896), 1667–1670. doi:10.1126/science.1157627

Paolacci, G., Chandler, J., & Ipeirotis, P. G. (2010). Running experiments on Amazon Mechanical Turk. *Judgment and Decision Making*, *5*(5), 411–419.

Peterson, R. A. (2001). On the use of college students in social science research: Insights from a second-order meta-analysis. *Journal of Consumer Research, 28*(3), 450–461. doi:10.1086/323732

Remus, W. (1986). Graduate students as surrogates for managers in experiments on business decision making. *Journal of Business Research, 14*(1), 19–25. doi:10.1016/0148-2963(86)90053-6

Rhodes, S. R. (1983). Age-related differences in work attitudes and behavior: A review and conceptual analysis. *Psychological Bulletin, 93*(2), 328–367. doi:10.1037/0033-2909.93.2.328

Richey, S., & Taylor, B. (2012). How representative are Mechanical Turk workers? Retrieved from http://themonkeycage.org/2012/12/19/how-representative-are-amazon-mechanical-turk-workers/

Saris, W. E., & de Pijper, W. M. (1986). Computer assisted interviewing using home computers. *European Research, 14*(3), 144–150.

Schultz, D. P. (1969). The human subject in psychological research. *Psychological Bulletin, 72*(3), 214–228. doi:10.1037/h0027880

Searles, K., & Ryan, J. B. (2015). Researchers are rushing to Amazon's Mechanical Turk. Should they? *Washington Post*, May 4. Retrieved from http://www.washingtonpost.com/blogs/monkey-cage/wp/2015/05/04/researchers-are-rushing-to-amazons-mechanical-turk-should-they

Sears, D. O. (1986). College sophomores in the laboratory: Influences of a narrow data base on social psychology's view of human nature. *Journal of Personality and Social Psychology, 51*(3), 515–530. doi:10.1037/0022-3514.51.3.515

Seng, Y. P. (1951). Historical survey of the development of sampling theories and practice. *Journal of the Royal Statistical Society. Series A, 114*(2), 214–231. doi:10.2307/2980977

Simons, D. J., & Chabris, C. F. (2011). What people believe about how memory works: A representative survey of the U.S. population. *PLoS ONE, 6*(8), e22757. doi:10.1371/journal.pone.0022757

Slade, L. A., & Gordon, M. E. (1988). On the virtues of laboratory babies and student bath water: A reply to Dobbins, Lane, and Steiner. *Journal of Organizational Behavior, 9*(4), 373–376. doi:10.1002/job.4030090409

Sparks, G. G. (1995a). A final reply to Potter, Cooper, and Dupagne. *Communication Theory, 5*(3), 286–289. doi:10.1111/j.1468-2885.1995.tb00111.x

Sparks, G. G. (1995b). Comments concerning the claim that mass media research is "prescientific": A response to Potter, Cooper, and Dupagne. *Communication Theory, 5*(3), 273–280. doi:10.1111/j.1468-2885.1995.tb00109.x

Tourangeau, R., Conrad, F. G., & Couper, M. P. (2013). *The science of web surveys*. Oxford, U.K.: Oxford University Press.

Zigerell, L. J. (in press). Understanding public support for eugenic policies: Results from survey data. *The Social Science Journal, 46*(4), 1–7. doi:10.1016/j.soscij.2019.01.003

CONDUCTING LONGITUDINAL RESEARCH ON AMAZON MECHANICAL TURK

Michael P. Hall, Neil A. Lewis Jr., Jesse Chandler, and Leib Litman

INTRODUCTION

Many questions that behavioral researchers and policymakers are interested in are inherently longitudinal (Bauer, 2004; Cohen & Manion, 1980; Willet, Singer, & Martin, 1998). For example, are people's political attitudes stable or malleable? What predicts relationship satisfaction over time? Does personality change as people age? What is the test-retest reliability of a psychological measure (Hall, Lewis, & Ellsworth, 2018)? Answers to these questions cannot be found with cross-sectional research designs; instead, researchers need to examine the same participants over time.

Among the many benefits of using Amazon Mechanical Turk for research is the relative ease with which researchers can conduct longitudinal studies. In this chapter we first provide an overview of both the benefits and the challenges of conducting longitudinal research. We then present two case studies that illustrate how the MTurk platform can make longitudinal research easier. Finally, we describe best practices in conducting longitudinal research, including how third-party platforms such as CloudResearch (formerly TurkPrime) can simplify the tasks researchers need to carry out in order to conduct longitudinal studies on Mechanical Turk.

WHY LONGITUDINAL RESEARCH?

Longitudinal research, by definition, involves observing, sampling, surveying, or obtaining some type of measurement from the same group of participants repeatedly over time. Longitudinal studies can be correlational, observational, experimental, or quasi-experimental. In addition to broadening the range of questions researchers can ask, longitudinal studies have several methodological advantages. For example, longitudinal studies increase statistical efficiency (Maxwell, 1998; Schmidt & Teti, 2005), address concerns of common method variance (Bagozzi & Yi, 1991; Campbell & Fiske, 1959), prevent cross-contamination of relevant variables (Ostroff, Kinicki, & Clark, 2002), and can help establish evidence of causality within a correlational framework (Granger, 1988).

Despite the statistical and methodological benefits of longitudinal designs, they also present a variety of challenges. In short, longitudinal studies are usually expensive, requiring both time and money (Ribisl et al., 1996). Logistically speaking, longitudinal studies are difficult to execute well and they are more complicated to manage than one-off studies or comparisons between two different cross-sectional datasets.

When conducting a longitudinal study, one concern typically takes precedence over all others: retaining participants. In fact, retention is so important that if too many participants are lost to attrition the entire study's value can be severely diminished (Ribisl et al., 1996). Participant retention is especially important at the end of the study, when analyses are being conducted and statistical power is critical. Power is directly affected by the number of respondents in the final wave of data collection, so researchers often over-recruit participants at Time 1 to allow for some attrition. The more time points in a study design, the more challenging and expensive it is to retain participants (Bauer, 2004; Laurie, Smith, & Scott, 1999).

Although attrition threatens researchers' ability to make causal inferences, keeping attrition low requires a substantial investment of time and resources. Especially before the advent of online data collection, maintaining contact with participants between study waves was a particularly onerous task. People move, contact information changes, and locating missing participants or bringing people back to the laboratory for subsequent measurements required considerable time and effort. For these reasons, common strategies for retaining participants included hiring a large staff to track and remind participants about upcoming study time points (e.g., National Center for Education Statistics, 2002), and paying participants enough money to motivate them to continue participating (Berk, Mathiowetz, Ward, & White, 1987; Berry & Kanouse, 1987). Although these methods help retain participants, they also exacerbate the other great challenge of conducting longitudinal research: cost. The

Internet in general and Mechanical Turk in particular can help alleviate concerns about resources and cost.

RETENTION, LONGITUDINAL RESEARCH, AND MECHANICAL TURK

In many ways, Mechanical Turk simplifies the work necessary to conduct a longitudinal study. Tracking and contacting participants can be as easy as gathering people's worker IDs and sending batch emails through MTurk's application programming interface. Maintaining participant records and organizing survey responses is simplified by stimulus development platforms, and the need to bring people into a laboratory or to schedule follow-up measurements is eliminated by the ability to send surveys or conduct interviews over the Internet.

As with any longitudinal research, minimizing attrition (and maximizing retention) is critical. Before Mechanical Turk started being utilized for longitudinal research, researchers had already worked out several factors that promote participant retention in longitudinal research. For instance, Ribisl et al. (1996) outlined eight factors for promoting participant retention, several of which are directly applicable to Mechanical Turk. Their recommendations include the following: having a project identity (e.g., a recognizable name and/or logo), teaching project staff the importance of tracking participants, using simple tracking methods, ensuring research participation is easy and rewarding, making a large effort to track participants early in a study, and tailoring tracking efforts to the demands of individual studies and participants as needed. Other important factors include considering the study experience; considering individual differences such as gender, age, or employment status; and considering incentives (Watson & Wooden, 2009).

Incentives, and in particular monetary incentives, have been the focus of much attention in longitudinal research. Although some longitudinal studies do not compensate participants, it is more common to do so than not. As such, considering how compensation affects participant retention is very important on Mechanical Turk.

Before Mechanical Turk, longitudinal researchers singled out a few pieces of wisdom when it comes to maximizing participant retention through incentives (Laurie & Lynn, 2009). First, cash incentives are more effective than gifts, and in general, higher incentives lead to higher response rates (Auspurg & Schneck, 2014). High incentives are particularly important for participants who may have a lower propensity to respond to a follow-up measurement (Laurie & Lynn, 2009). A second piece of wisdom for maximizing retention is that it's better to guarantee compensation unconditionally prior to the beginning of a survey, rather than compensating participants based on how much of a survey they complete (Auspurg & Schneck, 2014; Laurie

& Lynn, 2009). Finally, increasing compensation over time increases retention. However, whether these increases should be made slowly and in steady increments or infrequently is less clear (Laurie & Lynn, 2009).

Recently, researchers have evaluated how effective retention-maximizing techniques are on Mechanical Turk. Chandler, Litman, and Robinson (manuscript in preparation) conducted a meta-analysis to examine what predicts participant retention in longitudinal studies (i.e., at least two time points) on Mechanical Turk. These researchers examined many different predictors, including overall study length, length of interval between time points, duration of surveys, incentives, worker qualifications (e.g., number of MTurk HITs completed, reputation metrics), and whether researchers reminded participants of upcoming surveys, among many others. The results of the study indicated that retention increased when time between study intervals was shorter, when participants were reminded of upcoming surveys, when wages increased, when Time 1 wages were above average and Time 2 wages were even higher, and when workers were required to have high worker qualifications. Other researchers have also found that bonus payments—either for excellent work or additional work—and notifications to participants that the study is longitudinal up front are also important factors that increase retention (Stoycheff, 2016).

In the next section, we present two case studies of longitudinal research conducted on Mechanical Turk. Case study 1 covers the Michigan Climate Attitudes Study, which was conducted by two of this chapter's authors (Hall et al., 2018); and case study 2 covers an online, daily diary study conducted by Boynton and Richman (2014). In presenting these case studies, we hope readers will see how Mechanical Turk can facilitate longitudinal research and how each case study employed many of the retention-maximizing techniques discussed in this chapter.

CASE STUDY 1: CONDUCTING LONGITUDINAL RESEARCH ON MECHANICAL TURK OVER THE COURSE OF ONE YEAR: THE MICHIGAN CLIMATE ATTITUDES STUDY

Overview

The Michigan Climate Attitudes Study (MCAS) was a longitudinal study of American adults' beliefs about climate change and engagement in sustainable behaviors (Hall et al., 2018). In particular, the MCAS had several goals: (a) to use longitudinal methods to assess the relative stability (or lack thereof) of Americans' beliefs about climate change, (b) to determine significant predictors of Americans' climate change beliefs, and (c) to determine whether different types of climate change beliefs predict engagement in a variety of pro-environmental behaviors and support for sustainable climate policies. As with much longitudinal research, the core research questions that guided the MCAS were best answered with repeated observations of the same participants. Mechanical Turk provided a suitable platform for us to answer these questions because we had limited financial resources and sought to minimize participant attrition. In the end, the MCAS surveyed 600 geographically diverse Americans over the course of one year for less than $15,000.

Method

We used Mechanical Turk to recruit a sample of 600 American adults to be surveyed seven times over the course of one year—beginning in July 2014 and ending in July 2015. (Since the time of our study, Mechanical Turk has improved the location restriction feature, now enabling requesters to recruit participants from individual states. CloudResearch also offers more detailed geographic recruiting strategies, to be discussed later in this chapter.) Because a goal of the MCAS was to assess attitudes about climate change, it was essential to obtain a geographically diverse sample of U.S. respondents—to accurately represent the diversity of climatic experiences across the country.

Respondents' geographic location can be affected by the time a survey is made available (U.S. Census Bureau, 2015). This is because surveys that are launched in the morning on the East Coast will be less likely to be seen by participants on the West Coast, who are three hours behind. To maximize our chances of achieving geographic diversity, we posted four different HITs (each with 150 participants) on Mechanical Turk to coincide with 9 a.m. in each of the four U.S. time zones.

Over the course of the year, we surveyed participants six more times, with new surveys being sent out approximately every eight weeks. Each follow-up survey was available for five days before expiring. Participants were notified that they were eligible to complete a survey by email three times for each wave: once a few days before the wave to alert them of when the survey would launch, once on the day of the survey launch, and once the day before the expiration of the survey.

To ensure that only people who participated in our original survey could access each subsequent survey, we assigned our initial participants a "qualification." Qualifications on Mechanical Turk are a method of defining a group of MTurk workers according to a certain attribute (Paolacci & Chandler, 2014). The attribute of our qualification was that workers completed our initial study. By creating the qualification and adding it to each subsequent survey we conducted, we were able to restrict participation in subsequent waves to only those who completed the initial questionnaire (see Figures 3.24–3.29).

As with any longitudinal survey, maximizing retention was an important goal for the MCAS. To motivate our participants to complete as many follow-up surveys as possible, we devised a progressive payment schedule that increased rewards over time (see Table 9.1 for details). To further motivate participants, we notified them at the study's start as well as at each additional wave of data collection that completion of all surveys would result in a further bonus payment. By the end of the study, participants who completed every survey and received the bonus payment earned $28.50 for their participation, which entailed approximately two hours of survey-taking overall. Thus, the MCAS compensated workers at a rate of more than $14 per hour.

Results

Overall, our method yielded a geographically diverse sample of 600 participants (see Tables 9.2–9.4). Table 9.5 compares the geographic distribution of Time 1 respondents to the U.S. population according to the 10 ZIP code zones in the United States and each zone's share of the U.S. population according to the 2010 Census (U.S. Census Bureau, 2015). Overall, the representation of each ZIP zone in the MCAS

TABLE 9.1 ● PAYMENT SYSTEM FOR THE MICHIGAN CLIMATE ATTITUDES STUDY (MCAS)	
Time	Payment
1	$0.50
2	$1
3	$2
4	$3
5	$4
6	$6*
7	$7*
Bonus	$5
Total	$28.50

*Compensation for Times 6 and 7 were originally $5 and $6, respectively. However, we increased the compensation by $1 for each of these surveys because we were well within our budgetary confines and also hoped that increasing payments would be motivating to our participants. As a result, the number of participants who completed Times 6 and 7 each increased compared to previous time points.

TABLE 9.2 ● RACIAL IDENTIFICATION OF THE TIME 1 MCAS SAMPLE		
Race	N	Percentage
White	483	80.50
Hispanic	37	6.17
Black	36	6.00
Asian	46	7.67
Native American	6	1.00
Hawaiian / Pacific Islander	3	0.50
Other	2	0.33
Total*	613	102.17

*Includes individuals who selected more than one racial categorization.

TABLE 9.3 ● GENDER IDENTIFICATION OF THE TIME 1 MCAS SAMPLE		
Gender	N	Percentage
Male	370	61.67
Female	225	37.50
Prefer not to answer	5	0.83
Total	600	100.00

sample was quite similar to the actual geographic distribution of the United States. Two exceptions are ZIP zones 4 and 7, in which the MCAS sample does not perfectly match the U.S. population.[1] As can be seen in Table 9.2, demographic diversity paralleled that traditionally observed in MTurk samples (Casey et al., 2017).

Most important, our method was effective in achieving a high level of retention over time, as illustrated in Figure 9.1. Of the 600 participants who completed Time 1, 438 (73%) returned for Time 2. After that initial expected drop-off (Ribisl et al., 1996), retention remained high for the remainder of the study. From Time 2 onward, each follow-up survey was completed by an average of 426 participants, yielding an average retention rate of 95.2% for the five subsequent surveys. In addition, 291 participants (48.5% of the

---

[1] ZIP zone 4 includes Michigan, and we believe that we over-recruited from Michigan because potential participants who lived in Michigan were especially likely to complete our survey due to its title: Michigan Climate Attitudes Study. We have no intuition as to why ZIP zone 7 was under-represented in our sample.

TABLE 9.4 ● EDUCATION LEVEL OF THE TIME 1 MCAS SAMPLE		
Education Level	N	Percentage
< 9th grade	0	0.00
9th–12th, no diploma	5	0.83
High school/GED	66	11.00
Some college	173	28.83
Associate degree	52	8.67
Bachelor's degree	230	38.33
Graduate degree/professional	67	11.17
No response	7	1.17
Total	600	100.00

TABLE 9.5 ● GEOGRAPHIC DISTRIBUTIONS OF TIME 1 MCAS SAMPLE AND U.S. POPULATION (U.S. CENSUS, 2010)		
ZIP Zone	MCAS (percent)	U.S. (percentage)
0 (CT, MA, ME, NH, VT, RI, NJ)	6.67	7.53
1 (DE, NY, PA)	11.67	10.68
2 (DC, MD, NC, SC, VA, WV)	11.83	9.84
3 (AL, FL, GA, MS, TN)	13.83	13.79
4 (IN, KY, MI, OH)	17.50	10.44
5 (IA, MN, WI, MT, ND, SD)	6.50	5.35
6 (IL, KS, MO, NE)	5.17	7.61
7 (AR, LA, OK, TX)	7.33	11.77
8 (AZ, CO, ID, NM, NV, UT, WY)	6.17	6.83
9 (AK, CA, HI, OR, WA)	13.33	16.16

initial sample) completed all seven surveys and received the bonus payment at the end of the study. Overall, an average of 75.2% of the Time 1 sample (451 participants) returned for at least one subsequent survey between Times 2 and 7. Furthermore, of those who completed the second wave (Time 2), 95.2% returned for at least one subsequent survey.

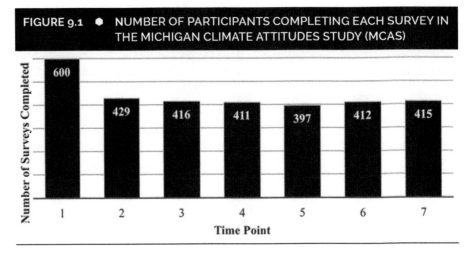

FIGURE 9.1 ● NUMBER OF PARTICIPANTS COMPLETING EACH SURVEY IN THE MICHIGAN CLIMATE ATTITUDES STUDY (MCAS)

The entire study cost $13,076 (including Amazon's service fee[2]), which is considerably lower than the alternative of using a panel survey company.[3]

Conclusions

We designed our study to overcome the barriers to retention and cost that are inherent in all longitudinal research. By doing so, we were able to answer substantive questions about Americans' attitudes about climate change. Given the success of these methods, our hope is that sharing them will encourage others to pursue more longitudinal research questions on Mechanical Turk, as such longitudinal research is essential for improving our understanding of a variety of social and behavioral phenomena.

Key Points About Longitudinal Research on Mechanical Turk Based on the MCAS

Participant Screening Criteria

When posting studies to Mechanical Turk, researchers can select from several screening criteria (called "Worker Requirements") to determine who is eligible to participate in the study. These selection criteria include restrictions based on location, the participant's "HIT Approval Rate"—the percentage of time other requesters have approved of that participant's work—and the "Number of HITs Approved," an indicator of how many previous MTurk tasks a particular participant has completed. We recommend using these features to improve the odds

---

[2] At the time we conducted this study, Amazon's service fee was a 10% commission. Since that time, the fee went up to 20–40%.

[3] A relatively "inexpensive" panel survey company provided a quote of $7 per participant for a *single session* survey with similar characteristics (e.g., length, demographics).

of recruiting high-quality participants in longitudinal studies—something we did in the MCAS. For example, if a researcher only allows participants who have previously completed more than 10,000 HITs, such participants are essentially professional survey takers. Hence, these participants should be easier to retain than more casual participants. Although experienced workers might help reduce attrition, however, there are questions about how much one can generalize from a sample of super experienced and knowledgeable research participants (so-called superworkers). For a more detailed discussion of this issue, see Chapters 7 and 8 and Stewart et al. (2015). Ultimately, this decision should be guided by the nature and purpose of one's study.

Study and Payment Transparency

For any longitudinal study, it is important for participants to know exactly what they are signing up for at the outset. We recommend making details about what will be expected from participants and how they will be compensated as clear and transparent as possible before participants have officially enrolled in the study. In the MCAS, we provided potential participants with clear details about the duration, expected time commitment, and compensation of the study before they accepted the first HIT.

Increasing Payments as Incentives

A key feature of our design was an increasing payment system, designed to sustain participant motivation. We paid competitive rates with our initial survey and increased compensation for each subsequent survey. Other researchers have achieved increasing payment schemes by holding the absolute payment amount constant, but decreasing the length of subsequent surveys, thereby increasing the hourly rate; this method is also effective for retaining participants (see Brandt, Wisneski, & Skitka, 2015). In addition to increasing payments, we also included a bonus payment as an extra source of motivation (Stoycheff, 2016): participants who completed every survey (time point) in our study were eligible for an extra $5 bonus payment, equivalent to an additional 21% of total study compensation. Our study design allowed participants to continue participating even if they missed a previous time point. We realize that not all longitudinal studies can allow participants to miss a time point, but our study benefits from this design. Regardless of whether participants can miss a time point, bonuses can provide an extra boost of motivation for participants to complete all study requirements.

Reminders and Ease of Study Access

MTurk workers, like anyone else, have busy lives and can understandably forget to complete a follow-up survey in a longitudinal study to which they committed. Therefore, we recommend (a) making follow-up surveys very easy to access and (b) using frequent and friendly reminders to participate. In our study, we contacted participants before the launch of a follow-up survey to give them advanced notice, upon the launch of that follow-up survey, and once more on the final day of each survey's availability to remind them of the survey's impending expiration. In each message, we included a link directly to the survey as well as exact search terms that would turn up the survey on the MTurk website. In many instances, participants told us these small steps were very helpful and appreciated.

CASE STUDY 2: CONDUCTING INTENSIVE LONGITUDINAL RESEARCH: AN ONLINE DIARY STUDY OF ALCOHOL USE

The goal of intensive longitudinal designs is to characterize change over time on an individual rather than a group level (see Bolger & Laurenceau, 2013). This necessitates not only a greater overall number of measurements than in a typical longitudinal study but also an increased frequency of measurement. Examples of intensive longitudinal designs include diary studies and experience sampling. For these types of studies, participants may be engaged on a daily basis or, in some cases, several times a day.

Recent advances in online technology in general, and mobile technology in particular, make it possible to collect attitudinal, behavioral, and biometric data remotely. For example, researchers studying disordered eating may ask participants to fill out a short questionnaire on their smartphone after each meal. Many such studies are, almost by definition, impossible to conduct in the laboratory, since the goal is to study people as they naturally engage in daily activities.

Participant recruitment and retention for intensive and time-consuming research is often difficult and stands as one of the biggest barriers to feasibility. For this reason, intensive longitudinal research is an area in which Mechanical Turk can be indispensable. Mechanical Turk is one of the most effective options for conducting intensive longitudinal research. Indeed, to our knowledge, Mechanical Turk is the best source of samples for recruiting and retaining participants for complex intensive study designs. Here, we illustrate the feasibility of conducting daily diary studies on Mechanical Turk. We describe a case study in which a two-week diary study of alcohol consumption was conducted with an online sample of drinking-age adults.

Method

Boynton and Richman (2014) used Mechanical Turk to recruit 518 participants to complete a two-week daily diary study of alcohol use. Participants were recruited as part of a larger online survey of personality and health. Initially, Boynton and Richman posted a HIT on Mechanical Turk inviting participants to complete a brief screener assessing basic demographic and health factors. Participants who were White, Black/ African American, Latino, or Asian/Pacific Islanders; were 21–65 years old; currently resided in the United States; and were able to speak and read English were invited to complete a follow-up survey in which they completed a series of social-personality and health-related measures. For the daily diary portion of the study, participants completed five-minute daily surveys about their alcohol consumption for up to 14 consecutive days. Each survey asked participants about their thoughts and behaviors (related to alcohol) from the previous evening. Participants were compensated for completing the screener/ baseline survey ($0.85) and daily diary surveys (up to $5.00 for perfect adherence). They received daily reminders to complete their survey.

Results

Of the 518 participants recruited, Boynton and Richman (2014) retained 369 participants for their two-week daily diary study (71.2% of their target sample). Those participants contributed a total of 3,145 daily observations, and the average number of completed daily measures was 8.5 ($SD = 3.9$).

Conclusions

Boynton and Richman's (2014) study provides another example of how Mechanical Turk can be used to recruit and successfully retain more than 70% of participants in a longitudinal design. In addition, the study shows the type of engagement that researchers can receive from participants (daily dairies across two weeks), while keeping research costs low (in their case, $5 per participant).

BEST PRACTICES FOR LONGITUDINAL RESEARCH

As described in the two case studies, Mechanical Turk can be used to conduct longitudinal studies, including those with multiple time points. The goal of such studies is often to maximize retention as much as possible. In this section, we describe specific strategies for retaining participants as well as various tools that simplify conducting longitudinal research on Mechanical Turk.

Maximizing Retention Rates

Chandler et al. (manuscript in preparation) examined factors that contribute to retention on Mechanical Turk by conducting a meta-analysis of more than 1,200 longitudinal studies run on CloudResearch, with a total of 36,361 participants across studies. The studies were conducted by different labs that had heterogeneous study designs and sampling practices, making it possible to measure how the variability in these practices is associated with retention rates.

The study found that the average retention rate was 68%. This value provides a rough benchmark against which researchers can evaluate retention in their own studies. However, there was also considerable variability around the average. More than 30% of studies achieved retention rates above 80%, and more than 10% had retention rates above 90%. Although most studies tended to have high retention, a considerable number of studies had very low retention, prompting questions about which factors are associated with high retention rates and whether these factors are under the researcher's control. Factors that significantly predicted retention were the length of time between sessions (longer intervals had lower retention), whether researchers contacted participants, higher wages, worker characteristics, and task characteristics.

Wages

Wages play an important role in increasing retention rates on Mechanical Turk. Six dollars per hour is an effective hourly wage for retaining participants at both the first and subsequent waves of data collection. Wages moderately above $6 per hour do not appear to significantly improve retention. However, we have conducted longitudinal studies that pay upwards of $8 per hour that have retained close to 100% of participants over multiple successive weeks. Thus, for studies in which minimizing attrition is critical, researchers should consider setting above-average hourly wages across all sessions, preferably with increasing wages across sessions, as described earlier.

Task Characteristics and Bounce Rate

A study's bounce rate is another significant predictor of retention. Bounce rates are a direct measure of workers' desire to work on a HIT after previewing its description. Bounce rates are useful as an indicator of retention because they likely capture a variety of reasons a HIT might be unappealing, such as if the procedure is difficult or the topic isn't of interest. Thus, although the bounce rate of a study provides little causal insight into what factors discourage retention, it is a good indicator of potential problems that need to be addressed. Researchers should monitor the bounce rate, as it predicts dropout both within-session and across longitudinal sessions. The average within-session bounce rate is 24%. Thus, if the bounce rate falls above this point, researchers should consider that the pay rate–to–difficulty ratio may not be optimal for achieving high retention rates in longitudinal studies.

Worker Characteristics

Worker characteristics have a large effect on retention. Put simply, the more experienced a worker is, and thus the more committed that worker is to earning money on Mechanical Turk, the more likely the worker is to complete all study sessions. Worker experience is indicated by the number of prior HITs completed.

Table 9.6 shows the relationship between worker activity level and the probability of completing Wave 2 in a longitudinal study. As the table shows, a strong relationship exists between activity level and retention. The most active workers, who have completed more than 5,000 HITs, are 60% more likely to participate in Wave 2 of a longitudinal study than are workers who have completed only a few HITs. Highly active workers are also much more likely to participate in high-paying HITs in general. Attracting these workers will likely require setting higher wages. At the same time, such workers have the highest probability of being nonnaive. Thus, researchers should weigh the advantages of maximizing longitudinal retention against the disadvantages of increased nonnaïveté (see Chapter 7).

TABLE 9.6 ● AVERAGE RETENTION AT WAVE 2 BASED ON WORKER ACTIVITY LEVEL (HITS COMPLETED)	
HITs Completed	**Average Retention**
1–10	21.20%
11–100	44.00%
101–500	55.80%
501–1,000	62.43%
1,001–5,000	69.28%
5,001–10,000	81.44%

USING API-BASED TOOLS TO SIMPLIFY LONGITUDINAL STUDIES

Mechanical Turk is a powerful platform for conducting longitudinal research. It allows researchers to select experienced and high-quality workers, contact participants to let them know about subsequent surveys, and monitor things that may increase attrition such as a study's bounce rate. Although Mechanical Turk has these capabilities, many tasks cannot be easily completed from the graphical user interface (GUI). Unless researchers know how to write code to interact with the application programming interface, their ability to implement many of the practices described here is limited.

In Chapter 4 we described third-party, API-based platforms that offer tools to improve Mechanical Turk's functionality for social science research. Longitudinal research is one of the best examples of when such tools can be helpful. Setting up longitudinal studies requires (a) specifying that a HIT is open only to specific workers on the basis of participation in previous studies, (b) matching participants across phases of a study, and (c) notifying participants that a HIT is available. Each of these steps can be difficult and time consuming using Mechanical Turk's GUI-based tools. To restrict HITs to specific workers from previous studies, Mechanical Turk's qualifications have to be created using CSV files, as discussed in Chapter 3. Workers can only be notified one at a time. And the process of matching workers across multiple datasets requires asking workers to report their worker IDs, which some workers fail to do. Below we describe how these steps can be easily accomplished with API-based tools.

Tracking Participants Across Waves of a Longitudinal Study

Because longitudinal studies have multiple phases, there are typically multiple data files that store the results from the different study waves. Worker IDs allow data to be matched across phases. CloudResearch facilitates the process of matching Worker IDs across multiple data files by automatically passing each worker's ID to platforms like Qualtrics via an embedded query string in the survey's URL (see Figure 4.5). Requesters can then automatically insert the Worker ID into data files.

Worker Notification

As shown by Chandler et al., manuscript in preparation, notifying workers that a follow-up study has been launched is the most effective way to increase retention. When a HIT is posted, many workers are not actively viewing their dashboard and may not become aware that the study is available. A short time later, the HIT will move down the dashboard queue and workers will be much less likely to see it. For this reason, unless workers receive an email notification, they may never know that the HIT has become available. This problem is compounded with longer intersession intervals. Third-party apps can significantly simplify this process (see Figures 4.10 and 4.11).

Contacting Participants

Longer intercession intervals are associated with lower retention rates. However, sending an email notification virtually eliminates this effect (Chandler et al., manuscript in preparation), showing that email notifications can offset what is perhaps the largest predictor of attrition in longitudinal studies. On CloudResearch, all workers can be notified that a study has been posted by simply clicking the Email Included Workers button on the dashboard (Figure 9.2). The notification automatically includes the HIT link.

FIGURE 9.2 ● USING CLOUDRESEARCH TO NOTIFY WORKERS THAT A WAVE 2 HIT IS READY

Maintaining Anonymity in Longitudinal Studies

The ability to directly communicate with workers is one of the most powerful features of Mechanical Turk, and it is not available on many other online data collection platforms. However, this is also a common source of confusion for institutional review boards. The collection of personally identifiable information, such as email, is not required to send notifications to workers. Instead, requesters notify workers based on their worker IDs and then Mechanical Turk routes the email to the appropriate workers. Emails and other personal information are stored securely on Mechanical Turk and are not available to the researcher (unless a worker replies to the researcher via personal email). This mechanism makes Mechanical Turk ideal for longitudinal research, as it allows for direct communication with participants, thus increasing retention rates, while maintaining anonymity.

SELECTIVE RECRUITMENT

A somewhat unique characteristic of Mechanical Turk is that longitudinal HITs can play a critical role in studies that selectively recruit specific groups of workers (Goodman & Paolacci, 2017). Mechanical Turk has recently added the ability to select workers based on various demographics such as gender and age. However, some research requires demographic and attitudinal variables that are not listed among the current MTurk qualifications. In such cases participants can be recruited via a two-step longitudinal process. At Time 1, a short survey is administered in which participants are paid a few cents for answering screening questions. At Time 2, a HIT is open to select workers based on the match of their responses.

Best practices for selective recruitment mirror the longitudinal best practices reviewed earlier. In particular, wages at Time 2, the intersession interval, and email contact can have a critical impact on the ability to recruit high numbers of selectively targeted workers. The intersession interval may be of particular relevance. To screen high numbers of workers, screening studies are often open for long time periods. Since the intersession interval is highly associated with retention rates, researchers should send invitation emails on a rolling basis, rather than wait until the entire screening process is complete. This may be particularly relevant for studies that aim to recruit rare and difficult-to-find participants, where the loss of even a few potential subjects may have important consequences on the study's power. Additionally, because HITs that are open for a long time are more likely to consist of low-active workers who are less likely to participate in follow-up HITs, shortening the intercession interval and sending at least one, or perhaps multiple, notifications will be particularly important for improving retention rates.

CONCLUSION

Mechanical Turk provides a powerful and robust environment through which to conduct longitudinal research. As this chapter has shown, researchers can conduct studies with multiple waves of data collection spread out over time or run studies that require daily responses from participants. In many studies, close to 100% of participants have been retained. However, when researchers do not employ longitudinal best practices, retention can be alarmingly low. Low retention is typically caused by poor user experience, long and uninteresting tasks, and low wages. Under normal circumstances, researchers can expect retention rates around 70%. However, when highly active workers are recruited, when the wages are sufficiently high, and when workers find the task enjoyable, dropout can be eliminated almost completely. Most researchers will find that conducting longitudinal studies on Mechanical Turk is most effective when using third-party, API-based tools. Many such tools for facilitating longitudinal and other complex research designs on Mechanical Turk are currently available.

REFERENCES

Auspurg, K., & Schneck, A. (2014). What difference makes a difference? A meta-regression approach on the effectiveness conditions of incentives in self-administered surveys. *Proceedings of the MAER-Net 2014 Athens colloquium (MAER-Net)*, Athens.

Bagozzi, R. P., & Yi, Y. (1991). Multitrait-multimethod matrices in consumer research. *Journal of Consumer Research, 17*(4), 426–439. doi:10.1086/208568

Bauer, K. W. (2004). Conducting longitudinal studies. *New Directions for Institutional Research, 121*(121), 75–90. doi:10.1002/ir.102

Berinsky, A. J., Huber, G. A., & Lenz, G. S. (2012). Evaluating online labor markets for experimental research: Amazon.com's Mechanical Turk. *Political Analysis, 20*(3), 351–368. doi:10.1093/pan/mpr057

Berk, M. L., Mathiowetz, N. A., Ward, E. P., & White, A. A. (1987). The effect of prepaid and promised incentives: Results of a controlled experiment. *Journal of Official Statistics, 3*(4), 449–457.

Berry, S. H., & Kanouse, D. E. (1987). Physician response to a mailed survey: An experiment in timing of payment. *Public Opinion Quarterly, 51*(1), 102–116. doi:10.1086/269018

Bolger, N., & Laurenceau, J. P. (2013). *Intensive longitudinal methods: An introduction to diary and experience sampling research.* New York, NY: Guilford Press.

Boynton, M. H., & Richman, L. S. (2014). An online daily diary study of alcohol use using Amazon's Mechanical Turk. *Drug and Alcohol Review, 33*(4), 456–461. doi:10.1111/dar.12163

Brandt, M. J., Wisneski, D. C., & Skitka, L. J. (2015). Moralization and the 2012 U.S. presidential election campaign. *Journal of Social and Political Psychology, 3*(2), 211–237. doi:10.5964/jspp.v3i2.434

Campbell, D. T., & Fiske, D. W. (1959). Convergent and discriminant validation by the multitrait-multimethod matrix. *Psychological Bulletin, 56*(2), 81–105. doi:10.1037/h0046016

Casey, L. S., Chandler, J., Levine, A. S., Proctor, A., & Strolovitch, D. Z. (2017). Intertemporal differences among MTurk workers: Time-based sample variations and implications for online data collection. *SAGE Open, 7*(2). doi:10.1177/2158244017712774

Chandler, J., Litman, L., & Robinson, Y. (manuscript in preparation). Maximum retention rates in longitudinal studies on Amazon Mechanical Turk.

Cohen, L., & Manion, L. (1980). *Research methods in education.* London, U.K.: Croon Helm.

Goodman, J. K., & Paolacci, G. (2017). Crowdsourcing consumer research. *Journal of Consumer Research, 44*(1), 196–210.

Granger, C. W. J. (1988). Some recent development in a concept of causality. *Journal of Econometrics, 39*(1–2), 199–211. doi:10.1016/0304-4076(88)90045-0

Hall, M. P., Lewis, N. A., Ellsworth, P. C. (2018). Believing in climate change, but not behaving sustainably: Evidence from a one-year longitudinal study. *Journal of Environmental Psychology, 56*, 55–62.

Laurie, H., & Lynn, P. (2009). The use of respondent incentives on longitudinal surveys. In P. Lynn (Ed.), *Methodology of longitudinal surveys* (pp. 205–233). London, U.K.: Wiley.

Laurie, H., Smith, R., & Scott, L. (1999). Strategies for reducing nonresponse in a longitudinal panel survey. *Journal of Official Statistics, 15*(2), 269–282.

Maxwell, S. E. (1998). Longitudinal designs in randomized group comparisons: When will intermediate observations increase statistical power? *Psychological Methods, 3*(3), 275–290. doi:10.1037/1082-989X.3.3.275

National Center for Education Statistics. (2002). *High school and beyond: Overview.* Washington, DC: National Center for Education Statistics.

Ostroff, C., Kinicki, A. J., & Clark, M. A. (2002). Substantive and operational issues of response bias across levels of analysis: An example of climate-satisfaction relationships. *Journal of Applied Psychology, 87*(2), 355–368. doi:10.1037/0021-9010.87.2.355

Paolacci, G., & Chandler, J. (2014). Inside the Turk: Understanding Mechanical Turk as a participant pool. *Current Directions in Psychological Science, 23*(3), 184–188.

Ribisl, K. M., Walton, M. A., Mowbray, C. T., Luke, D. A., Davidson, W. S., & Bootsmiller, B. J. (1996). Minimizing participant attrition in panel studies through the use of effective retention and tracking strategies: Review and recommendations. *Evaluation and Program Planning, 19*(1), 1–25. doi:10.1016/0149-7189(95)00037-2

Schmidt, K. R. T., & Teti, D. M. (2005). Issues in the use of longitudinal and cross-sectional designs. In D. M. Teti (Ed.), *Handbook of research methods in developmental science* (pp. 3–20). New York, NY: Wiley.

Stewart, N., Ungemach, C., Harris, A. J. L., Bartels, D. M., Newell, B. R., Paolacci, G., & Chandler, J. (2015). The average laboratory samples a population of 7,300 Amazon Mechanical Turk workers. *Judgment and Decision Making, 10*(5), 479–491.

Stoycheff, E. (2016). Please participate in Part 2: Maximizing response rates in longitudinal MTurk designs. *Methodological Innovations, 9*(2), 1–5. doi:10.1177/2059799116672879

U.S. Census Bureau. (2015). State and County QuickFacts. Retrieved from http://quickfacts.census.gov/qfd/index.html (Accessed September 25, 2015).

Watson, N., & Wooden, M. (2009). Identifying factors affecting longitudinal survey response. In P. Lynn (Ed.), *Methodology of longitudinal surveys* (pp. 157–181). London, UK: Wiley.

Willet, J. B., Singer, J. D., & Martin, N. C. (1998). The design and analysis of longitudinal studies of development and psychopathology in context: Statistical models and methodological recommendations. *Development and Psychopathology, 10*(2), 395–426. doi:10.1017/S0954579498001667

BEYOND MECHANICAL TURK

Using Online Market Research Platforms

Leib Litman, Jonathan Robinson, and Cheskie Rosenzweig

INTRODUCTION

In previous chapters, we discussed the profound impact Mechanical Turk has had on the scientific community. As described throughout this book, traditional sources of participant recruitment, such as the undergraduate subject pool, have significant limitations. Key among them from a methodological perspective is that undergraduate subject pools lack diversity and representativeness. They consist of younger participants who are more highly educated and less politically and ethnically diverse than the general U.S. population. This lack of diversity makes it difficult to impossible to recruit samples representative of the United States or to selectively target many hard-to-reach subgroups. Although Mechanical Turk has helped researchers reach a wider pool of participants, as a sampling frame, Mechanical Turk also suffers from limitations of size. This limitation makes it difficult to selectively recruit groups that are underrepresented on the platform, such as participants over age 50, and to recruit many other hard-to-reach groups.

In this chapter we describe alternative sources of online participant recruitment. We begin by describing online probability-based samples that do not suffer from the demographic limitations that Mechanical Turk has but are often prohibitively expensive. We next describe other alternatives to Mechanical Turk for data collection, with a focus on market research platforms. These platforms provide significant advantages over Mechanical Turk in terms of size and representativeness, but they can suffer from issues of lower data quality for some types of tasks. We describe several methods for improving data quality that will allow researchers to harness the substantial sampling power available through these platforms. The chapter concludes with a comparison of the strengths and limitations of Mechanical Turk and market research platforms.

LIMITATIONS OF MECHANICAL TURK

Although a significant number of research studies are now conducted on Mechanical Turk, the shift of social science from the laboratory to web-based recruitment is still in its infancy. Fundamental questions about best practices remain. For instance, which participant recruitment platforms are best suited for conducting online research? And under which circumstances are specific online platforms best matched for specific research questions? Mechanical Turk has helped researchers overcome many of the limitations of more traditional recruitment practices, but the platform has several of its own limitations, which have been discussed throughout this book and are reviewed here. Key among these limitations is a relatively small population, which makes it difficult to recruit hard-to-reach groups.

Small Population

As discussed in Chapter 6, Mechanical Turk has about 85,000 workers who participate in academic studies each year. In any one month, about 30,000 unique MTurk workers participate in close to one million assignments through CloudResearch, with active workers completing hundreds of studies each month. Although this participant pool is large enough to accommodate many studies, a much larger sample pool is required when the goal is to recruit hard-to-reach samples.

Representativeness

MTurk workers are significantly more diverse than the undergraduate subject pool in terms of gender, age, race, education, and employment. At the same time, however, the MTurk population is significantly less diverse than the general U.S. population along the same variables. The population of MTurk workers is less politically diverse, more highly educated, younger, and less religious compared to the U.S. population (Casey, Chandler, Levine, Proctor, & Strolovitch, 2017; Huff & Tingley, 2015; Levay, Freese, & Druckman, 2016). This lack of diversity leads to difficulty in recruiting certain demographic segments, most notably participants over age 50.

Limited Selective Recruitment

Mechanical Turk has basic mechanisms to selectively recruit workers who have already been profiled. However, Mechanical Turk is structured in such a way as to make it very difficult to recruit participants based on characteristics that have not been profiled (see Chapter 5). For this reason, although rudimentary selective recruitment mechanisms exist, there are significant limitations on the ability to recruit specific subgroups of workers. This problem is exacerbated by the relatively small size of the worker pool. It is much more difficult to find rare subgroups of participants in the relatively small pool of MTurk workers, compared to other opt-in panels that have access to tens of millions of participants. This problem is particularly apparent for cross-cultural research. The vast majority of MTurk workers are from the United States, Canada, and India, severely restricting recruitment from other countries.

In light of these limitations, a natural question is whether platforms other than Mechanical Turk can be used as sources of data. The answer to this question is that there are numerous candidate platforms, each with its own strengths and weaknesses in terms of panel size, price, usability, data quality, and representativeness.

ONLINE PROBABILITY-BASED PANELS

As discussed in Chapter 8, Mechanical Turk is an opt-in panel and, as a result, its population is biased by the opt-in process. In the world of online research, however, there are several panels that use probability-based survey methods to obtain representative samples over the Internet. Nationally representative probability samples are used for population-oriented research (see Chapter 8). The goal of such research is to make inferences about the population. Most studies in the social and behavioral sciences do not use probability samples because generating precise population estimates is not their goal. However, even researchers who do not use probability samples may find it of interest that probability sampling can be conducted online and that many platforms can be used to conduct such research. Indeed, some of these probability-based platforms have been used as benchmarks to assess the representativeness of data collected on Mechanical Turk, as described in Chapter 8. Additionally, some probability-based platforms offer grants to academics who conduct population-oriented research studies.

Online probability panels often begin with offline random-digit-dialing (RDD) to identify potential participants. After participants are contacted and recruited into the panel (Craig et al., 2013), they participate in online studies similar to the way they participate in opt-in panels.

Recruiting and maintaining a probability-based panel requires a high degree of effort and resources, meaning these panels are fairly expensive. The actual price per completion is difficult to estimate given variability among providers, the cost of survey creation that sometimes accompanies a provider's "service bundles," and the degree to which a researcher wants to target particular populations. Nevertheless, projects often cost anywhere from $25 to $150 per participant, making these samples prohibitively expensive for researchers without large funding sources.

Table 10.1 lists several online probability panels, the size of their participant pool, and some other panel features. As is evident from the table, several panels are quite small, often even smaller than Mechanical Turk. The size of these panels makes targeted recruitment difficult or impossible. Thus, representativeness often comes at the expense of other sample features that are of research value, such as recruitment of hard-to-reach groups.

Probability-based panels are often maintained meticulously. Participants are given a few surveys to complete in a specified period of time in order to increase the chances they will opt in to a given study. As part of the effort to obtain representative data, panel providers aim for high opt-in rates and low attrition. Response rates vary across sample providers, with some in the range of 11.5% to 13% (Understanding America Study, GESIS Panel) and others as high as 36.9% (AmeriSpeak). To minimize coverage bias, panel providers pay close attention to the opt-in rate both when participants join the panel and when they decide to participate in certain studies.

Many sample providers also give their users reports on the degree to which the demographics of a particular sample are similar to the U.S. population. Most panels will also provide weights, which can be used to compensate when the data do not perfectly match known population parameters. Additionally, many providers also use quota sampling for underrepresented groups to increase representativeness (see Chapter 8).

In some cases, grants are available for academic researchers who use online probability-based panels. For example, Time-sharing Experiments for the Social Sciences (TESS) runs a large-scale survey through the AmeriSpeak panel. Researchers can apply for grants to use this nationally representative, probability-based online panel, provided they are engaged in social science projects that "utilize experimental designs and seek to make a valuable contribution to knowledge."

Data representativeness is the key goal of online probability-based panels. Representativeness allows for generalizability with precision from sample to population, which is critical for the purposes of some, but not all, research. For more details on what studies are most likely to be affected by issues of representativeness, and whether or not Mechanical Turk is well suited for specific research questions, see our discussion of the fit-for-purpose framework in Chapter 8.

TABLE 10.1 ● ONLINE NATIONALLY REPRESENTATIVE PROBABILITY-BASED PANELS

Panel Name	Size	Sample Frame	Recruitment Method	Public Availability for Data Collection	Administration Method	Area of Representativeness
American Life Panel	6,000	Address-based sampling from U.S. Postal Service, RDD, selection from previous representative sample groups	Mail, phone, in person	Yes	Online	USA
ELIPSS	1,000	Random household sampling from U.S. Census	Mail, phone, in person	Yes, via proposal	Online	Metropolitan France
AmeriSpeak	26,000 households	Random selection from NORC's National Frame	Mail, phone, in person	Yes	Online and by phone	USA
Understanding America Study	6,000	Random postal code–based sampling	Mail, phone	Yes	Online	USA
CentERPanel, LISS	2,000 households	Address-based sampling from U.S. Postal Service	Mail, phone	Yes	Online	Netherlands
GFK KnowledgePanel	55,000	Address-based sampling from U.S. Postal Service	Mail, phone	Yes	Online	USA
GESIS Panel	4,700	Sampling from municipal population registers	Web, mail, phone, in person	Yes, via proposal	Online and by mail	German speakers domiciled in Germany

OTHER MICROTASK PLATFORMS

Prior to describing market research platforms, it is worth noting that there are several online platforms whose basic structure is similar to Mechanical Turk. Platforms such as Figure Eight (previously CrowdFlower), Microworkers, and Prolific are typically smaller than or similar in size to Mechanical Turk and can be used to collect data in the same general way Mechanical Turk is used. We are not aware of any methodological advantages of using these platforms over Mechanical Turk, although some researchers prefer some platforms over others. Notable differences exist between Mechanical Turk and some of these alternative sources of online recruitment. For instance, Figure Eight provides enterprise services, meaning that it works with companies that purchase services in bulk, rather than with individual researchers. At the time of this writing, Prolific's participant pool is based mostly in Europe, with around 35% of the sample based in the United States.

Research examining data quality on these platforms has found that some are of similar quality to Mechanical Turk, while others are of lesser quality (Peer, Samat, Brandimarte, & Acquisti, 2015). Some research has been conducted to compare naïveté levels on Mechanical Turk and other platforms (Peer, Brandimarte, Samat, & Acquisti, 2017) (see Chapter 7 for an in-depth discussion of nonnaïveté). However, these studies did not use sampling practices that avoid superworkers (discussed in Chapter 7), and it is thus difficult to draw conclusions from the outcomes of these studies.

ONLINE MARKET RESEARCH PLATFORMS

Although probability samples are able to overcome the lack of representativeness of Mechanical Turk, they do not help when researchers want to sample hard-to-reach participants. There is, however, another class of platforms that are significantly larger than Mechanical Turk and offer numerous qualitative advantages over Mechanical Turk. These are market research platforms, which were created to give market researchers the capacity to target specific segments of the population for the purpose of conducting online market research. Hundreds of such providers exist, and platforms have evolved over the past 30-plus years to meet the needs of the market research community.

The main advantage of market research platforms is their size and their ability to recruit respondents who cannot otherwise be reached on microtask platforms. Table 10.2 provides several examples of studies that can easily be run on market research platforms but would be difficult or impossible on Mechanical Turk. As such, market research platforms provide an indispensable and complementary source of online participants for social and behavioral science research.

Number of Participants	Selective Targeting
400	Hispanic participants from Ohio who are not using a mobile device; African American participants from Ohio who are not using a mobile device
900	Four different income brackets, equally split within Democrats, Republicans, and Independents
1,000	Muslims, Jews, and conservative Christians
25,000	General population
5,000	Five different income brackets within each state, matched to each state's unique U.S. Census–based income distribution
600	Currently purchasing car insurance
3,000	Nationally representative sample in France
4,000	Sample matched to the U.S. Census based on age, gender, race, ethnicity, and education
10,000	Participants in Australia
1,500	Participants who are currently living in Philadelphia, matched to the U.S. Census on gender, race/ethnicity, and income
400	African Americans age 18-25
800	Three-wave longitudinal study in Malaysia
1,000	Democrats who have children
800	Participants who work in marketing
700	Bicultural and bilingual Asian participants
300	Asian participants who lived in the United States and China for five years each
2,400	Participants with chronic pain and sleep disturbance
400	Equal distribution of Democrats, Republicans, and Independents living in Ohio and Michigan
1,900	Adult cigarette and e-cigarette users
900	Individuals currently in psychotherapy who have attended at least three sessions

TABLE 10.2 ● EXAMPLES OF SAMPLES RECRUITED THROUGH MARKET RESEARCH PANELS

In Chapter 1 we briefly introduced the market research industry—a multibillion-dollar industry, used mostly by corporations to query people's attitudes and opinions about products and services. In the late 1990s the market research industry saw a major shift toward online data collection similar to the one currently occurring in academia. Just as academic researchers are increasingly becoming aware of the advantages of online participant recruitment over the more traditional lab-based approaches, public opinion firms likewise realized that online research provides many of the same advantages compared to telephone and face-to-face interviews that, up to that point, were the staple methodology in those fields. The shift to online public opinion research created a thriving market of online participant providers who serve the needs of both opinion poll and market research firms. In the discussion that follows, we provide some background on market research platforms that is relevant to social and behavioral research. How are these platforms created and maintained? What are the advantages of and limitations to collecting data from them? Most importantly, do these alternative sources of online data collection meet the data quality requirements of research in social and behavioral sciences?

Participant Recruitment on Market Research Platforms

Companies that maintain market research platforms often use two approaches to reach online participants. The first consists of asking potential panelists to opt in to a panel. This can be through advertisements anywhere online or offline, which route participants to sign up to be part of a panel. Once people express interest in being part of a panel, they are asked to provide demographic information and to answer questions about their background, interests, and preferences. Panel companies use this information to make people who match a certain profile available for specific studies.

The second commonly used approach is called river sampling. In river sampling, people are recruited directly into a particular study as they surf the web (Baker et al., 2013). People might see an advertisement to participate in a survey while they are playing a video game or shopping. Sometimes people who are first recruited through river sampling choose to join an opt-in panel after completing a particular questionnaire. In both opt-in and river samples, participants are given incentives to take surveys, for example, by earning cash or reward points or by being entered into sweepstakes.

Advantages of Market Research Panels Over Mechanical Turk

The key advantage of market research platforms over Mechanical Turk is access to a very large and constantly replenishing pool of participants. Because of their size, market research platforms allow researchers to selectively recruit subgroups of people, including people from hard-to-reach populations.

Table 10.2 lists several examples of targeted samples that can be easily recruited through market research platforms but could be difficult and in some cases impossible to recruit on Mechanical Turk. These samples, which were all recruited via Prime Panels, are not available on Mechanical Turk because Mechanical Turk doesn't have (a) access to these populations, such as participants living in Australia; (b) access to these groups in high enough numbers, such as 25,000 participants from the general population; or (c) mechanisms for the selective recruitment of the target group, such as participants living in Philadelphia.

In addition to having the capacity to sample specific subgroups, another benefit of market research platforms is that they are more representative of the U.S. population than is Mechanical Turk. In one study that examined this issue directly, Chandler et al. (2019) compared the demographic composition of samples collected on Mechanical Turk and Prime Panels—a provider of market research samples that aggregates from multiple platforms—with the nationally representative ANES panel. The demographic characteristics of participants recruited from Prime Panels were more representative of the U.S. population than were MTurk samples. In particular, the Prime Panels sample was older, more religious, more likely to be married and have children, less likely to have a college degree, and more politically conservative—all areas in which the MTurk population is known to diverge from the general U.S. population (see Chapter 6).

Among the most striking differences between Mechanical Turk and Prime Panels were differences in age, religiosity, and political composition. For age, participants recruited on Prime Panels more closely matched the U.S. population than did those on Mechanical Turk. On Mechanical Turk, close to 90% of participants were under age 50, only 3.3% were older than 60, and almost none were older than 70. On Prime-Panels, however, close to 40% of participants were older than 50, 16.1% were older than 60, and 7.5% were older than 70. Thus, the age distribution on Prime Panels more closely matches the age distribution of the U.S. population.

In terms of religious attitudes, participants on Prime Panels were virtually indistinguishable from the U.S. population, whereas participants on Mechanical Turk were considerably less religious. For example, less than 14% of the ANES and Prime Panels samples reported being agnostic or atheist, compared to more than 40% on Mechanical Turk. Furthermore, compared to Mechanical Turk, Prime Panels participants were substantially more likely to identify as Christian and to say that religion is very important or central to their lives and that they consult God through prayer on a daily basis.

Finally, political orientation is another characteristic where Mechanical Turk differed from the U.S. population, but Prime Panels looked a lot like the representative ANES sample. For example, on Mechanical Turk, more than 55% of participants reported being liberal, compared to just 35% on Prime Panels and 36% in the probability-based ANES sample.

Demographic differences like those reviewed here are important because they can sometimes influence experimental treatment effects. This point is perhaps best illustrated by the study, discussed in Chapter 8, in which participants were asked their opinion toward abortion either before or after answering a question about God's opinion toward abortion. In a representative sample of the U.S. population, people's attitudes become less favorable toward abortion when the God-centered question was presented first. In a convenience sample of MTurk workers, however, the God-centered question does not influence participants' attitudes toward abortion. This is because MTurk workers are overwhelmingly nonreligious and are thus not affected by a God-centered prime. Prime Panels participants, by contrast, are much more representative of the U.S. population in terms of religiosity, and Chandler et al. (2019) found that the God-centered question affected their attitudes toward abortion in the same way as a nationally representative sample.

Such studies show that sample composition can be an important factor in the ability to detect some treatment effects. The more representative population on market research platforms may thus play a role in researchers' ability to replicate findings in some areas of the social and behavioral sciences. Because religious attitudes are correlated with multiple political and psychological outcomes, the strong skew of the MTurk population with regard to religious attitudes may present a potential threat to the external validity of some studies conducted on Mechanical Turk, particularly those whose outcomes are strongly correlated with religiosity.

The same point potentially applies to other variables—such as age, political orientation, education, income, and family composition—that are highly skewed on Mechanical Turk, particularly when these variables are correlated with outcomes of interest. For example, age is an important moderator of many psychological outcomes (e.g., Ng & Feldman, 2010; Rhodes, 1983) and political attitudes (e.g., Alwin, Cohen, & Newcomb, 1991; Oxley et al., 2008). Thus, studies that recruit participants from market research platforms, which more closely match the age distribution of the U.S. population, may have higher external validity when outcomes of interest are correlated with age.

At the same time, as discussed in Chapter 8, existing evidence suggests that the vast majority of experimental treatment effects replicate on Mechanical Turk despite the demographic differences between MTurk workers and the U.S. population. Significantly more research is needed in order to understand how the sample composition of various opt-in panels, including Mechanical Turk and market research platforms, can influence the outcomes and effect sizes of specific studies.

Finally, another advantage of market research platforms over Mechanical Turk is overall lower levels of nonnaïveté. Consistent with the notion that MTurk participants are increasingly becoming familiar with protocols that are commonly encountered in the social and behavioral sciences, Chandler et al. (2019) found that familiarity with common stimuli was significantly higher in a standard MTurk sample compared to Prime Panels. In particular, exposure rates to the Cognitive Reflection Test and the trolley dilemma on Mechanical Turk were 70% and 60.5%, respectively. On Prime Panels the exposure rates were 19% and 11%, respectively. Data also indicated that performance on the trolley dilemma and Cognitive Reflection Test was attenuated on Mechanical Turk due to overexposure to these stimuli.

It is important to note, however, that MTurk samples were recruited using standard sampling techniques. As described in Chapter 7, nonnaïveté can be easily reduced on Mechanical Turk by stratifying a sample based on activity level or using a maximum HIT completion requirement (see Robinson, Rosenzweig, Moss, & Litman, 2019). Thus, nonnaïveté levels on market research platforms are lower relative to Mechanical Turk only when the sampling strategies suggested in Chapter 7 are not used.

Data Quality on Market Research Platforms

As described earlier, one advantage of market research platforms over Mechanical Turk is that they provide access to larger pools of participants who are, as a whole, more representative of the U.S. population and more naive to common stimuli used in the social and behavioral sciences. However, market research samples also suffer from some very important limitations, the most important of which is low data quality.

The general framework for thinking about data quality on market research platforms is captured in Figure 10.1. Market research platforms are vastly larger than Mechanical Turk. Although the exact numbers of panelists are difficult to estimate, it is likely that the global pool is close to 100 million, with close to 20 to 30 million people in the United States. The MTurk participant pool, by contrast, is approximately 85,000 participants per year. Although the MTurk population is smaller, the proportion of highly attentive participants on Mechanical Turk is very high.

While the pool of participants is significantly larger on market research platforms than on Mechanical Turk, the proportion of inattentive participants is much larger too. Despite this drawback, market research platforms have a greater number of attentive participants than does Mechanical Turk due to the sheer size of the market research pool. Thus, market research platforms offer a significantly larger and more representative pool of attentive participants. However, the inattentive participants on market research platforms must be screened out in order to effectively leverage its potential. In the next section we describe screening techniques that have been used

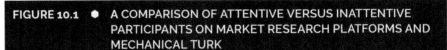

FIGURE 10.1 ● A COMPARISON OF ATTENTIVE VERSUS INATTENTIVE PARTICIPANTS ON MARKET RESEARCH PLATFORMS AND MECHANICAL TURK

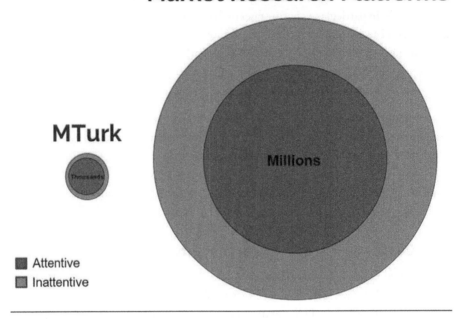

to sample participants on market research platforms and also discuss how screened market research samples compare to MTurk samples.

Screening Participants on Market Research Platforms

On Mechanical Turk, data quality is maintained by a reputation mechanism that is ingrained into the platform's very culture (see Chapter 2). This reputation mechanism keeps workers attentive for fear that they will lose out on high-paying HIT opportunities if they accumulate several rejections. Market research platforms, however, lack this robust reputation mechanism. Although market research platforms vary widely in their panel management practices, participants on these platforms are generally not ingrained into a larger working culture and do not necessarily have to worry as much about the long-term consequences of their reputation. For these reasons, the lack of a reputation mechanism may result in severe reductions in data quality on such platforms.

Consistent with these expectations, several studies that have examined data quality on market research platforms have found high levels of inattentiveness among participants (Chakraborty, 2014; Conklin, 2009; Courtright & Miller, 2011; Downes-Le

Guin, Mechling, & Baker, 2006; Hays, Liu, & Kapteyn, 2015; Kees, Berry, Burton, & Sheehan, 2017; Smith, Roster, Golden, & Albaum, 2016; Teitcher et al., 2015). Studies typically report that close to 30% of respondents do not read questions at all and may engage in straightlining, the practice of selecting the same response option for all questions. Kees et al. (2017) directly compared the data quality of a study on a market research platform to that of Mechanical Turk. They found that the pass rate of attention manipulation checks was strikingly lower on the market research platform. Whereas the pass rate on Mechanical Turk was more than 90%, only 50% of market research participants correctly answered attention check questions such as "Is Barack Obama the first president in the United States?" According to the study's authors, it is likely that people misread this question as ". . . the first Black president . . .?," because they were not paying close attention.

Due to legitimate concerns about data quality on market research platforms, researchers must take care to screen out inattentive participants. Implementing screening practices is considerably more important on market research platforms than on Mechanical Turk. MTurk studies show that, even in the absence of any attention checks, the reputation mechanism can be sufficient to ensure high data quality (e.g., Peer et al., 2015). On market research platforms, by contrast, the absence of screening mechanisms results in substantial data quality problems. A key question is thus whether the use of screening procedures sufficiently increases data quality on market research platforms.

This question was addressed by Chandler et al. (2019). In their study, a screener was used to vet participants on market research platforms for attention and basic English proficiency. The screener, which consisted of four Likert items, was positioned prior to the beginning of the study. About 35% of participants on market research platforms failed the screener, compared to only 4% of participants on Mechanical Turk. Participants on Prime Panels who did not pass the screener (but were nevertheless allowed to complete the study so that their data could be examined) had unacceptably low internal reliabilities on survey questions, low pass rates on attention checks in the survey, and standard experimental effect sizes that were smaller than typical. Prime Panels participants who passed the screener, by contrast, provided data that had internal reliabilities and standard experimental effect sizes similar to published norms. Specifically, in a series of four experiments—the "Asian disease" problem (Tversky & Kahneman, 1981), Mount Everest (Jacowitz & Kahneman, 1995), the trolley dilemma (Thomson, 1976), and political equality (see Mullinix, Leeper, Druckman, & Freese, 2015)—effect sizes were nearly identical on Mechanical Turk and Prime Panels. Effects in some of these experiments rely on participants' careful reading of specific wording that distinguishes one experimental condition from another. This indicates that participants who are recruited through market research platforms are as attentive to commonly used stimuli as MTurk workers, provided that extensive screening is used to route inattentive participants out of a study.

OVERALL COMPARISONS BETWEEN MECHANICAL TURK AND MARKET RESEARCH PLATFORMS

In order to obtain high levels of data quality on market research platforms, a large number of participants need to be screened out. These screens are intended to have a similar effect on data quality as the reputation mechanism on Mechanical Turk. While the use of such screeners is sufficient to obtain high levels of data quality for the purposes of most research studies, the kind of work that such participants are willing to engage with will still likely be qualitatively different from the kinds of work Mechanical Turk participants are ready to take on.

As discussed in Chapter 2, MTurk participants see themselves as workers who are willing to perform many different types of highly demanding tasks, including those that take many hours. Market research participants, by contrast, mostly see themselves as respondents in survey studies. Although they are willing to stay attentive and answer questions for short durations, few are willing to engage in the kinds of categorization and transcribing tasks that are standard on Mechanical Turk. For these reasons, Mechanical Turk provides better quality data on several types of tasks even after inattentive participants are screened out of market research samples.

Thus, while market research platforms provide significant advantages over Mechanical Turk in terms of offering a larger and more representative population and more flexible targeted recruitment, Mechanical Turk offers its own numerous advantages over market research platforms. Market research platforms typically limit study participation to under 20 minutes, whereas on MTurk participants can engage in studies over many hours. Additionally, participants on Mechanical Turk engage in open-ended responses, and have low dropout rates in longitudinal survey studies, especially when the right participants are recruited and best sampling practices are used (see Chapter 8). As a general rule, the level of in-depth engagement on Mechanical Turk significantly surpasses that of market research platforms. For these reasons, both market research platforms and Mechanical Turk offer unique advantages and should thus be viewed as complementary sources of online recruitment for different types of studies in the social and behavioral sciences.

There are also numerous structural differences between Mechanical Turk and market research platforms. On Mechanical Turk, researchers have more control over various study settings, allowing for direct communication with participants, while maintaining anonymity. Perhaps the biggest difference is in how compensation levels are set. On Mechanical Turk, researchers have more control over various study settings, and through third-pary platforms can directly communicate with participants while maintaining anonymity. On market research platforms, by contrast, researchers do not typically set compensation levels and often do not know how much participants are paid. Furthermore, compensation varies considerably across providers in terms of both type and amount. For example, SurveyMonkey gives 50 cents to the participant's charity of choice for participating in a study that lasts up to 20 minutes. Other platforms give gift cards or reward points. Yet others have their own point systems, and once participants have enough points they can redeem the points for either cash or gift cards. Researchers typically have no way of knowing or quantifying exactly how much participants would be paid in terms of cash value (see Antoun, Zhang, Conrad, & Schober, 2016). Institutional review boards may at times want to know about participant compensation, since some are more used to the transparent compensation process on Mechanical Turk. The overall process of market research platforms is similar to Mechanical Turk in that there are online participants who engage in studies for various rewards, but researchers using market research platforms typically do not have knowledge of what these rewards are.

Another important consideration is that market research platforms often collaborate with one another in order to increase reach and maximize the likelihood of finding hard-to-reach participants. Hard-to-reach samples can be recruited more easily by aggregating across multiple suppliers, as is done by Qualtrics and Prime Panels. Indeed, because many hard-to-reach participants are simply impossible to recruit without aggregating, much market research would not be feasible or would be prohibitively expensive without it.

There are numerous other minor differences between market research platforms and Mechanical Turk. For example, on market research platforms there is no need for a secret code. Once participants complete the study, they are automatically redirected to a landing page and their IDs are recorded in the system.

CONCLUSION

Mechanical Turk and market research platforms both offer unique advantages and have specific limitations. Among academics, Mechanical Turk is a much better studied and understood platform, perhaps the most well-researched and well-understood participant pool in the world. The MTurk worker pool has been studied extensively both in terms of the demographic and attitudinal composition of workers, and in terms of workers' behavior, such as participation rates in typical studies, sample composition across time of day, and follow-up rates in longitudinal studies. Much less is known about market research platforms in terms of both demographic composition and participant behavior. Significant research will be needed to examine all these questions in order to fully realize the value of these platforms for research in the social and behavioral sciences, as well as their potential to supplement Mechanical Turk as a source of participant recruitment.

From what is already known about market research samples, screening methods are essential for attaining high-quality data. Research indicates that when screening methods are used, market research platforms are a viable source of online participants, complementary to Mechanical Turk.

REFERENCES

Alwin, D. F., Cohen, R. L., & Newcomb, T. M. (1991). *Political attitudes over the life span: The Bennington women after fifty years*. Madison: University of Wisconsin Press.

Antoun, C., Zhang, C., Conrad, F. G., & Schober, M. F. (2016). Comparisons of online recruitment strategies for convenience samples: Craigslist, Google AdWords, Facebook, and Amazon Mechanical Turk. *Field Methods, 28*(3), 231–246.

Baker, R., Brick, J. M., Bates, N. A., Battaglia, M., Couper, M. P., Dever, J. A., . . .Tourangeau, R. (2013). Summary report of the AAPOR task force on non-probability sampling. *Journal of Survey Statistics and Methodology, 1*(2), 90–143. doi:10.1093/jssam/smt008

Casey, L. S., Chandler, J., Levine, A. S., Proctor, A., & Strolovitch, D. Z. (2017). Intertemporal differences among MTurk workers: Time-based sample variations and implications for online data collection. *SAGE Open, 7*(2). doi:10.1177/2158244017712774

Chakraborty, N. (2014). Online MR quality: Is ignorance bliss? Insights Association. Retrieved from https://www.insightsassociation.org/article/online-mr-quality-ignorance-bliss

Chandler, J., Rosenzweig, C., Moss, A. J., Robinson, J., & Litman, L. (2019). Online panels in social science research: Expanding sampling methods beyond mechanical Turk. *Behavior Research Methods, 51*(5), 2022–2038. doi:10.3758/s13428-019-01273-7

Conklin, M. (2009). What impact do "bad" respondents have on business decisions? Retrieved from http://www.markettools.com/downloads/WP_BadRespondents.pdf?

Courtright, M., & Miller, C. (2011). "Respondent validation: So many choices!" *Paper presented at the CASRO Online Research Conference*, Las Vegas, NV.

Craig, B. M., Hays, R. D., Pickard, A. S., Cella, D., Revicki, D. A., & Reeve, B. B. (2013). Comparison of US panel vendors for online surveys. *Journal of Medical Internet Research, 15*(11), e260. doi:10.2196/jmir.2903

Downes-Le Guin, T., Mechling, J., & Baker, R. (2006). Great results from ambiguous sources: Cleaning Internet panel data. *ESOMAR World Research Conference: Panel Research*.

Hays, R. D., Liu, H., & Kapteyn, A. (2015). Use of Internet panels to conduct surveys. *Behavior Research Methods, 47*(3), 685–690. doi:10.3758/s13428-015-0617-9

Huff, C., & Tingley, D. (2015). "Who are these people?" Evaluating the demographic characteristics and political preferences of MTurk survey respondents. *Research & Politics, 2*(3). doi:10.1177/2053168015604648

Jacowitz, K. E., & Kahneman, D. (1995). Measures of anchoring in estimation tasks. *Personality and Social Psychology Bulletin, 21*(11), 1161–1166. doi:10.1177/01461672952111004

Kees, J., Berry, C., Burton, S., & Sheehan, K. (2017). An analysis of data quality: Professional panels, student subject pools, and Amazon's Mechanical Turk. *Journal of Advertising, 46*(1), 141–155. doi:10.1080/00913367.2016.1269304

Levay, K. E., Freese, J., & Druckman, J. N. (2016). The demographic and political composition of Mechanical Turk samples. *SAGE Open, 6*(1). doi:10.1177/2158244016636433

Mullinix, K. J., Leeper, T. J., Druckman, J. N., & Freese, J. (2015). The generalizability of survey experiments. *Journal of Experimental Political Science, 2*(2), 109–138. doi:10.1017/XPS.2015.19

Ng, T. W. H., & Feldman, D. C. (2010). The relationships of age with job attitudes: A meta-analysis. *Personnel Psychology, 63*(3), 677–718. doi:10.1111/j.1744-6570.2010.01184.x

Oxley, D. R., Smith, K. B., Alford, J. R., Hibbing, M. V., Miller, J. L., Scalora, M., . . .Hibbing, J. R. (2008). Political attitudes vary with physiological traits. *Science, 321*(5896), 1667–1670. doi:10.1126/science.1157627

Peer, E., Brandimarte, L., Samat, S., & Acquisti, A. (2017). Beyond the Turk: Alternative platforms for crowdsourcing behavioral research. *Journal of Experimental Social Psychology, 70*, 153–163. doi:10.1016/j.jesp.2017.01.006

Peer, E., Samat, S., Brandimarte, L., & Acquisti, A. (2015). Beyond the Turk: An empirical comparison of alternative platforms for crowdsourcing online research. *ACR North American Advances.*

Rhodes, S. R. (1983). Age-related differences in work attitudes and behavior: A review and conceptual analysis. *Psychological Bulletin, 93*(2), 328–367. doi:10.1037/0033-2909.93.2.328

Robinson, J., Rosenzweig, C., Moss, A. J., & Litman, L. (2019). Tapped out or barely tapped? recommendations for how to harness the vast and largely unused potential of the mechanical Turk participant pool. *PLOS ONE, 14*(12), e0226394. doi:10.1371/journal.pone.0226394

Smith, S. M., Roster, C. A., Golden, L. L., & Albaum, G. S. (2016). A multi-group analysis of online survey respondent data quality: Comparing a regular USA consumer panel to MTurk samples. *Journal of Business Research, 69*(8), 3139–3148. doi:10.1016/j.jbusres.2015.12.002

Teitcher, J. E. F., Bockting, W. O., Bauermeister, J. A., Hoefer, C. J., Miner, M. H., & Klitzman, R. L. (2015). Detecting, preventing, and responding to "fraudsters" in internet research: Ethics and tradeoffs. *Journal of Law, Medicine & Ethics, 43*(1), 116–133. doi:10.1111/jlme.12200

Thomson, J. J. (1976). Killing, letting die, and the trolley problem. *The Monist, 59*(2), 204–217. doi:10.5840/monist197659224

Tversky, A., & Kahneman, D. (1981). The framing of decisions and the psychology of choice. *Science, 211*(4481), 453–458. doi:10.1126/science.7455683

11

CONDUCTING ETHICAL ONLINE RESEARCH

A Data-Driven Approach

Leib Litman and Jonathan Robinson

INTRODUCTION

While conducting a study in January 2017, we received the following email from a participant: "Thank you so much. I'm bordering on emotional thankful tears! It means so much!" The chain of events that led to this message began with confusion over a simple 60-cent bonus. In the study we ran, workers who completed certain tasks were eligible for a bonus. However, due to an incorrectly placed message at the end of the survey, this participant was under the impression that no bonus would be given. Even though the bonus was relatively small, the participant had become distraught not only because of the lost opportunity to earn money, but also, we suspect, because they felt unfairly treated and powerless. We quickly responded and reassured the participant that the bonus would soon be granted. Our short reply made the participant feel like someone cared about treating them fairly. Their email let us know how much our small act—a friendly email reply—meant.

This story and many others like it illustrates a fundamental principle of conducting online research. Online participants are real people who are emotionally and financially affected by the actions of researchers. Sometimes it is easy to forget there is a human on the other end of the Internet connection because online research lacks personal contact. But, when collecting online data, researchers should strive to treat participants as if they were participating face-to-face in a field experiment or lab study.

Treating online participants ethically has multiple challenges. It requires understanding both the culture of online ecosystems and the technical aspects of the platforms on which studies are conducted. The primary goal of this chapter is to provide information that will help researchers make informed ethical decisions when conducting studies on Mechanical Turk. We begin with a brief review of ethical principles that have historically guided behavioral research and how they apply to Mechanical Turk. Then, we cover three ethical issues specifically related to research on Mechanical Turk: how much to pay participants, whether it is acceptable to reject work, and how to maintain participant anonymity. Finally, we close the chapter with several recommendations for how researchers can conduct research on MTurk that is both ethical and shows respect for research participants.

HISTORICAL BACKGROUND

The ethical treatment of human subjects is integral to social science research. Ethical considerations affect almost every aspect of the research process from study design to data collection and post-study data management. The principles that guide research ethics have evolved over the course of the 20th century and continue to develop today. The need for the ethical principles that guide research to evolve is especially clear when considering the novel contexts in which research occurs today, such as online platforms.

The Nuremberg Code was the first post–World War II formulation of ethical principles for human experimentation, which resulted from the consideration of atrocities carried out by the Nazis. The Nuremberg Code consists of 10 points, some of which provide the foundation for today's ethical principles and federal regulations. The Nuremberg Code stresses the need for *informed consent*, an examination of *risk and benefit*, and the right of participants to *quit at any time*.

In the United States the revelations of abuses that took place in the Tuskegee clinical trials led to the formation of the National Commission for the Protection of Human Subjects of Biomedical and Behavioral Research. In 1979 the commission issued the Belmont Report with two stated goals. The first was to "identify the basic ethical principles that should underlie the conduct of biomedical and behavioral research." The second was to "develop guidelines which should be followed to assure that such research is conducted in accordance with those principles." In keeping with these goals, the Belmont Report is divided into two separate sections: (a) Ethical Principles and (b) Applications.

Items in the Applications section of the Belmont Report typically used the Nuremberg Code as a starting point. The Belmont Report then presented those applications within a larger theoretical framework relating to the ethical principles that were supposed to underlie the applications. For example, the specific application of *informed consent* was framed in the Belmont Report within a larger ethical principle of *respect for persons*. Respect for persons focuses on the foundational notion that every human being should be capable of *self-determination*, meaning that people need to be treated as *autonomous agents* capable of deliberation about issues that are important to them.

From the general principle of self-determination, several other specific applications arise, including that information needs to be presented in a *clear and comprehensible fashion*, that research has to be completely *voluntary*, and that participants must be given the opportunity to *stop the study at any time*. Another overarching ethical concept within the Belmont Report is that of *beneficence*, or making an effort to secure people's well-being. Out of this overarching ethical principle, which traces back to the Hippocratic Oath, the Belmont Report derives the application of *risk-benefit analysis*.

Taking the Belmont Report as its basic foundation, the U.S. Department of Health and Human Services developed the Code of Federal Regulation (45 CFR 46). Subpart A of the Health and Human Services code was later adopted by 17 federal agencies and is thus referred to as the Common Rule. Later modifications to the Common Rule became known as the Final Rule. In addition to these legal guides, various organizations, such as the American Anthropological Association and the American Psychological Association, have their own rules and guidelines that their members are expected to follow.

Although the ethical principles outlined above are familiar to most researchers, novel research environments such as Mechanical Turk and other online panels present situations and dilemmas that often have no direct precedent. In exploring these dilemmas, we are left to examine how the broader ethical principles of the Belmont Report—respect for persons, beneficence, self-determination, and risk-benefit analysis—apply to these novel contexts.

RISK OF HARM IN ONLINE RESEARCH

The first ethical consideration of any research study is the identification of potential sources of harm. What are the sources of potential harm in online research platforms, and how much risk do they pose to research participants? During its brief history, most online research has been considered to pose minimal risk (Kraut et al., 2004). The vast majority of online research studies consist of questionnaire instruments, vignettes, and measures of cognitive processes such as memory, attention, and reaction time. Engaging with such stimuli does not typically provoke more stress than a person might encounter in everyday life—the historical benchmark for assessing the magnitude of potential harm.

To examine how stressful it is to work on Mechanical Turk, we asked more than 10,000 MTurk participants the following question: "Do you find most MTurk surveys more or less distressing than typical things you encounter in everyday life?" Just over 93% of workers indicated that participating in MTurk studies is not more distressing than everyday life (see Figure 11.1). To ensure this result was not an artifact of the question wording, we asked the question in two different ways. In one version the question referred to the overall experience of participating in research studies on Mechanical Turk; in the second version the question referred specifically to the content of studies. In both cases, more than 93% of respondents indicated that MTurk studies were not more distressing than typical everyday experiences.

We later followed up with workers who indicated that MTurk work is more distressing than typical everyday experiences. Sixty percent reaffirmed this position, while the other 40% indicated that they no longer found MTurk work more distressing than everyday life. These results suggest that close to 4% of workers find Mechanical Turk reliably distressing. It is possible that the other 3% who initially said Mechanical Turk was distressing but then changed their minds may have been primed by a short-term aggravating experience or learned to avoid the

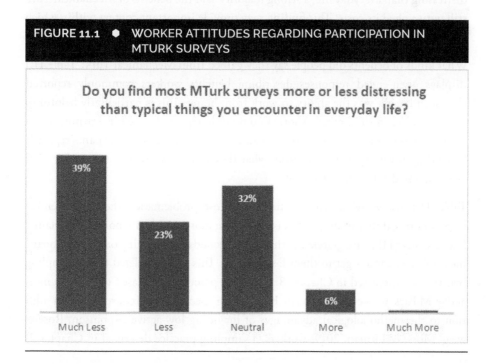

FIGURE 11.1 ● WORKER ATTITUDES REGARDING PARTICIPATION IN MTURK SURVEYS

Do you find most MTurk surveys more or less distressing than typical things you encounter in everyday life?

39%   23%   32%   6%

Much Less   Less   Neutral   More   Much More

more stressful aspects of Mechanical Turk work over time. Overall, these findings are consistent with other forms of online and offline research in the social and behavioral sciences, suggesting that participating in Mechanical Turk research poses minimal risk to the vast majority of participants.

At the same time, it is important to understand why a small minority of people consistently report that participating in studies on Mechanical Turk is distressing. To do so, we conducted a follow-up study to examine the most common sources of workers' distress and to assess workers' experiences from a cost-benefit perspective. Despite the stress that some workers may experience, what are the benefits for workers of having access to Mechanical Turk and do workers feel that the benefits outweigh costs?

In our follow-up study, we asked the 4% of workers who consistently reported that work on Mechanical Turk was more distressing than their everyday experiences to identify the most distressing part of working on Mechanical Turk. The most common answer was that HITs are hard to find. In fact, difficulty finding HITs was a more common complaint than low pay. Whereas 70% of workers reported finding HITs distressing, only 25% reported low pay as distressing.

What about aspects of Mechanical Turk that workers find beneficial? Overall, 75% of workers reported that the benefits of Mechanical Turk outweigh the costs. That is, among the 4% of workers who reliably reported that Mechanical Turk work is more distressing than everyday life, a strong majority said the benefits of Mechanical Turk still outweighed its costs. This finding may provide important context within which to interpret the reported distress.

What kinds of benefits did people say they gained from Mechanical Turk? Table 11.1 displays open-ended responses describing benefits workers commonly reported. One such benefit was the ability to work from home. This is particularly helpful to those who live in rural areas. Another commonly reported benefit is learning about interesting topics and trends in science and medicine. Indeed, participants reported benefiting in very specific ways from what they learn as workers. One worker even self-diagnosed a thyroid condition!

Table 11.1 shows what workers find the most problematic. These open-ended responses reveal that finding HITs is one of the most common reported complaints. Because most HITs are grabbed within a few seconds of appearing on the dashboard, most workers cannot get to them fast enough. This issue is related to the sampling bias that we discussed in Chapter 8. Sampling practices are biased toward the most active MTurk workers who accept HITs using specialized software. Thus, in addition to the methodological advantages of including low-active (Robinson, Rosenzweig, Moss, & Litman, 2019) workers (a sampling practice described in Chapter 7),

TABLE 11.1 ● POSITIVE AND NEGATIVE EXPERIENCES COMMONLY REPORTED BY MTURK WORKERS

Positive Experiences (besides money)	Negative Experiences
I find a lot of studies interesting and stimulating for my mind.	Avoiding rejections, getting rejections regardless of honest/good quality work.
Knowledge on some topics, (sleeping studies, mindfulness, etc.).	Most requesters are nice people, but some will just not respond or threaten people with blocks or rejections. Some requesters will lie about their pay rate.
Sometimes the studies can teach me new ways of thinking.	Finding requesters that don't reject for a simple mistake.
I've learned things, mainly about psychology but also general knowledge from different types of tasks.	Knowing you didn't miss an attention check, but getting a rejection anyway.
Sometimes, I actually learn about new topics and trends. At times it can be very educational.	Occasionally I'm asked to watch and comment on a video that is upsetting. I find some of the videos upsetting for personal reasons, and I'm even more upset that they don't contain a content disclaimer before I try them.
Every now and again I learn something that is fascinating, which causes me to read more about it.	Sometimes I have to look at and react to graphic pictures.
I can work from home, which I really prefer because I live in a rural area.	I dislike being asked to share certain personal information (again, insufficient warnings about this kind of content—I feel ambushed by it).
I have learned some interesting things along the way.	Unclear instructions.
I actually self-diagnosed my thyroid condition based on what I learned through a task I completed on MTurk.	AMT has hired so many workers that it takes as much time to find work as it does to actually do it. HITs literally disappear in milliseconds rather than hours.
How robots interact with the world, how machine learning works in cars, among other things.	Finding survey HITs to do is nearly impossible due to intense competition from others wanting to grab the same HIT. So in the end you end up with less to do unless you catch it first.

(Continued)

TABLE 11.1 ● *(Continued)*	
Positive Experiences (besides money)	**Negative Experiences**
	Good HITs being posted one at a time and disappearing instantly, not being able to make a living wage, underpaid work.
	I do thorough work and tend to take longer than the average MTurker as a result. Finding HITs where I don't have to worry much about a rejection, or that will pay appropriately for the time required takes a fair amount of time. To accomplish this, I have to utilize Chrome add-ons called MTurk Suite so that it can scan MTurk, to some extent filter out the available HITs, and afterwards I manually check each requester ratings on Turk Opticon or Turker View to determine if I should do the HIT. It's time consuming, and most of the time the good HITs are taken instantly, and I have to use MTurk Suite to keep retrying to catch the HIT, and hope that it does.
	Too hard to find good HITs these days.

Note: Representative open-ended responses of workers describing positive and negative MTurk work experiences. The responses included in this table are only from those workers who reported that MTurk work was more distressing than everyday life (4% of more than 10,000 workers polled).

sampling methodology may also have important ethical considerations. We address this issue in more detail later in this chapter.

Additional complaints by workers included low pay, seemingly unfair or arbitrary rejections, and the content of some surveys. In the discussion that follows, we first address the problem that survey content can pose to participants and then we explore best practices for setting wages and rejecting work.

RESEARCH ON SENSITIVE TOPICS

Some research on Mechanical Turk investigates sensitive topics such as trauma, sexual abuse, and drug addiction (e.g., Schnur et al., 2017). It is sometimes assumed that asking people about these topics or about their traumatic experiences will increase the risk of harm and may even retraumatize participants. However, the empirical litera-ture demonstrates that, for most people, participating in trauma-related research is not significantly more distressing than other things in day-to-day life (Cromer &

Newman, 2011; Newman & Kaloupek, 2004; Newman & Kaloupek, 2009). Indeed, even when rape victims and people with post-traumatic stress disorder (PTSD) are asked questions about their experiences, most report not finding the study upsetting and say they would still have participated if they had known what the study entailed (Griffin, Resick, Waldrop, & Mechanic, 2003).

A large literature on the experiences of sexual abuse and violence survivors (Black & Black, 2007; Black, Kresnow, Simon, Arias, & Shelley, 2006; Disch, 2001; Draucker, 1999; Edwards, Dube, Felitti, & Anda, 2007) shows that victims of trauma report that negative experiences while participating in survey research are minimal and that the benefits outweigh the costs in their view. As noted in a review of this literature, "Contemporary evidence . . . indicates a general absence of harm and, in fact, a generally positive experience for most research participants including those who previously have been exposed to traumatic stress or developed PTSD" (Newman & Kaloupek, 2009). Furthermore, "the risks associated with asking about abuse are overstated and inconsistent with actual data" (Gleaves, Rucklidge, & Follette, 2007, p. 236).

These findings are generally consistent with reports of MTurk workers. As described earlier, the vast majority of MTurk workers do not find participation in studies distressing, and of those who do, the vast majority say the benefits outweigh the costs. At the same time, for those workers who are distressed, 55% report that the content of surveys is one source of such distress. As shown in Table 11.1, content that participants reported as distressing included stimuli depicting gore and assault, graphic pictures including pornography, excessive violence, being made to watch videos with upsetting content, and being asked for personal information. Including such content in research studies is particularly distressing when no warning is given beforehand. Close to 60% of workers who reported being distressed by such content also said they would not be distressed if clear warnings were included.

A DEEPER DIVE INTO CONTROVERSIAL AND COMPLEX ISSUES

Although the content and procedures of most MTurk studies pose minimal risk of harm, several aspects of the research experience are unique to Mechanical Turk and require closer consideration. In the rest of this chapter we examine three issues we feel have received the highest level of attention: (a) how much should workers be paid, (b) whether and under what circumstances it is acceptable to reject work, and (c) anonymity.

ECONOMICS OF MECHANICAL TURK: CONSIDERATIONS FOR SETTING WAGES

How much to pay people for online studies is one of the most debated questions concerning the ethical conduct of research on Mechanical Turk. Although Mechanical Turk describes itself as a place for people to make money in their spare time, several MTurk workers report relying on MTurk as either full- or part-time employment. Furthermore, some research reports describe unfair treatment of MTurk workers (e.g., Fort, Adda, & Cohen, 2011; Marder & Fritz, 2015). Various researchers have claimed that MTurk workers make unacceptably low wages, with some estimates putting the median wage at close to $2.00 per hour (Hara et al., 2018). This debate has led some observers to conclude that researchers should be obligated to pay at least a minimum wage or more for MTurk work (e.g., Silberman et al., 2018).

However, many reports about wages on MTurk have been based on relatively small samples, have not examined important moderators of wages, or are not based on wages from academic research studies, which may differ from nonacademic studies in important ways. In this section we present wage data from a large multiyear database in order to describe the distribution of wages, how wages have changed over time, and how wages are affected by important moderators. Our goal is to present data that may inform practice.

FIGURE 11.2 ● MTURK WAGE INCREASES OVER TIME

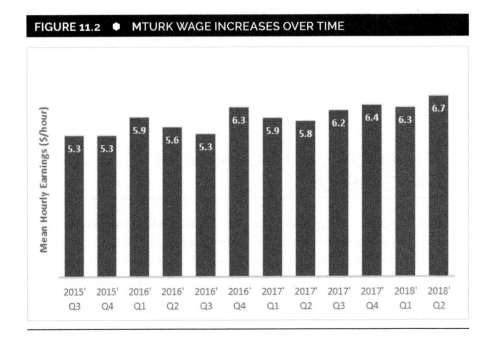

Mechanical Turk as an Economic Ecosystem

As in traditional marketplaces, wages on Mechanical Turk are driven by market forces. Requesters set prices and workers choose whether to work on tasks or not. CloudResearch (formerly TurkPrime) has collected data on more than 18 million completed tasks from 2015 to 2018. Across all of these tasks, the mean wage was $6.10 per hour. As shown in Figure 11.2, wages on Mechanical Turk are not stagnant. There has been a steady and consistent rise in wages from around $5.25 per hour in 2015 to about $6.70 per hour in 2018. This increase shows that even though requesters can set arbitrarily low wages, market forces have led to wage increases over time.

Importantly, the mean hourly wage does not fully capture the considerable complexity and variability of MTurk wages. Several additional factors are relevant for understanding the effective hourly wage across different Mechanical Turk tasks and workers.

Task-Based Wages

HIT payments on Mechanical Turk are set based on the task rather than on hourly wages. For this reason, the mean hourly wage of a HIT is not an indication of each worker's wages. There is significant variability in wages from one worker to another, depending on how quickly each person completes the task. For example, tasks that take 10 minutes to complete on average will be completed faster by some people and slower by others. Thus, each worker's effective hourly wage will differ substantially for the same task.

Within-HIT hourly wage variance shows that the average within-HIT standard deviation is $3.30 per hour. This means that, within any specific HIT, there is considerable variability in hourly wages across workers. Workers differ significantly in how quickly they complete HITs, creating large individual differences in earned wages.

Several factors predict workers' wages. One of the most significant factors is experience. Experienced workers are better at finding high-paying HITs and tend to work on such HITs almost exclusively. Experienced workers are also much faster at completing HITs. Because experienced workers tend to complete tasks faster than inexperienced workers, they are able to earn significantly more per hour.

CONSIDERATIONS OF ETHICS AND METHODOLOGY

Every researcher who runs a study on Mechanical Turk has to decide how much to pay participants. This decision has surprising methodological implications. Although the question of wages in general, and that of the minimum wage in particular, has received significant attention, there has been virtually no discussion regarding the implications of such decisions for sampling methodology.

Several studies (e.g., Buhrmester, Kwang, & Gosling, 2011), including our own (Litman, Robinson, & Rosenzweig, 2015), have shown that wages generally do not influence data quality on Mechanical Turk. However, data quality is not the same as sample composition. As we have seen throughout this book, wages have a profound influence on sample composition and dropout rates. When studies pay more than $6.00 per hour, over 65% of the sample will consist of superworkers (see Table 7.1). Thus, higher wages will affect both sample composition and wage equity.

From the perspective of sample composition, increasing wages makes it much more likely that the majority of participants in a study will be highly active superworkers. Because superworkers look for high-paying HITs and use tools to automatically accept such HITs, studies with high wages are likely to attract a large portion of experienced workers (see Table 7.1). At the same time, the increased participation of superworkers crowds out less active and inexperienced workers, who are the people earning the lowest wages on MTurk. This means that without an intervention to prevent superworkers from flooding into a study, increases in wages are likely to have an ironic effect, disproportionately increasing the earnings of superworkers, many of whom already may make more than $20.00 per hour (TurkerView, 2019).

For this reason, we believe that the ethics of wages cannot be considered in the absence of a parallel consideration of sampling methodology. Fortunately, the overrepresentation of superworkers can be addressed by setting quotas. As Figure 7.1 shows, the composition of superworkers in a sample is usually between 35% and 65%, depending on the pay. Thus, one approach to limiting superworkers is to set a quota of 30% across all pay scales, leaving the other 70% of HITs to other participants (see Robinson et al., 2019). Using quotas in this manner will ensure that increases in wages are distributed throughout the MTurk worker pool.

Another methodological consideration related to pay rate is dropout. Setting low wages significantly increases dropout, which can increase sample bias overall and can be particularly pernicious in randomized experimental designs (Zhou & Fishbach, 2016). Across studies, the dropout rate can be as high as 60% for studies with low hourly wages, compared to just 12% for high-paying studies (see Table 7.3). Low wages are also especially likely to increase dropout in longitudinal studies. Thus, although researchers are free to set arbitrarily low wages, participants are also free to not participate in or to drop out of such studies, which is exactly what workers tend to do.

Basic market forces have tended to make researchers increase wages over time (see Figure 11.2), and this trend will likely continue. We believe that fully understanding the connections among low wages, dropout rates, sample composition, and data quality will make researchers avoid low wages even more. At the same time, it is important for researchers to remember that a subclass of semiprofessional superworkers tend to make higher-than-average wages due to their speed and efficiency. Furthermore, without an intentional intervention, these superworkers are most likely to benefit from higher wages to the detriment of others. Thus, we advocate for changes in sampling practices, like quota sampling, that help ensure rising wages are distributed more evenly among MTurk workers.

Gender Disparities

Perhaps one of the most surprising findings to emerge from an examination of wage data on Mechanical Turk is the existence of systematic gender and race disparities. What is surprising is not so much that these disparities exist—after all, gender-based wage gaps are ubiquitous in traditional labor markets (e.g., Blau & Kahn, 2017)—but that they exist on a platform where workers are supposed to be anonymous. Unlike other gig-economy platforms, workers on Mechanical Turk do not create personal profiles, advertise pictures of themselves, or interact with requesters in ways that expose their identity unless they choose to. On an anonymous online platform, systematic wage disparities would seem to be a puzzle.

However, research reveals that just as higher paying HITs are more likely to attract superworkers, they are also more likely to attract participants who are younger, male, and more highly educated. Litman et al. (2019) examined wages across a span of four years, during which time more than 100,000 HITs were run on Mechanical Turk. A robust and persistent gender wage gap was observed that accounted for 4.7% of wages. The study looked only at HITs in which the requesters did not know the demographics of workers, including their gender. Additionally, the study controlled for covariates, including experience, age, income, education, family composition, race, number of children, time of day, day of week, task length, and 13 types of subtasks. The wage gap persisted even after these variables were controlled for. Indeed, separate analyses that examined the wage gap within each subcategory of every control variable showed that the wage gap is ubiquitous, persisting within each of the 90 examined subgroups.

Although the cause of the gender pay gap on Mechanical Turk is not entirely clear, what is clear is that the online sampling environment produces gender pay inequities similar to those observed in more traditional labor markets. These disparities occur when many mechanisms known to produce the gender wage gap in traditional labor markets are not at play in the online microtask environment. Such findings have important implications for online participant recruitment in the social and behavioral sciences, and they present both a challenge and an opportunity for researchers using online platforms.

Unlike traditional labor markets, online data collection platforms have built-in tools that can allow researchers to easily fix gender pay inequities. For example, researchers can simply use gender quotas to fix the ratio of male and female participants for every study. Simple fixes like this not only will produce more equitable wage outcomes but also are most likely advantageous for reducing sampling bias due to gender being correlated with pay. Thus, although there is a ubiquitous discrepancy in wages between men and women on online microtask platforms, such disparities have relatively easy fixes in online gig economy marketplaces such as Mechanical Turk, compared to traditional labor markets where gender-based pay inequities have often remained intractable. As with the superworker bias, gender and racial wage gaps on Mechanical Turk can be addressed by setting quotas.

REJECTING, BLOCKING, AND EXCLUDING WORKERS

As research participants, MTurk workers are unique in that their status as participants runs in parallel to their role as members of an online community that functions independently of scientific research. The dual status of workers as both research participants and platform members poses several questions. What is the nature of an MTurk worker's relationship with the researcher? Is it that of a participant to a researcher, an employee to an employer, or some combination of both? Employees are traditionally required to complete work for which they are paid and to meet some agreed-upon standards of quality. Research participants are traditionally expected to complete studies more or less as volunteers and, in accordance with the principles of research ethics, are free to withdraw from a study without penalty at any time. Does this mean it is unethical to reject work on Mechanical Turk? Is withholding payment considered a penalty? If so, are researchers obligated to pay participants even if they do not complete a study, or if they do not adequately complete a task? These are some of the difficult questions we turn to now.

Rejecting HITs

The question of whether or not to reject a HIT, and thus to withhold payment, arises when a worker does not complete a HIT according to some standard of effort or attention that is taken as common practice on the platform. For example, common sources of concern are workers who do not pass attention checks, who respond down the middle on surveys, or who do not provide answers to a required open-ended question (see Chapter 5). MTurk rules allow requesters to reject submitted work without stating a cause, meaning researchers have to set their own rules for rejecting workers. When work is rejected, not only do workers go unpaid, but the rejection also has a negative impact on their reputation, possibly making them ineligible for future HITs. Yet from the perspective of an employer-employee relationship, rejecting such work aligns perfectly with how the platform is intended to function.

However, the obligations of the researcher to MTurk workers as research participants may be in conflict with this function. Concerns over the implications of rejecting workers have led many institutional review boards (IRBs) to require researchers to pay all participants who complete a study, independent of their responses. As such, the position of many IRBs is that MTurk workers should never be rejected.

Figure 11.3 shows the distribution of rejections across more than 5,000 researchers. Overall, only 0.3% of all submitted assignments are rejected. Almost 49% of all requesters never reject any work. An additional 38% of requesters reject less than 1% of submitted assignments. Thus, close to 87% of researchers either never reject work or do so at an extremely low rate.

FIGURE 11.3 ● HIT REJECTION PATTERNS AMONG ACADEMIC REQUESTERS

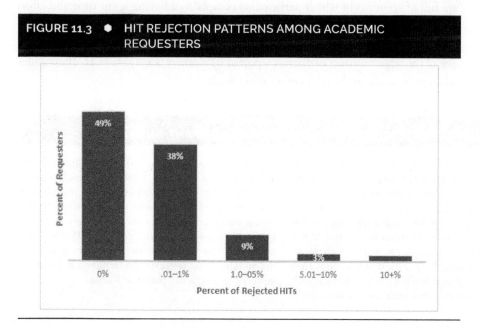

At the same time, there are some requesters who reject work at a much higher rate. Over 2% of requesters reject more than 10% of all submitted work, and some requesters reject more than 50% of all submitted assignments. This pattern of rejections shows that by and large academic requesters reject submitted work very infrequently. At the same time, some requesters reject work at a very high rate.

Arguments against Rejecting HITs
Uncertainty in Defining Quality

Outside of academic research studies, Mechanical Turk is typically used for tasks in which it is easy to verify whether the work was done correctly. However, in the majority of social and behavioral research studies, participants engage in tasks where determining attentiveness is inherently difficult. For example, it is difficult to know how carefully participants read survey questions. MTurk workers rarely if ever straightline, making easy-to-detect markers of inattention rarely useful in practice. In addition, attention manipulation checks correlate with each other at fairly low levels (see Chapter 5) and are not always reliable indicators of attentiveness or effort.

Adding to the complexity of this issue, attention manipulation checks are sometimes used in questionable ways. The reliability and validity of most attention checks are rarely assessed empirically. Many researchers rely on their intuition to determine what kinds of catch trials are appropriate and often use attention checks that are hard to pass even by well-meaning and attentive participants. Worker forums are full of accounts in which participants complain of having spent time and effort on completing a research study, only to be rejected for either unknown or dubious reasons (see Box 11.1). As discussed earlier in this chapter, being rejected unfairly is one of the largest sources of distress reported by workers (see Table 11.1). These issues raise concerns about the ethics of rejecting work.

BOX 11.1 INAPPROPRIATE REJECTION OF AN MTURK PARTICIPANT: AN EXAMPLE

My favorite ones were a batch that was something simple like click the best caption for an image. Had like a 60 min timer and paid like 7 or 8 cents for one or two clicks. Of course I filled my queue. I got rejections for "taking too long" on the hits. When I explained to them that some of the hits sit in the queue while I'm working on other hits, they explained they were doing a study that timed how long it took workers to do a simple task and rejected anyone that took over 3 minutes. I explained the queue system and that people aren't doing hits one at a time usually. He apologized, took down the study and told me if it screwed me over too much take it up with mturk. I laugh when I think about it now. It was about 50 rejections but I never do any more for one requester that would take me below 99%, especially new ones and this the situation that reminds me to not do too many for any one single requestor at a time.

Correlation Between Rejections and Demographics

Another concern about using attention checks to reject participants is that pass rates appear correlated with socioeconomic status, education, and other demographic factors. Although this issue has not been studied in detail, rejection rate data on Mechanical Turk show that certain demographic groups are more likely to be rejected than others.

Data from more than 18 million completed assignments recorded in the CloudResearch database show that younger workers and those over age 60 are most likely to be rejected. Additionally, participants who have only a high school education and those who finished less than one year of college are also significantly more likely to be rejected.

The rejection criteria used by researchers are unknown. However, to the extent that participants are rejected for failing attention checks, it may be that certain groups of participants are better prepared to perform well on such tasks. Mechanical Turk is a competitive environment in which wages are maximized by completing tasks quickly. Workers are constantly attempting to complete as many tasks as they can and to perform those tasks as quickly as possible. Processing speed, reading comprehension, and educational preparedness likely play a role in the ability to pass many of the tasks used by researchers to identify quality responses. It is not surprising, then, that participants with a low level of education will be less likely to pass such tasks.

Remember that the rejection discrepancy across demographic groups in academic research studies is a relatively small problem on Mechanical Turk. First, as noted earlier, only 0.3% of all tasks are rejected. Second, participants without a high school degree submit only 1% of all HITs on Mechanical Turk. Likewise, participants over age 60 are the least common group on the platform. However, the pattern of rejections on Mechanical Turk across demographic groups may be pointing to a larger methodological problem with the use of attention checks and other markers commonly used to assess data quality.

Specifically, the pattern of rejections points to a larger selection bias created by a tendency to disproportionately screen out certain demographic groups. Very little work has been done to date to understand the scope of this problem, how it arises, and what may be done to address it. For the present purposes, we want to point out that using overly stringent attention checks likely biases the sample against low education and elderly participants—the very people who are the hardest to find online and who contribute the most to sample diversity.

Arguments for Rejecting at Least Some HITs
Protecting the Health of the MTurk Ecosystem

Although the practice of accepting all submitted work protects each participant from potential mistreatment by the researcher, it has negative consequences for the well-being of the platform as a whole. As discussed in depth in Chapter 2, the rejection mechanism plays multiple roles in the MTurk ecosystem. In addition to protecting the individual requester from having to pay workers who did not complete their jobs, it protects the entire ecosystem from bad actors. When workers are rejected, their reputation is downgraded in addition to their not being paid. For workers who may try to game the system, multiple rejections downgrade their reputation to the point where they become ineligible for most HITs. Research has shown that workers with low reputation ratings are indeed much more likely to provide random data in psychology studies (Peer, Vosgerau, & Acquisti, 2014). Thus, rejecting such workers protects the research community as a whole by keeping bad actors from participating in research studies. When such workers are not rejected, their reputations remain intact and their fraudulent behavior is continuously reinforced.

How such problems can threaten the health of online participant platforms was demonstrated briefly in August 2018. During that time, researchers noticed a spike in bad-quality data—something that was seldom encountered previously on Mechanical Turk. As researchers started communicating with each other, it became clear the issue was widespread. In a short period of time, researchers discovered that the problem was arising from non-U.S. workers who were able to create U.S.-based accounts on Mechanical Turk (Moss & Litman, 2018). These workers used virtual private networks (VPNs), also commonly referred to as "server farms," to access studies in the United States. Several studies, including studies conducted by our research team (Moss & Litman, 2018), clearly showed these workers were providing random responses on survey questions and open-ended items. This issue spiraled out of control quickly, as popular media articles made unsubstantiated claims that Mechanical Turk was ruining social science with bad-quality data (Dreyfuss, Barrett, & Newman, 2018; Stokel-Walker, 2018).

Although the situation was brought under control quickly by identifying and blocking the offending worker accounts, this problem could have been prevented, or at least significantly minimized, if researchers rejected workers who they knew for certain were providing fraudulent data. Such workers would have quickly seen reductions in their reputation metrics, which would have made them ineligible for most academic research studies. However, because researchers were prevented from rejecting workers by their IRBs, the reputation mechanism could not be leveraged to extinguish this fraudulent behavior, leaving both the MTurk ecosystem and the entire research community exposed and vulnerable to fraud.

Do researchers and IRBs have an ethical responsibility to protect the research ecosystem from fraudulent actors? This is a complex question that arguably should be approached from the perspective of a risk-benefit analysis. The benefit conferred to society by scientific research is one of the foundational principles of the Belmont Report. Thus, the principle of beneficence may extend not only to the research participant but also to the larger society the research is aimed to benefit. It is thus important to consider this issue from a perspective that seeks to minimize risk both to participants and to the research process as a whole.

Protecting the Integrity of High-Paying HITs

Most research studies on Mechanical Turk are short and thus pay relatively little. The financial consequences of paying several workers who may have been inattentive are relatively minor. However, a growing number of studies on Mechanical Turk pay workers substantial compensation, sometimes totaling more than $500. Such studies require extra protection because without accountability they are certain to attract fraud. Having to pay all workers, independent of whether the task was completed properly, will make running such studies online impossible.

Autonomy

Finally, another issue relevant to the conversation about rejecting work is autonomy. At least some ethical theorists take the position that paid research participants should be held accountable to meet study requirements. Indeed, this argument is based on the notion that research participants should be treated as independent autonomous agents. The ethical principle of autonomy is one of the foundational concepts in both the Nuremberg Code and the Belmont Report. It stresses the need to treat research participants as autonomous agents, meaning they are free to act in whatever way they choose.

The concept of autonomy can be interpreted in several ways. Some researchers and IRBs have interpreted autonomy to mean that participants are free to act in any way they want. Under this interpretation, if a participant chooses to respond randomly and not to meet the basic requirements of a research study, that is in line with the participant's autonomous choice.

Others, however, have stressed that the principle of autonomy does not imply that participants can act with complete indifference to the fate of others. In the words of Edwards (2005), "Consent must conceptually involve some commitment to the project on which consent is based and, along with it, certain responsibilities to oneself and to others. . . . There are at least minimal standards of decency and respect to uphold on both sides."

Under this conception, when workers sign a consent form they agree to follow the basic requirements of the study. They are of course free to withdraw from the study at any time if they feel like it is not something they want to do. But the basic assumption of participation and reimbursement is predicated on the agreement that participants will follow the study's instructions and abide by the general rules that govern requester and worker interactions on Mechanical Turk. Having such expectations is in the best interest of all MTurk workers, since the absence of oversight may lead to decreased use of the platform and thus to the loss of participation opportunities for hundreds of thousands of people.

PRACTICAL ADVICE FOR REQUESTER-WORKER INTERACTIONS

The issues outlined previously pose challenging ethical dilemmas. Here, our aim is not to take a strong position on these issues. Instead, our goal is to suggest practices that in our view minimize the risk and maximize the benefit to participants, researchers, and the ecosystem as a whole.

Keep Rejections to a Minimum

Rejections should be made sparingly. For most studies in the social sciences, researchers should almost never reject more than 2% of workers. This rejection rate is consistent with the practices of more than 92% of academic requesters on Mechanical Turk, who reject fewer than 2% of submitted assignments (see Figure 11.3). By and large, online academic studies are relatively short, consisting of survey instruments and experimental manipulations. The overwhelming majority of participants are attentive to such stimulus materials. It is thus highly unlikely that more than a few participants should be rejected in most studies.

At the same time, there are exceptions to this rule. Some participants are inattentive and do not read instructions. Some research tasks are more demanding than others. The potential for fraud exists within all online platforms. When researchers can clearly demonstrate that a participant responded randomly or gave no effort to the task, a rejection may be warranted. In other situations, researchers might consider excluding or blocking workers.

Exclude Questionable Workers, Block Fraudulent Workers

As just mentioned, rejections should be made sparingly and when researchers have clear evidence that a worker has not given an honest effort to complete the HIT or has engaged in foul play. What should researchers do in situations that are less clear-cut? How can researchers make sure a worker who gave questionable effort does not wind up in a future study? We suggest using internal qualifications (see Chapter 3) to place the worker on an exclude list. Using an exclude list allows the researcher to make workers whose performance raises red flags ineligible for the study. Third-party platforms have features that make creating and using exclude lists easy (see Figure 4.10).

Importantly, researchers should recognize the difference between excluding and blocking workers. Researchers who wish to keep questionable workers out of future studies sometimes use Mechanical Turk's blocking feature. As described in Chapter 2, one potential problem with this feature is that many workers have reported that their account was suspended after they received blocks from multiple requesters. For this reason, we recommend that researchers use Mechanical Turk's blocking feature only in the most extreme cases of fraud.

Protecting Complex and High-Paying Studies

Although most online studies follow a relatively simple survey format, some studies are difficult, require participants to follow highly complex and lengthy instructions, involve unusual levels of effort, and offer high rates of compensation. Such studies may ask participants to provide detailed open-ended essay responses, to download and use an app, or to interact with others. For such studies, it is not uncommon for much larger percentages of workers not to follow instructions. Failing to reject the work of participants who do not adhere to task demands would result in much higher levels of fraudulent responses and would prevent such studies from being conducted at all. Hence, we recommend the following practices to reduce the rate of poor responses in such studies.

Pilot the Study and Solicit Feedback on the Clarity of Instructions

For complex studies, researchers should extensively pilot the study to understand the incidence rate of bad responses prior to launching the full study. If the rate of bad responses is higher than 2% or 3%, significant effort needs to be allocated to improving the instructions and clarifying the rejection criteria. We also suggest asking participants for feedback about the clarity of instructions. We often find that participants are not sure of the requesters' expectations. Allowing participants to provide feedback can often bring clarity to this issue.

Provide Clear Instructions

In one study, we paid participants upwards of $15 for open-ended responses based on reading several articles. We found that many responses did not meet our criteria in a pilot study. We then revised the instructions to include specific criteria for what we considered to be an adequate open-ended response. These criteria included a minimum number of words, a minimum number of sentences, at least one specific reference to the article participants were supposed to read, and a clear rationale linking the article content to the open-ended essay. Additionally, we provided a concrete example of an acceptable response.

We then piloted the study again and found that workers' responses were significantly improved. We additionally found that workers appreciated having specific criteria so that they knew exactly what to do.

Provide Opportunities to Resubmit the HIT

We also recommend giving workers an opportunity to redo the study, if possible. For studies where a second submission is possible, we recommend emailing workers whose submitted work does not meet the study's criteria, explain why, and offer an opportunity to try again. This applies primarily to complex tasks rather than to survey or experimental studies, where this would not typically be a viable option.

Best Practices for Minimizing Rejections

To summarize, we recommend the following approach to minimizing the number of rejected workers:

1. Most studies should not reject more than 2% of workers.

2. Reject workers who provide clearly fraudulent data but only when clear participant-level evidence for random responding is available.

3. Rather than rejecting work, prevent workers from participating in future studies by assigning qualifications.

4. Pilot complex studies to gauge data quality and rejection levels.

5. Engage in iterative piloting to improve instructions.

6. For complex studies, provide clear performance criteria.

7. Place the performance criteria both on the HIT instruction page and on the first page of the survey.

8. When possible, offer workers who do not meet performance criteria an opportunity to redo the study.

ANONYMITY

One thing that initially made Mechanical Turk so attractive to researchers was the ability to interact with participants anonymously. Anonymous survey research often is exempt from certain IRB requirements or receives expedited IRB status, making it much easier to collect data in a way that maintains ethical standards. But there are some challenges to maintaining participant anonymity.

Worker IDs

All participants on Mechanical Turk are assigned a unique alphanumeric string referred to as a worker ID. This worker ID is used to keep track of which participants complete a study, to send messages to participants, and in general to engage with participants in every way that is enabled by the MTurk interface. Worker IDs are an attractive feature because they allow for data collection to be anonymous while enabling researchers to keep track of participants, to prevent duplicate completions, and to invite participants for longitudinal follow-up.

In the process of a standard MTurk study, different data files are collected. The majority of behavioral researchers use third-party platforms for hosting their MTurk studies. For example, if researchers are conducting a study looking at personality traits using the Big Five and are also collecting demographic information, they will typically use a third-party platform such as Qualtrics to collect their data. Any sensitive information that is collected in the course of a study—for example, the sexual orientation of participants—is stored on Qualtrics and not on Amazon Mechanical Turk. Importantly, by default the Qualtrics data file does not contain information that can directly link the study data with the worker IDs.

Separately, on Mechanical Turk there is another data file with information about each worker who completed a study. This data file can be downloaded as a CSV file containing a list of all the worker IDs and other study-related information, including the start and end time of the study and how much each participant was paid (see Figures 3.22 and 3.26). Because the worker IDs and the data for the study are stored in separate data files, the personally identifiable information that is collected as part of the study can still be said to be protected since there is no way to link information from the Qualtrics data file to the CSV file.

A more problematic scenario emerges when it is necessary to collect worker IDs and insert them into the study data file. This can be necessary for multiple reasons. One common reason for collecting worker IDs is for payment purposes. For example, many researchers give bonuses based on performance. To do this, it is necessary to keep track of which worker ID is associated with each participant's data. Another common reason for collecting worker IDs is for follow-up in longitudinal studies. For studies in which workers participate in multiple waves, researchers need worker IDs in order to invite participants to subsequent sessions and to link data in the longitudinal datasets across participants.

Similar procedures are required in order to conduct targeted recruitment studies. A common practice on Mechanical Turk is to conduct two-wave studies in which participants are asked about specific criteria in the first wave and are later targeted for selective recruitment in later waves.

Indeed, including worker IDs in data files is often indispensable, and third-party platforms provide ways to automatically insert worker IDs in data files by embedding them in the URL (see Figure 4.5).

Studies that require worker IDs to be collected face the problem that the same Qualtrics data file will contain sensitive information and worker IDs. This problem is compounded by the fact that worker IDs have not been fully anonymized in the past (Lease et al., 2013).

Worker IDs of MTurk participants have in the past been the same as the IDs associated with their Amazon user profile. This means that worker IDs could be traced to the Amazon profile containing information about an individual's shopping history, address, picture, and other personally identifiable information.

For worker IDs to be traced to an Amazon account, users need to allow for their account information to be viewable publicly. It is not known what percentage of participants did that. However, for those participants who did make their account information public, their Amazon worker IDs were traceable directly to the personally identifiable information on their Amazon accounts. For example, Lease et al. (2013) showed that certain worker IDs could simply be entered into a Google search and the individual's full profile as it existed in their Amazon account would be revealed. Mechanical Turk has fixed this problem, and worker IDs are no longer linked to workers' Amazon profiles. However, this issue highlights the need to treat worker IDs with care.

An additional problem can sometimes arise when workers email researchers from their personal email accounts. Workers commonly contact requesters to inquire about a study. The emails sent by workers are almost always sent from their personal accounts. These emails often contain the worker ID, actual name of the worker, and their email address, thus linking the worker ID to personally identifiable information.

Best Practices for Managing Worker IDs

When a researcher adds worker IDs to their data file, several steps can be taken to protect the data. A linking file can be created that contains the worker IDs and random alphanumeric strings. The strings can then be added to the data file, circumventing the need to store the worker IDs in that file. The linking file should be kept on a separate computer. This way if the computer with the Qualtrics data file is lost or compromised, there will be no way to link the personal data to the worker IDs. Third-party apps can automatically add such strings to the data files instead of using worker IDs (see Figure 4.13).

Overall, Mechanical Turk provides a powerful infrastructure that enables researchers to have close contact with their research participants on the one hand, while maintaining anonymity on the other. Worker IDs should not be treated as being completely anonymous, and considerable care should be taken to protect the sensitive information that is collected in the course of a study. While linking worker IDs to study data is often unavoidable, researchers should consider using replacement IDs instead. This goal can be achieved by using either linking files or third-party tools.

BEST PRACTICES FOR CONDUCTING ETHICAL RESEARCH ON MECHANICAL TURK

Even though online research studies pose minimal risk to most participants, researchers should still follow best practices in order to minimize the potential of harm, distress, and inconvenience to workers. In this section we outline several best practices that apply to Mechanical Turk research. These best practices are divided into two sections that cover general guidelines applicable to all studies and guidelines for studies with sensitive content.

Some of these practices were described in earlier parts of the book and are repeated here to highlight their importance for the ethical treatment of online research participants.

Best Practices for All MTurk Research

Pilot Studies Before Launching

This advice may sound obvious, but some researchers do not pilot studies before launching them. Piloting studies makes sense both so that researchers can catch any errors in the instructions, study programming, or technical details (e.g., redirecting workers to an external web page) and so that researchers can accurately estimate the time it will take workers to complete the study. With an accurate estimate of how long the study takes, it is possible to set a fair compensation rate. We recommend running a pilot study with 20 participants prior to launching the full version.

Let Workers Know When They Will Be Asked to Do Things Out of the Ordinary

For most academic HITs, workers expect to complete a survey or experiment. Any time researchers ask workers to do something extra or out of the ordinary, workers should be informed in the HIT instructions so that they can decide whether it is something they want to do *before* accepting the HIT. If a worker accepts a HIT and then finds they are required to do something they would rather not do, they must decide whether to complete the task or abandon the HIT, which can affect their ratings and waste time.

Examples of things that should be disclosed in the HIT instructions are (a) if workers will be asked to download a file or app onto their device, (b) if workers will be asked to engage in a dyadic study with a partner, (c) if workers will be asked to engage in a video chat or to create a recording of themselves, or (d) if the study is overly tedious in some way. There are, of course, other situations where workers should be informed about what they will be asked to do. As a rule, we recommend disclosing anything that may catch workers off guard or cause multiple people to return the HIT after they find out what they will be asked to do. In line with the ethical principle of respect for persons, give people the information up front and let them decide whether they want to participate or not.

Pay People for Completing Screeners

Time is money, and that's certainly true on Mechanical Turk. When researchers set up a demographic questionnaire or other screener to determine worker eligibility, ineligible workers should not be terminated without being compensated. Although it may not seem like a big deal to have workers answer four or five questions for a single study, when many requesters engage in the same behavior, workers spend a lot of time doing things for free.

Instead of terminating workers who do not meet eligibility criteria, researchers can run a screener study to determine worker eligibility before launching the actual study. By separating the screener from the actual study, you can compensate workers a small amount for answering your screener and remove the temptation for workers to "guess in" to the study by answering the screener multiple times until they find the right eligibility criteria. Once researchers have a list of workers who meet their criteria, the workers can be placed on an include list (see Figure 4.10) and sent an email to let them know the study is available.

Pay a Minimum of 12 Cents a Minute, Preferably More

For standard behavioral science studies, we recommend paying a minimum of 12 cents per minute. Although pay on Mechanical Turk is a controversial topic, we believe a minimum of 12 cents per minute keeps studies affordable for most academic researchers while leaving ample room to increase pay for more demanding tasks (e.g., lots of open-ended responses, dyadic studies, or longitudinal studies). Because Mechanical Turk leaves compensation entirely up to requesters, researchers who want to pay more than a baseline of 12 cents a minute should simply do so.

Pay Workers as Soon as Possible

Researchers should pay participants as soon as possible. This may not always be easy, since approving work often requires checking data quality first. But researchers should be mindful that waiting for payment is burdensome to participants. Payment should be automated whenever possible.

Treat Worker IDs as Personally Identifiable Information

Collecting worker IDs should be standard practice. Without worker IDs, it is impossible to match workers to their data. Worker IDs can also be used to determine who is eligible or ineligible for studies. If some workers are not attentive, do not properly follow the instructions, or in some other way provide bad data, their worker IDs can be used to exclude them from future studies. In addition, worker IDs are essential for longitudinal research, in which data cannot be analyzed without matching worker IDs or some other identifier across datasets.

Worker IDs are not completely anonymous, however. This means worker IDs should be treated with the same caution as personal data.

Best Practices for Research on Sensitive Topics

Although most research participants are not harmed by survey content, it is possible for researchers to underestimate the potential harm of any specific research study. For this reason, when asking questions of a sensitive nature, researchers should consider taking the following steps to minimize the probability and magnitude of risk of harm.

Allow Participants to Skip Questions

Researchers should consider allowing participants to skip sensitive questions. Skipping questions is highly uncommon among MTurk workers. Allowing participants to skip questions can therefore be an effective way to minimize potential harm with little to no negative consequences for data quality.

Include Assessments of Potential Distress at the End of Pilot Studies

Because it is easy to underestimate the potential harm of any specific study, researchers may consider adding questions to assess participants' reactions to potentially sensitive items at the end of a pilot study. By assessing any potential harm prior to launching the full study, researchers can minimize risk to participants. Collecting such data is not necessary in the vast majority of cases for reasons outlined previously. However, if there is no published research on the risk of harm in a researcher's domain of interest, conducting a pilot study is likely warranted to determine whether any additional protections may be necessary.

Provide Support Materials

Researchers should provide participants with a list of support websites and hotlines at the end of the study.

Be Extra Careful About Confidentiality

For questions with sensitive content, it is particularly important to ensure anonymity and confidentiality.

CONCLUSION

With technology and platforms like Mechanical Turk, social and behavioral scientists have quickly gained access to millions of people who may serve as potential research participants. Although the prospects for research are exciting, technology within the social sciences faces many of the same ethical challenges and moral dilemmas that technology outside of the sciences faces. We have covered some of these issues in this chapter—setting fair pay, managing the relationship between MTurk workers and researchers, and maintaining anonymity—but several other issues are worthy of discussion and are beyond the scope of this chapter. We look forward to the discussion of such issues within the academic community.

To close, we would like to note one reason researchers can be optimistic about the prospects of finding solutions to the ethical issues that surround conducting research on Mechanical Turk: many of the aspects of Mechanical Turk that workers list as the most distressing (see Table 11.1) are the result of researcher behaviors that are easily changed. For example, workers list finding HITs, being rejected without explanation, and being asked to do things within HITs that they are uncomfortable with as some of the most common sources of stress. Fortunately, requesters can distribute HITs more evenly using quotas; rejections can be accompanied by an email explaining the reasons for the rejection; and workers can avoid many situations they are uncomfortable with when researchers clearly explain what workers will be asked to do within the HIT instructions. Small changes like these, we believe, can have a big influence on the experience of workers. Like the example we opened this chapter with, sometimes the difference between a good and a bad outcome may be simple human kindness and taking the time to use technology in a positive way. Academic requesters on Mechanical Turk are already leading the way in resolving many ethical issues, and we are confident that they will continue making positive changes moving forward.

REFERENCES

Black, M. C., & Black, R. S. (2007). A public health perspective on "The ethics of asking and not asking about abuse." *American Psychologist, 62*(4), 328–329. doi:10.1037/0003-066X62.4.328

Black, M. C., Kresnow, M.-J., Simon, T. R., Arias, I., & Shelley, G. (2006). Telephone survey respondents' reactions to questions regarding interpersonal violence. *Violence and Victims, 21*(4), 445–459. doi:10.1891/0886-6708.21.4.445

Blau, F. D., & Kahn, L. M. (2017). The gender wage gap: Extent, trends, and explanations. *Journal of Economic Literature, 55*(3), 789–865. doi:10.1257/jel.20160995

Buhrmester, M., Kwang, T., & Gosling, S. D. (2011). Amazon's Mechanical Turk: A new source of inexpensive, yet high-quality, data? *Perspectives on Psychological Science, 6*(1), 3–5.

Cromer, L. D., & Newman, E. (2011). Research ethics in victimization studies: Widening the lens. *Violence Against Women, 17*(12), 1536–1548. doi:10.1177/1077801211436365

Disch, E. (2001). Research as clinical practice: Creating a positive research experience for survivors of sexual abuse by professionals. *Sociological Practice, 3*(3), 221–239. doi:10.1023/A:1011526211933

Draucker, C. B. (1999). The emotional impact of sexual violence research on participants. *Archives of Psychiatric Nursing, 13*(4), 161–169. doi:10.1016/S0883-9417(99)80002-8

Dreyfuss, E., Barrett, B., & Newman, L. H. (2018). A bot panic hits Amazon's Mechanical Turk. *Wired.* Retrieved from https://www.wired.com/story/amazon-mechanical-turk-bot-panic/

Edwards, S. J. L. (2005). Research participation and the right to withdraw. *Bioethics, 19*(2), 112–130.

Edwards, V. J., Dube, S. R., Felitti, V. J., & Anda, R. F. (2007). It's ok to ask about past abuse. *American Psychologist, 62*(4), 327–328. doi:10.1037/0003-066X62.4.327

Fort, K., Adda, G., & Cohen, K. B. (2011). Amazon Mechanical Turk: Gold mine or coal mine? *Computational Linguistics, 37*(2), 413–420. doi:10.1162/COLI_a_00057

Gleaves, D. H., Rucklidge, J. J., & Follette, V. M. (2007). What are we teaching our students by not asking about abuse? *American Psychologist, 62*(4), 326–327. doi:10.1037/0003-066X62.4.326

Griffin, M. G., Resick, P. A., Waldrop, A. E., & Mechanic, M. B. (2003). Participation in trauma research: Is there evidence of harm? *Journal of Traumatic Stress, 16*(3), 221–227. doi:10.1023/A:1023735821900

Hara, K., Adams, A., Milland, K., Savage, S., Callison-Burch, C., & Bigham, J. P. (2018). A data-driven analysis of workers' earnings on Amazon Mechanical Turk. *Proceedings of the 2018 CHI Conference on Human Factors in Computing Systems*, 449.

Kraut, R., Olson, J., Banaji, M., Bruckman, A., Cohen, J., & Couper, M. (2004). Psychological research online: Report of Board of Scientific Affairs' Advisory Group on the Conduct of Research on the Internet. *American Psychologist, 59*(2), 105–117. doi:10.1037/0003-066X.59.2.105

Lease, M., Hullman, J., Bigham, J. P., Bernstein, M. S., Kim, J., Lasecki, W., . . .Miller, R. C. (2013). Mechanical Turk is not anonymous. *SSRN Electronic Journal*. doi:10.2139/ssrn.2228728

Litman, L., Robinson, J., Rosen, Z., Rosenzweig, C., Waxman, J., & Bates, L. M. (2019). The persistence of pay inequality: The gender wage gap in an anonymous online labor market. *PsyArXiv* doi:https://doi.org/10.31234/osf.io/jq589

Litman, L., Robinson, J., & Rosenzweig, C. (2015). The relationship between motivation, monetary compensation, and data quality among US- and India-based workers on Mechanical Turk. *Behavior Research Methods, 47*(2), 519–528. doi:10.3758/s13428-014-0483-x

Marder, J., & Fritz, M. (2015). The Internet's hidden science factory. *PBS NewsHour, 11*.

Moss, A. J., & Litman, L. (2018). After the bot scare: Understanding what's been happening with data collection on MTurk and how to stop it [blog post]. Retrieved from https://blog.turkprime.com/after-the-bot-scare-understanding-whats-been-happening-with-data-collection-on-mturk-and-how-to-stop-it (Accessed February 4, 2019).

Newman, E., & Kaloupek, D. G. (2004). The risks and benefits of participating in trauma-focused research studies. *Journal of Traumatic Stress, 17*(5), 383–394.

Newman, E., & Kaloupek, D. (2009). Overview of research addressing ethical dimensions of participation in traumatic stress studies: Autonomy and beneficence. *Journal of Traumatic Stress, 22*(6), 595–602. doi:10.1002/jts.20465

Peer, E., Vosgerau, J., & Acquisti, A. (2014). Reputation as a sufficient condition for data quality on Amazon Mechanical Turk. *Behavior Research Methods, 46*(4), 1023–1031.

Robinson, J., Rosenzweig, C., Moss, A. J., & Litman, L. (2019). Tapped out or barely tapped? Recommendations for how to harness the vast and largely unused potential of the Mechanical Turk participant pool. *PLOS ONE, 14*(12), e0226394. doi:10.1371/journal.pone.0226394

Schnur, J. B., Chaplin, W. F., Khurshid, K., Mogavero, J. N., Goldsmith, R. E., Lee, Y. -S., . . .Montgomery, G. H. (2017). Development of the Healthcare Triggering Questionnaire in adult sexual abuse survivors. *Psychological Trauma: Theory, Research, Practice, and Policy, 9*(6), 714–722. doi:10.1037/tra0000273

Silberman, M. S., Tomlinson, B., LaPlante, R., Ross, J., Irani, L., & Zaldivar, A. (2018). Responsible research with crowds: Pay crowdworkers at least minimum wage. *Communications of the ACM, 61*(3), 39–41.

Stokel-Walker, C. (2018). Bots on Amazon's Mechanical Turk are ruining psychology studies. *New Scientist*. Retrieved from https://www.newscientist.com/article/2176436-bots-on-amazons-mechanical-turk-are-ruining-psychology-studies/

Zhou, H., & Fishbach, A. (2016). The pitfall of experimenting on the web: How unattended selective attrition leads to surprising (yet false) research conclusions. *Journal of Personality and Social Psychology, 111*(4), 493–504. doi:10.1037/pspa0000056

INDEX